"**A** compelling and fascinating account...I was riveted."
—Dominick Dunne

"*Sexual Violence* is so clearly the account of a dedicated, compassionate, and inspired public servant that within moments of opening this compelling and important book, the reader has forgotten that she is a lawyer." **—Fran Lebowitz**

"A fascinating behind-the-scenes account of the revolution that Linda Fairstein has brought in the prosecution of sex crimes against women. This is a story about heinous crimes and horrible tragedies, told with uncompromising candor and clarity. Yet we come away hopeful in knowing that victims of rape finally have a powerful advocate in the criminal justice system. Justice is at long last being served." **—Ellen Chesler**

"Linda Fairstein is one of the genuine bright spots in New York's criminal justice system, a fair and tough-minded player on the side of the angels. *Sexual Violence* is powerful stuff, and very well-written. Mystery writers will be stealing from it for years." **—Lawrence Block**

"Recommended to every woman in America."
—Kathie Lee Gifford

"Vividly chronicles Fairstein's twofold commitment: convicting rapists and providing services to survivors...She's shown that one prosecutor can make a hell of a difference." **—*Glamour***

SEXUAL VIOLENCE

Our War Against Rape

Linda A. Fairstein

BERKLEY BOOKS, NEW YORK

SEXUAL VIOLENCE

A Berkley Book / published by arrangement with
William Morrow and Company, Inc.

PRINTING HISTORY
William Morrow and Company edition published 1993
Berkley trade edition / June 1995

ISBN: 0-425-14780-0

BERKLEY®
Berkley Books are published by The Berkley Publishing Group,
200 Madison Avenue, New York, New York 10016.
BERKLEY and the "B" design
are trademarks belonging to Berkley Publishing Corporation.

PRINTED IN THE UNITED STATES OF AMERICA

10 9 8 7 6 5 4 3 2 1

For
Samuel Johnson Fairstein, my father,
and
Justin N. Feldman, my husband,
wise and gentle men

PREFACE

T HE ONLY JOB I wanted when I graduated from the University of Virginia School of Law in 1972 was to work as an assistant district attorney in New York County. At that time, there were about 160 lawyers on the staff, 7 of whom were women; in 1993, of the 600 lawyers prosecuting crimes in New York County, half are women. In 1972 the Manhattan District Attorney's Office was considered the best in the country. Its reputation has been even more greatly enhanced during its seventeen years under the leadership of Robert M. Morgenthau.

I did not seek the position then, as many young lawyers do now, because of an interest in stemming the tide of sexual violence or a commitment to women's issues. When I entered the legal profession, there was not a specialized unit devoted to this kind of work anywhere in America, nor was there any prosecutor with expertise in the field. Rape and related offenses were rarely tried in our courtrooms. Rape victims were stigmatized by a society that did not understand the crimes. Our criminal justice system, laboring under archaic and unjust laws inherited from the British centuries ago, was completely unresponsive to their needs.

7

PREFACE

My professional interest was in public service. I wanted to practice law and be part of an office dedicated to delivering justice to the community it served. When I was fortunate enough to receive the appointment I coveted, like all of the other entering lawyers I pledged to remain in the post for four years, as the district attorney requested. Now, more than twenty years later, it is impossible for me to imagine any work more challenging or more rewarding than the prosecution of sex offenses.

The person responsible for the growth and evolution of this innovative force is Robert Morgenthau, the district attorney of New York County. From the beginning of his tenure in 1976, he recognized the need to dedicate resources and special attention to crimes of sexual violence. With his characteristic integrity and vision, he has gradually and continually expanded the size of the unit, which now has more than twenty experienced senior attorneys; added satellite divisions to specialize in child abuse (both sexual and physical) and domestic violence; encouraged our participation in training lawyers, advocates, and medical personnel both locally and across the country; advocated legislative reform on issues related to sexual assault; and educated the public about this long-misunderstood subject by urging my colleagues and me to speak to community groups, students of all ages, and other law enforcement agencies about the nature of crimes of sexual violence and their survivors. While a handful of cases are sensationalized by the media every year, Mr. Morgenthau has made every effort to ensure that each one of the hundreds of individuals victimized in Manhattan has access to the very best legal and counseling services, whether the victim goes forward in the criminal justice system or must properly be referred to another agency. Prosecutors all over America have imitated the model Morgenthau has developed—and more of them should—but no one can equal his sincere and responsible commitment to this area.

In 1975, the same year Robert Morgenthau was elected to the position of district attorney, Susan Brownmiller's definitive study of sexual assault, *Against Our Will—Men, Women and Rape,* was published. This great work traces the history of sexual force, from biblical references and literary allusions through victim interviews and descriptions of wartime experiences. The book was written as feminist attention to these issues was finally beginning to help revolutionize the way these crimes were treated within our courts. It was written before there was a sex crimes unit anywhere in the country.

My purpose in writing this book takes another direction altogether. The last two decades have witnessed extraordinary change in this field, and it has been my good fortune to come to the law at exactly the time when cases of sexual violence coming to trial became a possibility and a reality. We have not yet, as Brownmiller urges at the end of her book, denied rape a future. But we have started to make great progress in removing the veil of secrecy from these crimes and in attacking them vigorously and creatively in the courtroom.

There are scores of topics that are not covered here and need to be discussed or debated. Pedophilia, incest, battered women, the naming of victims by the media, civil suits against offenders or negligent third parties, male rape, and new sciences like DNA technology are among the many which should be explored in depth in future works. But my efforts are aimed at describing the work that has been accomplished so recently and persuading readers that the system *can* be made to function more comfortably and successfully for victims of these crimes.

In the cases I describe, I have altered the crime locations and the names and occupations of the victims and witnesses involved, to respect their privacy rights, but the circumstances are accurate. The case I follow through the court process, the midtown rapist trial, is not presented because it required very great legal skills. Any reader can tell that. I chose this case precisely because most stranger rape cases *are* quite likely to result in convictions, and survivors of this kind of rape can emerge from the trial and conviction of their attackers without suffering further abuse from the legal system. It is my earnest hope that with increased attention to this field throughout the next decade, victims will be encouraged to come forward more readily, and the devotion of services—nationwide—to their needs will become a reality.

I decided to write about the pioneering work of the Manhattan District Attorney's Office Sex Crimes Unit, and the corresponding efforts of the New York Police Department, in response to the frequent questions I am asked about the system's treatment of rape survivors and the many misconceptions the public still holds about the success of rape investigations and trials. Since my career commenced at the exact moment of extraordinary change in the legal process in this very area, I have interlaced the story of my own involvement as a prosecutor in this work, and I hope that some of the younger readers will be attracted to the enormously satisfying and fascinating world of public service in the law enforcement community.

Finally, you may wonder why I find this work, which must seem quite grim and depressing, such a deeply satisfying position. First and foremost is to be able to deliver service to the survivors of this devastating crime, and to do it with the quality and compassion that most of them do not expect. The frontline workers—police officers, detectives, nurses, doctors, and advocates—see the victims in far greater distress long before I get to meet them, and they make my job easier in this respect, because their intervention has already started the recovery process. To be part of a process that is attempting to achieve justice for crimes in which that result was long denied, and to practice law in a field where legislation *and* attitudes are still constantly evolving, is a rich reward and confirms all the ideals I held when I wanted to enter public service.

CONTENTS

11

CONTENTS

INTRODUCTION

For too many centuries, rape and other acts of sexual assault have been better known by the myths that have arisen to describe these crimes than by facts and truths. Their occurrences have been drastically underreported, the survivors long ignored by the legal and medical communities, and the nature of the criminality little understood by a general public willing to confuse sexual violence with consensual activity. Rape remains the only crime in which the victims—most often women, but frequently men and children—are stigmatized by others for their victimization and blamed for their participation in an act committed by forcible compulsion.

The debate has long raged about whether these crimes have been misnamed as "sex" crimes. There is no doubt that rape and its related violations are crimes of *violence.* They have nothing at all to do with sexuality as we experience it in our social lives, by consent. However, rape is unlike every other kind of violence because it is accomplished through sexual acts, and thus the sexual element is inescapably the most distinctive feature of this crime.

There is nothing pleasant about being struck in the eye by a man's fist. Nor does a day go by when police departments in every city of this country don't respond to domestic disputes in which a husband or a boyfriend hits a woman with a frying pan or kitchen chair or bedroom lamp—all of which can cause serious physical injury. I am not for a second minimizing the gravity of such attacks—all are violent and often life-threatening. But each of those assaults differs dramatically in nature from the assault in which men, who could use any of the above weapons to cause injury, choose instead to use as the weapon a penis—and with it to violate the most private and personal part of a woman's body. That is a crime of *sexual violence,* which is what sets it apart from every other kind of criminality. That is *my* view, though it is not shared by everyone who has studied or worked in this field.

The last two decades have witnessed extraordinary change in dealing with crimes of sexual violence: Legislative reform has been passed throughout the country; innovative police and prosecutorial units have been created and expanded; medical and psychological services have been established; scientific techniques like genetic fingerprinting have gained acceptance as investigative tools; and some of the blanket of silence has lifted to allow discussion of this intimate violation. But the pervasive nature of the age-old myths often overshadows this progress that has been made so recently. Since crimes of rape continue to occur with such frequency, it is critical to separate the fiction from fact and to shatter those myths that have so often discouraged victims from participating in the criminal justice system.

In 1969, *The New York Times* reported that although more than one thousand arrests were made in New York City for rape that year, only *eighteen* men were convicted of the crime. By 1975, at the end of the first year of operation of the newly formed Sex Crimes Prosecution Unit in the Manhattan District Attorney's Office, that figure had more than tripled in New York County alone. By the mid-1980s there were hundreds of sex offense convictions in our office—more than three hundred felony convictions each year for sexual assaults and related crimes, with both adult and child victims—and corresponding hundreds throughout the other boroughs. The long-overdue reforms and the commitment of people in support services and law enforcement who have devoted extraordinary human resources and great imagination to the investigation of these sensitive cases have had an enormous impact on this increase of convictions.

At the time I joined the Office of the District Attorney of New York County in 1972, New York remained one of the last states in the country to require corroboration—independent evidence—of every material element of a victim's description of her sexual assault. The word of a victim of armed robbery, physical assault, attempted murder, or any other crime could alone sustain a conviction. But when the charge was rape, the prosecutor had to present proof of more than the victim's testimony on all these three critical issues: the identification of the assailant—and obviously, this is *not* a crime that occurs in broad daylight with many witnesses, as bank robberies or muggings often do; the sexual nature of the attack—even though the crime is defined by penetration of the victim, not whether the defendant ejaculates and completes a sexual act; and the element of force—so that if a woman had wisely submitted to the threat of a weapon or physical violence and was not injured, that factor was automatically not corroborated. Thus, in this most intimate of all assaults, the crime least likely to be witnessed by anyone, the overwhelming percentage of victims were legally barred from ever presenting their stories to a jury.

The historical basis for that corroboration requirement was an opinion written by the Lord Chief Justice of the King's Bench in England, Sir Matthew Hale, who articulated the notion that because rape is a charge so easily made and so difficult for a man to defend against, it must be examined with greater caution than any other crime. He imparted that wisdom in 1671—and it controlled our country's laws for the next three centuries. Even in 1972, when our legislature was moving to eliminate that archaic requirement, a *New York Times* editorial called it "abhorrent" that any man could be convicted of rape solely on the unsupported charge of a woman.

Small wonder that myths about the difficulty of undertaking prosecutions had evolved. They were based on centuries of bad law, and the fact that until twenty years ago rape victims had virtually been denied access to the criminal justice system.

Once the laws began to change, the problem shifted slightly. The victim was entitled to her day in court, but prosecutors had no experience trying these cases. They had to learn how to better investigate rape complaints in the earliest stages, while memory and evidence were still fresh, to anticipate and successfully prepare for what would become the customary defenses, and to understand the issues unique to these crimes that would be raised time and time again. Progress in this has been uneven across the country.

The media attention to rape has been a two-edged sword. Hardly a month goes by without a newspaper or government study announcing an increase in reported figures of crimes of violence against women. Until quite recently, sensationalized tabloid headlines blared the only coverage of sex crimes, especially if the cases involved serial stalkers or celebrity defendants. And sadly, the occasional magazine pieces that appear on rape still echo the myths about the criminal justice system. The stories are written by people interested in and committed to resolving the problems of rape and its survivors, but not by professional investigators or prosecutors.

On the other hand, in the last few years, responsible articles about the nature of sexual assault crimes (whether stranger or acquaintance rape cases), the kind of trauma sustained by survivors, the prevalence of child abuse, and the voraciousness of sexual predators or recidivists have appeared as features in newspapers, magazines, and television documentaries. The public is made aware that a world-famous athlete like Mike Tyson can be convicted of rape, an articulate schoolgirl triumphing over the defense that she must have been "asking for it" because she went to his room at three in the morning. It is no longer fair to say that the system doesn't work: Laws have changed, and although public attitudes about the nature of this crime have been harder to change than the laws, we must continue to educate and inform, to explode the myths and prevent their propagation, which has darkened the subject of rape for far too long.

We have made very little progress in the effort to eradicate the crime of rape. That will not begin to happen until we undertake serious research to gain a real understanding of why it occurs—and there are many different reasons—with such alarming frequency in this society. And as long as there is sexual violence to deal with, it is time for people to understand that victims of it *can* be treated with dignity and with respect in the courtroom. In the jurisdictions, like New York County, that have dedicated significant resources to learning how to investigate and prosecute these cases, we have accomplished extraordinary results in the course of a very few years: The conviction rate of rape cases has soared within the last seventeen years, in trials for both stranger and acquaintance rapes, and we have fought to make victims more comfortable as they journey through the system.

The doors that were barred to survivors of sexual assault for so long have been opened, albeit only recently. By examining the changes that have been effected, the distinctions between the great variety of cases, the services now available and those that desperately need to be provided, we can continue to fashion more successful weapons in the struggle to vanquish sexual violence.

The diverse group of lawyers and police officers with whom I have had the privilege of working throughout these past twenty years have shared one common trait: They have cared passionately about the victims of sexual assault, and about making the criminal justice system work for them. The

INTRODUCTION

stories in this book—not about well-known individuals or people familiar from sensational headlines—which show this caring, explain the changing nature of the prosecution of sex crimes, and underscore the need for more attention to be devoted to this unique, violent, and intimate crime.

CHAPTER ONE

THE MIDTOWN RAPIST STRIKES

At about three p.m. on May 24, 1985, Lois Lusardo decided that she was hungry. She was a twenty-year-old college student majoring in accounting at Queens College. To pay her expenses, which were modest because she still lived with her parents in Bayside, she worked three afternoons a week at a children's wear manufacturer's showroom and shipping office on Thirty-first Street, just off Fifth Avenue. She kept the books up to date, answered the phone on occasion, and prepared the weekly paychecks for the signature of the company treasurer.

On this particular day, Lois had come directly from her classes to the fifty-year-old building where the Kids Will Be Kids Company had its offices on the eighteenth floor, overlooking a large and grime-encrusted air shaft. Breaking her usual pattern, she had not stopped for a salad at the deli next door to the office but had just taken the elevator to her floor and walked down the hall to her work area. She nodded at Sol, the chief salesman, greeted his junior assistant, Leslie, and waved at Raymond, the cleaning man, then sat down at her desk and started to go through the day's disbursements.

Lois worked at the numbers for two hours until she could

no longer ignore the growl of her stomach. She looked at her watch and assured herself that there would be no lines at the deli, that she could quickly get a snack and a soda and then return to her desk. She switched off her calculator, replaced the cap tightly on her felt-tipped pen, and announced to her co-workers that she was going to get something to eat, offering to bring back anything anybody wanted.

As the others shook their heads, Lois said she would see them in a few minutes, turned into the hallway, and walked to the elevator bank. She pressed the down button and counted the money in her jacket pocket—five dollars and change—which was more than enough for a midafternoon refreshment.

The elevator door slid open with the usual sound of a ping and a red arrow lighting the down signal, and Lois stepped into the empty car, pressing the lobby button. The descent began but stopped almost immediately on the sixteenth floor. When the doors opened, Lois was confronted by a slim, well-dressed man a bit older than she, who, without ever stepping forward onto the elevator, stared at her for a second, then grabbed the edge of the opened door with his left hand, dropped the briefcase he had been clutching in his right hand, and removed a large folding knife from the waistband of his pants.

The first words the man spoke were "Give me your money and your jewelry." Lois knew she was trapped in a four-by-four cell and looked over the shoulder of the man for help from workers she assumed had to be nearby. To her amazement, the entire sixteenth floor was vacant space, the dusty remains of some corporation that had gone out of business.

She reached into her pocket and gave her pathetic amount of cash to the robber, as well as her gold chain necklace and the watch her parents had given to her for her high school graduation. Surely he would let her go, she thought, after having given him all that she had.

"Okay, get off the elevator," he said.

"I have to go," Lois stammered. "They're waiting for me."

"You don't have to go anywhere. You're coming with me," and the soft-spoken man wearing a dark blue baseball cap pulled down on his forehead stepped forward toward Lois, keeping his back against the surging elevator door, and put his arm around her shoulder and the cold point of his knife against her neck as he took her off the car and on to the silent emptiness of the sixteenth floor.

He held her in that manner as he walked her several yards away to a door marked LADIES' ROOM. It was locked and that angered him; he let go of his captive and forced the door open with his knife. Lois's blood froze and she tried to control the feeling of hysteria rising within her as she realized he was taking her into an even more secluded space where they were less likely to be discovered by anyone.

She tried to talk with him, she told him that she had given him everything she had, that her boss was waiting for her in the lobby, that she could get him more money from her office, that . . .

"Shut up. You know what I want you to do," he said. And by this time he had dragged her into the first toilet stall and locked the metal door behind them. He pushed her back against the wall and they stood face-to-face, the fluorescent light outlining her attacker as he faced her, with barely a foot between them.

"No, I don't." Her answer was true. She was hoping that he did not want what she feared he did.

The man raised the knife to her neck. "Do you want me to hurt you?"

"No," she responded, trembling uncontrollably.

"Do you want me to kill you?"

Again, "No."

"You know what I want you to do."

Then he grabbed her by the arm and shoved her onto

21

the toilet seat. He replaced the knife in his pocket, unzipped his pants, and exposed his penis as Lois whispered, "Please, please just let me go. I won't ever tell anybody, please."

There was no response from the man, who began to touch Lois, moving his hands over her breast and reaching down to feel her vagina. He placed his penis against Lois's mouth, and when she refused to comply with his demands, crying that she had never done that before, he stopped, stepped back, and again held up the knife: "If you don't listen to me, maybe you'll listen to the knife."

Like women everywhere, Lois had heard stories from friends and had read countless articles and news accounts about women who had been killed resisting armed assailants. She did not want to be one of those statistics. More urgently, she felt completely powerless and vulnerable, isolated in a filthy toilet stall on an abandoned floor of the very building in which she worked, with a maniacal stranger standing over her, threatening her life with a knife. One thing was very clear to her: She was in no position to make any choices.

"Get up," he commanded. She obeyed his direction to stand and remove her blouse, skirt, and underwear. Then he unlocked the stall, pulled her to the area in front of the bathroom sinks, and made her get down on her back on the cold tile floor.

The man lowered his body on top of hers, not even taking the time to pull down his trousers, still clutching the knife in his hand as it rested against Lois's left ear. She was paralyzed with fear and disbelief as she felt the man enter her body with his penis.

"Move, damnit, move for me," her attacker directed as his agitation increased and he pushed himself back and forth against her rigid body. Lois was frozen and didn't respond, but that didn't matter much to her attacker. Within moments he ejaculated inside her, and the young woman's tears streamed down her cheeks and onto the head of the stranger whose face was nestled in the space between her shoulder and her neck.

He got up almost immediately and told Lois to get back into the stall and get dressed. She heard him go to the sink and run the water to wash his hands.

"That watch," he asked her, "how much is it worth?"

"I don't know."

His footsteps approached the stall and Lois saw his arm reach over the top of the door and return it to her.

"I know you're going to call the police—"

"No, I promise I won't," she interrupted, still fearful that he would kill her because she had had such an opportunity to memorize his face and clothing, to describe and identify him.

"I'm going to leave now. When you hear the elevator, when you hear that noise it makes when the doors open and close, you wait five more minutes and then you can go."

He walked to the bathroom door and as it closed behind him, Lois collapsed onto the toilet seat and broke into open sobs. Seconds later he came running back into the room, calling to her, "Hey, did I leave my newspaper in there?" Beside her, on the floor, was the *New York Post*, so Lois slid it out to the rapist, who said, "Thank you," as he bent to pick it up before taking leave a second time, almost half an hour after he had first encountered the hungry student in the empty elevator car.

She waited there far longer than the man had suggested, praying that he would be gone and she would not have to see him again. Then she unlocked the door of the stall, amazed that she could still walk and move like a normal woman, went to the sink to try to wash off the semen that coated her lower body, and put her clothes on.

Still terrified, she peeked out of the door of the ladies' room and looked in both directions down the hallway. There was no one in sight. Unable to get back on the elevator that had delivered her to her tormentor, Lois walked up the two flights of stairs to her company's suite of offices and pushed open the heavy door.

"There was just something about me," she later recalled.

"The minute I walked into the room, everyone looked up, and Raymond called out, 'What happened? Where have you been?' "

She swept past them and sat down in her cubicle, where once again she was unable to control the sobs that welled up inside her. Her friend Leslie was the first to approach the shaken and forever changed young woman. Lois Lusardo looked up at her and said, "Would you call the police, please? I've been raped."

CHAPTER TWO

ANOTHER DAY AT THE CRIMINAL COURT BUILDING

My OFFICE is on the eighth floor of the Criminal Court Building at 100 Centre Street in lower Manhattan. It is a massive, ugly gray courthouse built in the 1930s as a WPA effort, and a familiar sight to television viewers across the country, since it served as the backdrop against which Kojak posed at the end of every episode. The grim interior would come as a surprise to most people who rarely get to see behind the scenes of the seventeen floors of corridors, stretching two blocks in length, and housing the cramped work cubbyholes of hundreds of judges, assistant district attorneys, Legal Aid Society lawyers, and probation officers. Its north end connects by tunnel to the newly remodeled Tombs, where prisoners await their court appearances to determine whether they regain their freedom or take the bus ride to Rikers' Island, the New York City Jail.

Although I have served as an assistant district attorney for more than twenty years, the room in which I work is no larger or any fancier than those of my six hundred other colleagues. The only distinction earned here by seniority is that instead of sharing an office with two or three other "rookies," I have my own eight-by-eighteen-foot cubicle, with a single window that faces another government building across the narrow side street. I am a corridor away from the office of Robert Morgenthau, who has been the district attorney of New York County since 1975 and with his executive staff oversees the investigation and prosecution of all crime that occurs on the island of Manhattan.

It is from this room that I run the Sex Crimes Prosecution Unit (SCPU) of the New York County District Attorney's Office. Every day, adult women, adolescent, child, and occasionally male victims—all survivors of some form of sexual assault—arrive at our offices to be interviewed and questioned about the traumatic event that has altered their lives, in some respect, forever.

They first meet with me in the small, narrow room that has been my home for a quarter of my tenure in the office. Despite an effort to decorate the walls with cheerful prints and photographs, the room remains, like most city offices, a drab collection of old and battered pieces of furniture—a desk, several unmatched leather chairs, two bookcases of different vintages, and as many tall five-drawer file cabinets as can possibly be squeezed into the room at a given time. And like most city-issued supplies, everything—down to the worn carpeting—is a dull shade of gray.

Most of the time there is additional clutter in the room, as exhibits from completed trials or complex investigations—the maps and charts of rooftops, parks, housing project stairwells, and apartment interior diagrams documenting the violent landscape of Manhattan, the territory over which we have jurisdiction—lean against file cabinets and on top of bookcases, awaiting transportation to the larger storage space or archives in the basement of the cavernous building.

The top of my desk is covered with a bright green blotter, rarely more than a sliver of color because of the accumulation of manila folders that house hundreds of case files, white legal pads filled with notes of witness interviews, police reports, memoranda from prosecutors in the unit, seized property inventories, letters from victims praising colleagues in the unit who have successfully completed trials of their cases, angry letters from victims whose assailants have not yet been apprehended, mug shots of suspects being sought in serial rape cases, medical records of survivors, and every other kind of detritus of the world of criminal law.

The files concerning every sexual assault complaint remain on my desk top while the case investigation is open and active. When a case has been completed, John Dalton, my invaluable assistant since I was named to the unit in 1976, takes the folders around the corner to the larger office where my two paralegals work. There, in endless rows of file cabinets, on paper and on microfiche, is the history of sex offenses in this county for the last two decades: thousands and thousands of complaints and cases, sexual assaults and attempts to commit them, abuses of every sort—criminal or not—indexed and cross-referenced by the names of survivors and assailants. While it is rare to see the same victim twice throughout that twenty-year period of time, it is a well-documented fact that sex offenders are the most recidivist of criminals and more frequently repeat their violent acts than any other category of criminal. So it is that our files are replete with names of assailants my colleagues and I have prosecuted and convicted of rape, who have been sentenced to substantial prison terms, and who have been released on parole to rape again.

The number of files and amount of paperwork in my office and other offices, in storage and archives, reflect the staggering incidence of sexual assault that occurs in this city. Not a day goes by without at least one survivor—and often as many as five—coming forward to detail to us new examples of man's inhumanity, usually, to women.

To keep pace with this volume of sexual violence, and with a goal of one day conquering it, Mr. Morgenthau has continued to expand the unit and create corresponding specialty teams to deal with the specific problems of each category of prosecution. There are two dozen assistant district attorneys, all of them senior staff members with felony trial experience and extraordinary sensitivity, who are assigned to the Sex Crimes Prosecution Unit. More than a decade ago, Mr. Morgenthau established the Child Abuse Unit, in which another eight assistants specialize in sexually and physically abused infants and children, cases that present entirely different issues because of the victims' ages, their inability often to verbalize the events, and their developmental level—all of which affect their prospects as witnesses at trial. There is also, under the umbrella of dealing with crimes of sexual violence, a Domestic Violence Unit to handle the reports of physical and sexual abuse that occurs in spousal, familial, and common-law relationships.

What, then, is the attraction to this particular kind of work? The crimes are reported with increasing frequency each year. The criminals, with rare exceptions, can be counted on to repeat their crimes. When most survivors present themselves to us, they have little hope of success in the criminal justice system, even today. The reward my colleagues and I share is to be able to give to those victims what they least expect and most deserve: a just verdict in the courtroom, and a more comfortable path navigating the criminal justice system.

When I learned of the attack on Lois Lusardo in her midtown office building, it was exactly ten years after I as an assistant district attorney had tried my first rape case. The trial was assigned to me after I had been in the office three years, and that case changed the direction of my career and taught me firsthand some of the sad truths about this category of crime. I would like here to describe that first experience and the lessons it provided for me.

In the fall of 1975 I was working in a section of the office called the Major Felony Project, a bureau designated to prosecute the most violent crimes, and often, the offenders with lengthy criminal histories. The bureau chief was a wonderful trial lawyer—one of only two women in the trial division when I joined the office—named Joan Sudolnik, who is now an Acting Justice of the Supreme Court of the State of New York (which in New York State is the trial court where felony cases are prosecuted).

Joan had supervised my first ten felony trials throughout that year, and as my classmates and I became more comfortable in the courtroom, she moved us from single-witness cases (mostly robberies or physical assaults involving one individual's identification of another as the issue at the trial) to more complex cases like arson or kidnapping or attempted murder. On one of my intake days, Joan suggested that I take the rape complaint that had come into the unit to be drawn up and charged.

As with most crimes, my initial contact as an assistant district attorney was with a police officer who appeared in the complaint room of our offices early on a Friday morning, having made an arrest the previous evening. We sat down together in one of the small cubicles designated for interviewing police, and he started to explain the facts of the case. The victim had not accompanied him because she had spent most of the night waiting to be examined and treated in the emergency room of Lenox Hill Hospital and had just been released to return home at six o'clock in the morning.

As the officer told me the victim's story and his version of how the arrest "went down," it was quite obvious why the case had been fed to me, a relatively junior member of the team, even though the charge was such a serious one. It was so clear-cut and uncomplicated that I did not see any legal issues, and I could not conceive of any possible defense. The facts were straightforward and it seemed to need only some compassion and care for the survivor to get to a conviction of the accused. Did I have a lot to learn!

Lisa Marino was twenty-four—just four years younger than I was at the time—and had been employed at an investment brokerage firm on Wall Street since her graduation from college a few years earlier. She had worked late on a Thursday evening before heading uptown by subway to the studio apartment she had just moved into on the Upper East

Side of Manhattan. It was a bit after ten o'clock when she got to the express stop at Eighty-sixth Street and Lexington Avenue, and the area was still busy with the coffee shops and newsstands that stayed open most of the night in that part of town. As Lisa walked toward her small studio in a walk-up on Eighty-fifth Street on that cool fall evening, she was thinking about whether or not she had the energy left to open a can of tuna fish for a late supper or would just collapse into bed.

Although there wasn't much on her mind, Lisa never noticed that a young man followed in her footsteps as she turned off well-traveled Lexington Avenue on to the side street and mounted the eight front steps of the building. She opened the vestibule door with her key, stopped and emptied the bills from her mailbox, and didn't pay any attention as the heavy door swung slowly on its air spring behind her. It was after Lisa had rounded the staircase between the first and second floors that she heard a pounding noise and looked over her shoulder to see a husky young man coming up the stairs two at a time—with the gleaming blade of a knife extending from his right hand.

The terrified young woman ran up the next flight clutching her apartment key tightly, well aware that her only hope for safety was getting into her apartment *alone*. She didn't stand a chance. Her stalker overtook her in the third-floor hallway that led to her door, grabbed her in a choke hold from behind, and held the knife across the front of her throat as he told her not to scream or he would kill her.

Following his directions, Lisa unlocked the door—praying for the arrival of a neighbor or visitor—and was dragged into the isolation of her tiny home and watched in disbelief as her attacker, still holding her by the neck, sliced her telephone cord with his knife.

She feared the worst, as she had every reason to, and the thoughts that raced through her mind filled her with nausea, in addition to panic. "When he's finished with me, he'll kill me anyway. No one will find me here for days—I should have stayed with my roommates in the old apartment." She tried to calm herself down and force herself to think of every piece of advice she had ever read in a women's magazine feature about rape and self-defense. Talk to him, she decided, maybe he won't hurt me if I can talk him out of this whole thing.

He's so young, Lisa thought, when he finally loosened his hold on her neck and turned her around to face him. Tall and muscular, but with a baby face and sprouts of adolescent-looking facial hair. He can't be old enough to know what sex is, she tried to convince herself—and then went to work trying to convince him of that as well.

"I'll give you my money—I know that's what you want—it's in my wallet," she started tentatively.

"Later for that," he said, grinning.

"My boyfriend will be home any minute," wishing, more than she ever had before, and for a better reason, that she actually had a boyfriend. "Please take what you want and go before he gets home . . . please."

"He'll have to wait for me tonight. He'll have to have seconds."

Lisa couldn't believe how cool the kid was, staring her straight in the eye and smiling directly in the face of her fear, and with his free hand running his fingers back and forth across her breasts.

Don't cry, she told herself, whatever you do, don't cry, but she found that she had no more control over that than she did over anything else that was going on within her own home.

"You're beautiful—I seen you on the street tonight and I said I had to have you. Take off your clothes. Stay quiet and I'll put the knife away. Make a sound and the knife goes right into your eye. Understand?"

She understood perfectly.

Lisa Marino undressed in front of this total stranger, who stood inches away from her, staring at her body with his arms folded and the ever-present knife in hand.

"On the bed."

She didn't bother talking to him anymore. She didn't see the point.

The youth just unzipped his pants, climbed on top of Lisa's body, and put the knife on the floor below the bed while he rubbed against her until he penetrated her vagina. For the two minutes until he ejaculated, he kept telling Lisa that she was beautiful and that he loved her, and asked her if her boyfriend did "it" as good as he did.

The stranger stood up then, picked up Lisa's underpants and wiped his penis with them before throwing them on the floor and zipping his fly. He opened her pocketbook and went through her wallet, removing the seventeen dollars that was supposed to see her through until the next day's paycheck, and also taking one of her business cards.

"You got tokens too?" he asked, and found them in the bottom of the bag before she could answer.

"I be back another time, beautiful," he said, and laughed as he walked out and closed the door behind him.

Lisa wasted no time. She put on her terry cloth bathrobe and went into the common hallway to try to get help. At that exact moment, Jim Carson, a neighbor she had seen occasionally but never spoken to, was walking up from the third-floor landing to the fourth, with his two cocker spaniels on leashes.

Before she could compose herself to speak, Carson looked at her and asked, "Are you okay?"

"No, no I'm not. I've just been attacked and I have no phone. Can you call the police for me?"

"Did the guy just leave?"

Lisa nodded.

"I mean I just came up the stairs past a kid who was going out—yellow T-shirt, jeans, really dirty-looking. Him?"

"Yes." Lisa continued nodding.

"Here, hold these," Carson said, throwing the dog leads at Lisa and turning to run back down the narrow staircase.

"No, no, don't do that!" she screamed after him. "He's got a knife!"

And as Carson took off down the stairs, Lisa broke down anew at the idea she had unwittingly involved someone else in her tragedy and exposed him to a knife-wielding criminal.

The late-night commotion in the hallway of the small building brought neighbors to their peepholes. The wife of the elderly couple in 3A saw Lisa through hers and opened the door, offering assistance and shelter. Lisa accepted the invitation to come in with the two dogs in tow and used the phone to call 911 and report both the rape and the ongoing chase to the police.

A team of three anticrime officers—precinct police who patrol in plainclothes and unmarked cars—had been working in the area on a 6:00 P.M. to 2:00 A.M. shift and had stopped at Papaya King on the corner of Eighty-sixth Street for a hot dog and fruit juice dinner to break up their tour. They were standing at the counter, not many yards away from the subway entrance, when they all saw a "situation" headed in their direction. A scruffy-looking teenager was running fast, chased by a thirtyish buttoned-down type who was shouting "Police!" at the top of his lungs as he ran.

Neither of the runners could have known that the three eaters, also dressed in sweatshirts and jeans, were plainclothes officers. The cops joined the chase and stopped the youth in his tracks, at gunpoint. Carson, incredulous at his luck, caught his breath and told the cops what little he knew about the events preceding their timely arrival.

The group went back to Eighty-fifth Street, and Carson found Lisa inside the open door of apartment 3A. One of the cops led the trembling young woman back with him to the sidewalk, where, barely fifteen minutes after he had left her—and with no trace of the smirk that had highlighted his face—Lisa identified James Morales as the man who had raped her.

When the same officer to whom the identification had been made finished giving me the summary of the events, I drafted the simple complaint that formally charged Morales with the crimes he had committed. I also took from him the telephone number to reach Lisa Marino so I could call her later in the day to introduce myself, explain the steps that would follow, and schedule a meeting for her in my office to arrange the presentation of the case to a grand jury the very next week.

Late that afternoon, when my bureau mates and I talked about the cases each of us had picked up that day, I outlined the facts of the Morales case.

"A rock-crusher," moaned Mike Guadagno. "You'll never get a trial out of that case." He meant, of course, that since I had such a good complaining witness and such overwhelming evidence against the defendant, the rapist would probably plead guilty to the charge. I would not get to try the rape case.

At that point, the only issue seemed to be what had happened to the knife that Morales had held to Lisa's throat and with which he had threatened to put out her eye. He didn't have it when he was stopped by the police, just a couple of blocks from the crime scene. Carson had explained that Morales had been walking away from the building at a casual pace until he got up close to the kid and called to him to stop, at which time the suspect had bounded away. We prosecutors were all used to cases in which assailants dropped their weapons during a chase or threw them into the street or a sewer when being followed—and the reality was that most of the weapons were never found again, even if the officers had a chance to double back over the trail of the chase to look for them.

"You've got a ground ball, Fairstein," a second colleague assured me, using another of the favorite expressions for a no-contest case.

I felt even more confident about that call after meeting Lisa Marino in my office the next Monday morning. She arrived there at 8:30 that day accompanied by her older brother, and I tried to put them both at ease by answering all the questions they had before I got under way with what I needed to know.

"Where is he now?" was Tom Marino's first concern.

"He's in jail, but . . ." And the "buts" in these cases are the most difficult things to explain to victims of every violent crime. Most of them have to do with the meaning of bail in our system, that its purpose is to ensure the appearance of a defendant for court dates until the conclusion of his case, for he is presumed innocent until the jury decides otherwise. Of great weight are the defendant's "roots in the community"— whether he lives in this jurisdiction; with whom and for how long; whether he goes to school or is employed here; and whether or not he has a criminal record. In this case, I was fairly certain that bail would be granted.

Indeed, a criminal court judge set Morales's bail at ten thousand dollars, denying my request for an amount ten times greater based on the heinousness of the crime. I had argued that *no* amount of money could ensure the youth's return since the prosecution had such a strong case. As far as Morales's "roots" in the community went, he was sixteen years old, just now eligible for prosecution as an adult. He lived with his parents, who appeared in court on his behalf, seemed to be decent people, and who both held jobs that provided them with a modest income. The judge relied primarily on *their* community stability in his decision to grant low bail, despite the fact that the defendant was an unemployed high school dropout with no other verifiable ties.

My arguments to the judge that it was Morales who had been charged with these criminal acts, not his parents, and their responsibility to the court was not at issue while *his* was, had not met with any success either.

Like most victims and their loved ones, Lisa and Tom Marino were astounded at the possibility that Morales could be granted bail and be back out on the street immediately. Lisa contended, "But he knows where I live—I can't go back there again, I'll never feel safe." And like millions of others in her same circumstance, Lisa began to absorb the fact that her victimization did not end when her assault did. If the mental anguish was not sufficient to disrupt her life completely, then the practical inconveniences would certainly add to the load.

We three spent about twenty minutes together, after which I asked Tom if he would mind stepping out into the waiting area. He seemed to understand that Lisa would probably be more candid about her ordeal if she were not trying to spare his feelings and subject him to the painful details of the assault.

Lisa got through the questioning very well, and we went upstairs shortly after I explained the process to her to the ninth-floor rooms in which the grand juries are convened every day. With me as the interrogator—and without the presence of the defendant—she bravely faced the twenty-three jurors and once more recounted the facts of the case. Since these proceedings occur without a judge and a defense attorney, the examination lasted only ten minutes, mercifully, without any cross-examination.

James Morales was indicted for rape in the first degree, robbery in the first degree, and burglary in the first degree.

We would talk often, I assured her, and I would update her regularly on the progress of the case. I anticipated that if there were to be a trial, it would take place within three or four months.

"But what will he say?" she asked. "Will he deny that he did it? Will he say it never happened?"

I could not imagine what he would say any better than Lisa could, so I refused to guess and told her that as soon as his lawyer gave me any information about his plea I would pass it along to her. She was not to worry about the trial—that would be *my* task—and she was so credible, intelligent, articulate, and open that I could not foresee a single problem.

Morales was represented by a lawyer his parents had hired whom I had never encountered before. He had been practicing law for more than thirty years, but rarely in the criminal courts, so I was not able to get much scouting information about his ability or style. When we first met to conference the case, he didn't give much away about his client's defense other than to assure me that he was going to fight it vigorously every inch of the way.

Still to my surprise, the trial started exactly four months after the arrest, with the opening statements from both of the lawyers. I laid out the facts of the case as I expected to present them through my witnesses. My adversary gave no details at all, other than to assert his client's innocence and to announce that Morales would certainly take the witness stand on his own behalf and tell his own story of the events of the night in question. We were all puzzled, and I still could not figure what the kid could say for himself in light of the evidence we had.

Lisa Marino was a superb witness. She was direct in response to all of my questions, looking at the jurors despite her obvious discomfort and trying to impress upon them the certainty of the observations she made at the most critical moment of her young life. She had been determined to get through her testimony without tears, and she found that the most difficult part of her appearance was being in the courtroom barely ten feet away from the beast who had held her life in his hands for the brief time she had been his captive and he had molested her.

The cross-examination was distinctly unpleasant. Morales's attorney was snide and sarcastic, often making improper asides to her responses as he stood next to the jury box, many of them not even audible to the judge. Lisa was clearly rattled and tried to remain composed as she assured the man that she was certain about the time she had left work, even though her position did not require that she punch a time card, and adamant that she had not gone home to change out of her business clothes before walking back to Eighty-sixth Street and running into Morales. He pushed her hard on a number of facts that did not seem to be central to the case, and despite my objections to the questions, my opponent was given the latitude to ask most of the things he needed to get his job done.

I was beginning to get an idea of what he was trying to prove.

After Lisa's three hours on the stand, the People's case went on with testimony from Jim Carson, the three anticrime officers, and the laboratory experts who had identified seminal fluid on Lisa's underwear—the pair she claimed her assailant had used to wipe himself after the attack. The next day, having presented all of our evidence, I rested our case.

James Morales took the witness stand. The first time I heard him speak was when he raised his hand to take the oath to tell the truth.

His lawyer took him through the basic steps—his name, age, residence with his family, no prior history of involvement with the law—skipping over his dismal school record and his failure to hold a job. The kid looked so benign in the courtroom, dressed up in a sports jacket and tie, the "let's make the rapist look like an altar boy" image that prosecutors see all the time, and that often impresses the jury.

Then the second injustice began. Morales started to weave a tale that even *he* seemed so uncomfortable with that I could not believe it was not scripted for him by someone else. He told us that he had left his home on East 116th Street early on the evening in question to go to a movie at 7:30 at one of the many theater complexes lining East Eighty-sixth Street not far from the subway station. It was a karate film—a safe choice, since there was always at least one of those playing there then in any given week. And after the movie, between 9:30 and 10:00 P.M., as he walked to the uptown subway station, he first saw Lisa Marino. He didn't know her name, of course, but he couldn't believe his luck because she called out to him to stop as he strolled past the doorway in which she was standing.

She looked real pretty, Morales said, and so he stopped to see what she wanted. She was a prostitute, he discovered, and she offered him the opportunity to have sex with her, any way he wanted to do it. And although he had never been with a prostitute before—he would never have considered such a thing, he assured the jury—this girl looked so different, so special, so unlike the kinds of girls who hang out all up and down the stretch of Eighty-sixth Street (a fact not to be lost on any jurors familiar with that neighborhood) that he had really been tempted. Then he remembered about the money—because he wasn't working at the moment, his mother had given him twenty dollars when he left the house, and all he had left was seventeen, his change after the movie (and of course, an amount that covered the robbery accusation).

So he told that to the girl, who laughed and took his arm and told him that she would give him his first one for nothing, that she would rather be with a strong young man who could give her some pleasure than with some drunken old guy who had bad breath and not much energy. Besides, she told him, she knew he'd be back.

Morales took the jury back to Lisa's apartment, described the athletic sexual encounter and told them that she had even given him a business card, explaining that she worked in a stuffy office all day and any time he wanted to plan to "party"—for a price—he should call her at work, but never leave a message with anyone.

Then, he explained, her intercom rang as the door buzzer was pressed downstairs, and she panicked. She was no longer the sweet-faced girl he had met on the street as she shrieked at him to put his clothes on and get out of her apartment. She wasn't expecting anyone and was afraid that a friend from the office had dropped by unexpectedly and would catch her in this other side of her life.

As he dressed, Morales said he had noticed that Lisa was crying, mumbling that she should never have done this, and that she practically pushed him out of the door and into the hallway. He remembered passing the guy with two dogs on the staircase and figured he was the one stopping for a nightcap with the girl. He couldn't believe it when he saw the guy coming after him, and even worse, when the police stopped him. And no, of course he never had a knife. What knife?

My first cross-examination of a rapist was less than brilliant. Although there was neither truth nor much logic to this kid's story, it had been so neatly tailored to fit the facts to which Lisa had testified on the direct case that it was difficult to find inconsistencies within it.

When court ended, I returned to my office to prepare my summation. The first call came from Lisa Marino, who, like most victims in criminal cases, was not allowed to be present during the testimony of other witnesses. "What did he say? Did he admit he raped me?"

What an enormous sense of failure I felt in not having accomplished the latter, which I knew was so important to Lisa. But even more distressed was I at the prospect of telling her that the defense in the case was not simply that she had consented to intercourse with Morales—the age-old defense fallback—but that *she* was guilty of prostitution, according to him.

She was devastated. "How can the judge let him do that?"

I tried every explanation I could give her, with assurances that we all knew the story was completely incredible, but it was truly a blow that took the heart out of her.

Morales's lawyer had saved a lot of his steam for his closing argument. He neatly patched all the pieces of his client's story into Lisa's outline—accounting for his presence in her apartment, the amount of money found on him by the police, the business card also in his pocket, the knife that was never produced in court, and the fact that he was seen walking, not running, from the scene of the supposed crime.

Then he launched into his pitch. Appearances are deceptive, he told the jury, and we have all learned that it is impossible to judge a book by its cover. Lisa Marino may have appeared to fit the role of a rising young Wall Street worker, but how can we *ever* know from what dangers, what kind of excitement other people derive their pleasures, their thrills? Just because she looks so good, so proper, doesn't mean that when she leaves the pressures of her downtown job she isn't looking for some other form of relief and intoxication.

After all, he argued, trying to strike a chord that was one of the most useful things I learned that day—since I have rarely tried a case in which it hasn't been raised directly or by innuendo—we know very little and we understand even less about each other's sexuality. Like most defenders of rapists, my adversary tried to steer the jury away from the idea of these acts as *violent crimes* and toward the idea that the charges have something to do with human sexuality. Not one of the people sitting in the jury box, he urged them, knew anything more about Lisa Marino than her brief appearance had afforded them—what "turned her on," sexually, was anybody's guess.

Then, to my complete astonishment, he walked to my counsel table and picked up from it one of the pieces of evidence I had introduced at the trial: the victim's underpants. They were the only item of clothing from the night of the crime that had been shown to the jury and admitted into evidence. The panties were bikini style and were patterned in a leopard-skin print.

The lawyer dangled the underwear in front of the jurors, demanded of them to consider the type of woman who would purchase and wear *that* kind of panties: "Not a businesswoman, not a lady . . . but a hooker!"

I was about to go berserk! It was imperative that I listen carefully to his arguments in order to respond to them in my own closing remarks, but I was furious at his comments. Was it possible that anyone would buy that nonsense in this century?

Jury verdicts in criminal trials must be unanimous. I needed the vote of all twelve jurors to convict Morales. My adversary would also have a total victory with twelve votes, but it would be a triumph for him, in as simple a case as this, if even one juror accepted his story and caused a mistrial. One believer would "hang" the jury—that's all it would take.

My summation was very traditional and based on the evidence and credibility of the prosecution witnesses. I also had less professional thoughts, counting on the probability something other than white cotton underwear when she entered the room to begin deliberations. At the end of my hour, the judge charged the jurors on the law of the various crimes they had to consider and explained their duties to them. The group retired to deliberate.

Morales's lawyer tried to make small talk with me while we waited for a verdict, but I was so upset at the perjurious nature of his case that I was unable and unwilling to chat with him.

"Look," he said, "you know and I know what happened, but give me any group of people large enough and there is bound to be someone in it who will believe *anything* about a beautiful young woman and her sexuality."

I decided to leave the courtroom and wait in my office.

Fortunately, this group of twelve intelligent citizens was not quite large enough for the purposes envisioned by my adversary, and within several hours they announced that they had agreed upon a verdict. The defendant was guilty of the rape, burglary, and robbery of Lisa Marino.

I called her at once with the good news, at last. She was ecstatic, grateful, relieved—and very angry about the nature of the defense case. But she expressed to me the great satisfaction she had derived, quite unexpectedly, by coming face-to-face with her assailant and being believed by a group of total strangers. The experience of the trial, she said, had strengthened her, and the outcome made worthwhile everything she had endured since the night of the attack.

We shared one additional disappointment. On the date of the sentence, the judge imposed a prison term of four years, with no minimum time. I had not expected the maximum sentence (twenty-five years), despite the severity of the crime and its impact on Lisa Marino, simply because I knew Morales's youth and lack of criminal history would benefit him on this first conviction. It did surprise me, however, that the judge granted him youthful offender treatment, an optional feature, that meant he would not have the stigma of a criminal conviction and that therefore, incredibly, this arrest would not even be a part of his permanent record. Worse yet, the judge decided that Morales would not have to begin to serve his time in jail until *after* the appeal of his case was heard by a higher court. That process could take years!

My work in the Major Felony Project went on as usual, and eight months later I appeared in Part 30 of the Supreme Court, the part in which most of my assorted cases were calendared. On my way out of the room at the end of the morning, I was startled to see James Morales seated on the rear bench of the large courtroom, next to his father. I turned back around and went to the D.A.'s counsel table in the front well of the courtroom, where I picked up the day's schedule, a list of the cases, with more than fifty felony arrests, that would be heard that day, all for the purpose of the arraignment of each defendant on an indictment.

Scanning the several pages of names, I stopped dead at number thirty-seven: "James Morales—Rape in the First Degree—Section 130.35 of the Penal Law." The file jacket with the case summary and write-up was on the table and included the bail recommendation suggested by the assistant district attorney who had picked up the case at intake. It was, again, a knife-point rape of a woman Morales was alleged to have followed off the street and attacked under the stairwell of the ground-floor landing of her building—a woman whose victimization would have been spared had Morales, justly convicted, been imprisoned when his sentence had been imposed in the first case.

Even though he had already been convicted of three of the most serious crimes in the penal law, his fingerprint check at the time of the new arrest showed no "priors"—because he had been granted youthful offender status on the first case and was therefore deemed to have no record.

I remained in the courtroom for the next half hour until he was arraigned so that I could inform the judge about his history. At long last, James Morales was remanded to the prison system without bail and began to serve the sentence imposed in Lisa Marino's case.

The last lesson I learned from my first rape trial, then, was the real problem of rapists' recidivism. Lisa Marino had done everything required of her by the system and James Morales had been fairly tried and convicted by a jury. For what earthly reason did a second woman have to be sexually assaulted by a convicted rapist? I could give her no answer.

One of my colleagues convicted the defendant at the trial of his second case, and he was sentenced to a prison term of six years, to be served concurrently with the four years he was doing for our first conviction.

CHAPTER THREE

NO PLACE FOR A WOMAN

Mr. District Attorney.

That was the name by which Frank Hogan had come to be known throughout the country. He succeeded Thomas Dewey as the Manhattan D.A. in 1943 and served in that position for more than thirty years. Hogan revolutionized the prosecutor's office by taking it out of the political arena, making his legal staff appointments by merit rather than clubhouse associations and favors. He was known and admired for his integrity, and it was in his office that all young lawyers interested in public service and litigation dreamed of working.

In 1972, as I was about to graduate from law school at the University of Virginia, I was among those dreamers. The only job I wanted was to be an assistant district attorney in Mr. Hogan's office. But the odds were not in my favor. At the time I applied for the job, there were 7 women among the 160 lawyers working for Frank Hogan.

In my three years of law school, I studied property and torts and tax and trusts and estates, all required courses at that time. To me, it was everything exhilarating and challenging. Even commercial courses like secured transactions

45

had a certain intellectual demand which was appealing. But when I sat in the classroom for lectures on criminal law, procedure, and evidence I knew I had found what I wanted to do.

Monrad Paulsen, the dean of the law school and an expert in the field of criminal law (he had co-written the text used in most of the law schools across the country) was my professor in my first two criminal law courses. His explanation of the procedures and purposes of the justice system was dazzling. The simplicity of the purpose of the criminal law—the protection of the individual within the context of the protection of society—and the complexity of the procedures of the criminal law were a hypnotic combination.

Dean Paulsen encouraged my interest in the New York District Attorney's Office and was well aware that I would have to pursue it aggressively; no one would come to Virginia to recruit me. "It's a long shot," he soberly cautioned me, "but fight for it if that's what you want." At that point in time, Mr. Hogan had been Manhattan's district attorney for twenty-nine years. The biggest problem I faced, as Dean Paulsen explained it to me, was that Hogan held a number of distinctly "traditional" views of the role of women in the field of law enforcement. Primary among those was that he didn't really think they belonged in his office prosecuting violent crimes.

The response to my application was an invitation to come to New York for a series of interviews with members of the hiring committee. I drove up in April and was screened by lawyers from the Homicide and Supreme Court bureaus—smart young men who grilled candidates with questions about our interest in the field, our ability to withstand the pressure of courtroom trials, and hypothetical problems with issues of law and ethics.

Those interviewers passed me along to one of the handful of women on the staff. Sybil Landau, a talented member of the Appeals Bureau at the time and now a law school professor, spent another half hour asking more questions and discussing recent Supreme Court decisions. But she spent just as much time telling me what life was like in the office. I learned that it was only in the last few years that any of the women had been *allowed* to try cases in the criminal courtrooms. For the most part, they had been assigned to the bureaus that handled appellate arguments or did grand jury presentations, but they rarely handled jury trials—and never for serious crimes like rape or murder. (One looks today at Mr. Morgenthau's staff of more than six hundred assistant district attorneys—almost half of whom are women—and it is difficult to describe to the incoming applicants how limited the prospects were in 1972.)

If my interviewers had been trying to dull my interest or frighten me off, they had failed dismally. I was excited and intrigued and impressed, and wanted the job more than anything I had ever wanted in my life.

Within several days of my return to school, the head of the hiring board called to tell me that they were interested in me, but that Mr. Hogan would not meet with me himself until there was an opening available on the staff. Weeks and weeks went by, until I finally had a call from Mr. Hogan's assistant, Ida Van Lindt—still today Mr. Morgenthau's assistant, and a great friend to me—inviting me back for an interview with the district attorney.

That first meeting is as vivid in my mind as the appointments I had yesterday. I remember the sleeplessness the night before, how nervous I was on the ride into Manhattan from my parents' home in nearby Mount Vernon, and even my indecision about what to wear. Mr. Hogan was a genial and charming gentleman—and his quiet manner and shock of white hair gave him more the appearance of a leprechaun than of a legend of law enforcement. He came from behind the desk in the corner of his enormous office and sat facing me in a leather chair, talking mostly about my family and my personal background.

"You went to college at Vassar, I see."

"Yes," I responded.

"Majored in English literature, did you?"

"Yes." He was, I thought, obviously familiar with my résumé and I assumed that was a good sign.

He looked at me for a long while and then sighed. "Miss Fairstein," he said, "we deal with criminals here. Real ones, not the ones you read about in books or see on TV. These people stab with real knives. Their victims bleed. They kill people for no reason. Some of the people we prosecute are desperate, hardened, hate-filled people.

"I look at you," he went on, "and I see a young woman from a good family, educated at the best schools, with absolutely nothing in your background to prepare you for what you would be exposed to in a place like this. Then I think of the people in the holding pens behind the courthouse. It's tawdry, Miss Fairstein, it's very tawdry. Frankly, I have to tell you that I think this is no place for a woman like you."

I continued to try to argue my case, politely explaining all the reasons about which I thought he was mistaken and my long-standing desire to be engaged in public service and my eagerness to work in that office. He seemed to be listening, smiling occasionally, but the overall tone of the interview after he had announced his reservation was discouraging. When he ushered me out of his office, he told me I would hear from him after he had made his decision. I left the building completely dejected and certain that I would never see him again.

It was not until after my graduation from law school that I received the telephone call I had feared would never come. Mr. Hogan got on the line to tell me that there would indeed be an opening to begin work in the fall, and I was to come into the office immediately to fill out the paperwork and begin my background security investigation.

I celebrated for days.

At the time I entered the Office of the District Attorney of New York County to begin my assignment there, it was divided into a number of different bureaus. Young lawyers, each having made a commitment to Mr. Hogan to remain in the office for four years, started in one of the "junior" bureaus and rotated through the rest of the divisions.

The usual route consisted of an initial assignment in the Complaint Bureau, where we interviewed citizens who came in to us by the hundreds with complaints about crimes, usually petty thefts or consumer frauds, and were unable to get action from any other investigative agency; then on to the Indictment Bureau, where we presented witnesses in felony cases—serious crimes like robbery, assault, and rape—to grand juries every day of the week to obtain indictments in cases that would thereafter be prosecuted in trial courts by more experienced assistants; next to the Criminal Court Bureau, where we tried misdemeanor cases, the less serious crimes, punishable by less than one year in jail or a fine; and finally, after about two or three years, we were each assigned to one of the "senior" bureaus. Among those were the Homicide Bureau, which was responsible for all of the murder cases (and to which no woman had ever been assigned at the time I joined the office); the Supreme Court Bureau, which tried the felony cases that had been indicted by grand juries; the Special Narcotics Bureau, which handled all drug prosecutions; and the Appeals Bureau, in which assistants did all the appellate work for the office, including arguments before the Supreme Court of the United States.

After several months working as a trial preparation assistant in the fall of 1972, I joined the group of twelve office "classmates" of mine who had also come on staff in the preceding weeks and were in the first rotational step in the Complaint Bureau. There were no other women in that dozen. Fresh out of law school, we all shared the sense of excitement to be working in the criminal justice system—and in that premier office—and to be in a position to offer assistance, even in some small way, to the troubled citizens who found their way to us on a daily basis.

My first few months, then, were absorbed with hours of training sessions led by our supervising attorneys, who lectured to us on the law as well as about office procedures. In between the interviews we conducted throughout the day, most of us kept abreast of the calendars of the Supreme Court and spent whatever free moments we had watching portions of some of the thirty or more trials being conducted in our building every single day. No training ground could have been more fertile than 100 Centre Street, with skilled lawyers—prosecutors and defense attorneys—working on an endless array of fascinating cases, many with complex legal issues, some of which we were familiar with from newspaper headlines, but thousands of others that never made it to the news yet were every bit as interesting.

Most of the cases that came to us in the Complaint Bureau were resolved without arrests or prosecution. Many of the matters involved complaints that would today be handled by a consumer protection organization, but since very few such groups existed at that time, we tried to mediate the disputes when possible.

And sometimes, sadly, we remained a "court of last resort" for bizarre situations that really had no solution, or for which there was no other referral agency. It was common practice, as part of the friendly rivalry that existed between police and prosecutors, for station house desk officers to get rid of chronic complainers by telling them to take their cases to the D.A.'s office. We, the Complaint Bureau staffers, were the ones who had to entertain this variety of "walk-ins."

One of our more colorful regulars was an elderly woman who lived with her daughter and son-in-law on the Upper West Side, and whom the police chose to describe as "dotty" or a bit delusional. Every few months she appeared at her local precinct, and shortly thereafter at our office, to report that Martians, whom she believed to be inhabiting an adjacent apartment, were flashing signals at her through the ceiling and walls in an effort to read and control her brain waves. Needless to say, she was never able to get the police to investigate the matter to her satisfaction.

Among my colleagues was a terrific assistant named Ed

Broderick, who had been in the bureau for a few months before our group arrived, and had probably resolved more complaints than the dozen of us all combined. He listened compassionately to the woman, who appeared in his doorway several times a week after getting her first sympathetic ear. He also spoke to her daughter to make sure she was getting adequate psychiatric attention and care. Then he offered his solution. He handed the grateful, and amazed, woman a small box of paper clips and explained to her that by stringing them together from end to end, attaching them to her belt and letting them reach to the floor, it would have the effect of grounding the signals from the Martians and she would be free of their interference. She was delighted, and from that point on came to Ed's office periodically, with the ever-present chain of paper clips, to express her pleasure at how well the technique was working.

Our most important work was, of course, never that simple and rarely produced such satisfactory results.

For once we began to master the elements of the various crimes detailed in the penal law, we were given the next assignment of duty in what was called the "complaint room."

Room 450 of the Criminal Court Building was a cavernous area in the courthouse divided into a long string of cubicles, each inhabited by a typist, a typewriter, and a couple of chairs. Every time an arrest was made in Manhattan, for any crime whatsoever, the police officer wound up in the complaint room for the purpose of having his arrest papers reviewed by an assistant district attorney.

It was the task of that assistant, a member of the Complaint Bureau, to determine whether the charges were appropriate and, if so, to draft a criminal complaint so the defendant could be brought before a judge and arraigned on that charge.

Every day there was a group of typists assigned to Room 450, and every day several hundred police officers waited in the hallways for their turn to enter one of the cubicles. On a good day, four assistants covered this duty—walking from

51

one area to the next to interview cops and their civilian witnesses in order to dictate the legal language that would create a proper and sufficient document in the courtroom. On a bad day, usually on the busy weekends and holidays, only two of us had to manage the same territory.

The first time I went down to observe the procedures in the complaint room, I had the same experience that most of my colleagues had encountered in years past. It was so busy that after a few hours of my watching my classmates sprint from case to case, someone suggested that I pick up one of the manuals that listed samples of all the charges and get to work. "Don't just stand there and watch—make yourself useful."

The assistants who worked in Room 450 wrote up anywhere between fifty and one hundred cases on any given day. On my first outing, with a great deal of guidance, I slowly cranked out four affidavits.

The range of those four cases was typical of the variety of complaints that we see every day. My very first one was the arrest of a prostitute for grand larceny. As I entered the cubicle and picked up the police reports to review them, the officer introduced himself and presented me to the "victim" of the crime, a thirty-four-year-old businessman from Little Rock, Arkansas. The man had finished his dinner meeting, called home to say good-night to his wife, then picked up a companion on Eighth Avenue and taken her to the hotel room of her choice. Although he had given her the fifty dollars up front and paid for the room for one hour, she had also been able to "roll" him—go through his pants he had left on a chair while he used the bathroom—and she relieved him of another seven hundred dollars in cash.

He sheepishly went on to explain to me that not only did she get the cash, she also got his wedding ring. With much embarrassment, he said that he had removed and pocketed the ring earlier in the evening when he was at a fancy midtown bar, hoping to be able to charm a young woman, not a professional hooker, into bed by pretending to be single. He would never have put the police to this much trouble, he whined apologetically, for only the money, but he just couldn't go home and account for the missing wedding ring.

The young woman was arrested at her usual post, the same corner where he had picked her up. The cash was stuffed inside the leg of one of her boots, and she was wearing the gold band on her right hand. "Can you identify it?" the cop asked. "Of course" was the prompt response. "It's got 'Only you, forever' inscribed inside it." This was not a victim with whom I "bonded."

In the next booth was a corrections officer from the Tombs. He had arrested one of the inmates earlier that day for assaulting another prisoner with an ice pick. The defendant, who was in jail on an arson charge, had fashioned what looked like an ice pick from a metal bedspring in his cell and used it to stab someone else during an argument. The prisoner who had been injured refused to press charges, fearing reprisal from his comrades, and not wanting to be placed in the isolation of protective custody. The assailant was arrested, though, because this officer had been an eyewitness to the attack.

I was catching on to the technique and moved to my third complaint. The arresting officer was a rookie cop who had completed a busy tour of duty late the night before. He left the station house and walked down the block to a parking lot that belonged to the police department to get into his Camaro for the ride home. To his surprise, a man was seated behind the wheel, trying to jump-start the cop's car. The rookie asked what the man was doing, and the thief, apparently unaware that all the cars in the lot belonged to police officers, answered that he was just borrowing the car from a friend. Once in the station house, he was searched and found to be in possession of "burglar's tools," a kit that had seventy-seven car keys on a ring inside it. None of them right for a quick enough getaway.

The day ended with another surprise. The last detective with whom I spoke had arrested a well-known actress, then starring in a Broadway musical, for possession of an unlicensed pistol. He had been summoned to the theater when a caller reported that there was a dispute between two women, one of whom was armed. The actress claimed that she had mistaken the real gun, which was not loaded, for a stage prop and did not know it was real. The detective did not believe her story—especially once he noticed her husband's initials engraved on the side of the pistol.

I went upstairs to the bureau to meet with my supervisor and review the day's work. I felt that I had finally begun my "lawyering" and had had my first taste of dealing with witnesses, which I loved.

CHAPTER FOUR
UP THE LADDER

THAT FIRST WEEK of complaint room duty had been my assignment in April 1973, five months after my arrival in the office. By the July Fourth weekend, I was the most senior in the group of young lawyers staffing the busy room—and I had my first exposure to a crime of sexual violence.

As the complaint room "supervisor," I scanned each of the arrest reports prepared by the officers who came in during those long, hot summer days. The progress of cases through the district attorney's office was likened at that time to a conveyor belt assembly routine. That is, one of the young prosecutors had the first contact, which consisted of interviewing the arresting officer who brought in the case within hours of the arrest. Often, he or she was accompanied by the victim of the crime, who was also questioned in the complaint room. Based on those brief interviews, the junior assistant drafted the charges against the defendant. If the evidence brought before us was legally insufficient to sustain the charge, or if police procedures had been patently improper—like an illegal search of an individual or his home—it was our duty to dismiss the charges immediately.

Those complaints that were drafted proceeded to the

next step along the conveyor belt. The officer took his paperwork to the criminal courtroom on the first floor of the building and waited his turn for the judge to call the case. The defendant was produced from the holding pens to be "arraigned" on the charges and then the judge made a determination about the prisoner's bail.

For the cases that were charged as felonies—the most serious crimes in the penal law, punishable by substantial terms in state prison—the officer and his witness had to return to the courthouse within seventy-two hours of the arraignment. Then they would meet with a different assistant district attorney, who would reinterview each of them in order to present their testimony at a preliminary hearing. That hearing, conducted by a judge, took place in the presence of the defendant, and the witnesses were subject to cross-examination by the defense counsel. At the conclusion of the hearing, the judge determined whether "probable cause" existed to hold the defendant for the action of the grand jury. If so, the case then passed into the hands of yet another assistant, whose duty was in the Indictment Bureau.

Within three weeks after the hearing, the witness or victim testified again before the members of the grand jury, who voted on whether the evidence was legally sufficient to establish "reasonable cause to believe" that the defendant committed the crime with which he was charged. No defendant can be brought to trial for a felony in New York State unless first indicted by a grand jury.

The actual trial of the case was assigned, of course, to a senior attorney on the staff—the fourth prosecutor on the conveyor belt—who was obliged to repeat much of the process, reinterviewing each witness and learning the facts and details of the case.

This system, which worked such a terrible hardship on survivors of sexual assault especially, by forcing them to repeat such intimate details to so many different questioners, was not changed in our office until 1974, when the Sex Crimes Prosecution Unit was created. It was one of the most innovative and effective changes inaugurated by Robert Morgenthau when he restructured the entire office in 1976, to mandate that all felony cases were processed "vertically"—that is, assigned at the intake stage in the complaint room to a single senior assistant, whose duty it became to then handle *every* stage in the prosecution of the case. Such a measure is not only far more efficient for case management, but also much friendlier to the traumatized victims of serious crimes, who are able to establish and maintain a relationship with one lawyer throughout the life of the case.

I can recall with clarity a day in the summer of 1973 when my role in the complaint room was still only the initial step in the course of every complaint. I remember laughing with the first officer who arrived on the morning of July Fourth. He had arrested a defendant in possession of a small amount of an illegal drug, and when I questioned the cop about whether the defendant had made any statements, he told me the defendant had reached out his hands to surrender to the cuffs being placed on him, saying, "I don't know what this country is coming to when a man can be incarcerated on Independence Day!"

I walked from typist to typist, dictating complaints as the officers appeared, following the language in the manual for every standard criminal charge. After completing eight or nine misdemeanors, I entered a booth and asked the waiting detective, "What have you got?" For the first time, I heard the response: "Rape. First-degree rape. The worst."

I had never worked on any aspect of a rape case, and my only connection with this one—which would soon be in the hands of more senior attorneys for each of the successive court proceedings—would be to do the initial interviews and draft the complaint.

"Is the victim here?" I asked.

"No. She's at New York Hospital. She had to be admitted, she's been in almost a week."

Although I did not know it at the time, I came to learn that the overwhelming number of rape cases occur with no demonstrable physical injury done to the victim. Injury is not an element of the crime. So common sense made me assume that the police would suggest emergency room treatment for the victim to determine her well-being after the attack, to test for exposure to venereal disease, and even to collect evidence for a criminal proceeding. I was surprised to hear that the woman had been admitted to the hospital for a week.

The detective told me the story. Eleanor Smith was eighty-two years old. She lived alone in an elegant apartment on Beekman Place and took special pride in the fact that she was able to care for herself without being dependent on family and friends.

On a hot afternoon at the end of June, Mrs. Smith returned home from her marketing to keep an appointment she had made to have her windows washed, as she did every few months. The management of her luxury building had made all the arrangements, as usual, and when the doorbell rang at two o'clock she greeted the young man who had arrived with all of his gear.

As Harold Scott went to work on the large window with its splendid view of the East River, Mrs. Smith poured a cold soda for him, then settled on the living room sofa to listen to an opera recording and read the newspaper. Half an hour later, Scott emerged from the kitchen holding one of Mrs. Smith's carving knives, which he had lifted from its rack on the wall. He came up behind her chair and literally pushed her out of it onto the floor. Her scream, she later told the detective, was an involuntary reaction to being startled by the fall, and the fear that she had injured her once-fractured hip.

For the first minute that Eleanor Smith was on the floor with her own knife in Scott's hand held above her face, she said it never once occurred to her that his demands would be sexual. She told him where her pocketbook was and offered him the jewelry she had on, just to leave her alone and not to hurt her. Scott lifted her skirt and tore at her corset. Eleanor Smith began to understand.

She also became frantic. Her crying made Scott angrier, and he slapped her several times in an effort to shut her up. Then she began to plead with him while his hands fumbled with her clothes, telling him that she couldn't have sex with him, that she hadn't had intercourse since her husband died thirty years before. Nothing reached Scott, and ignoring Eleanor Smith's muffled cries, he raped her on the floor of her living room for more than twenty minutes. He got up, replaced the knife on the kitchen counter, and walked out of Eleanor Smith's apartment, leaving all his equipment behind him.

Mrs. Smith was unable to move. She remained on the floor for almost one hour, with excruciating pain in her bad hip and her heart palpitating wildly. When at last she worked herself onto her feet, she was relieved to find that her hip was bruised but unbroken, and she sat on her sofa and began to sob. She waited several hours, sitting in the same place until the sky darkened in the late evening, before making the decision to call the police.

"But why?" I questioned the detective. "Why did she even think twice about that?"

"I asked her the same thing. She broke down when I was talking to her—all I could see was my mother—I put my arms around her and just held her till she stopped. Finally, she told me she was too embarrassed to tell anyone."

"Embarrassed?"

"Yeah," he went on. "She didn't think anyone would believe that a thirty-year-old man would have any sexual interest in an eighty-two-year-old woman. She kept repeating that she couldn't imagine that she could be the object of anyone's sexual desires, and she did not want anyone else to say that about her!"

"What did you tell her?"

"Everything I could think of that the department teaches us. That rape is motivated by anger and power and control. That it's a crime of violence—with sex as the weapon, not sex the way she thinks about it. She's a brave lady, and she's doing much better now. Everyone has been terrific to her. Imagine living eighty-two years, never hurting a soul, then having this happen? I think I could kill the guy myself."

The detectives had driven Eleanor Smith to the hospital, where the doctors had decided to admit her to be better able to monitor her condition, since she had a history of heart trouble.

I never met Eleanor Smith, nor had any further contact with Scott's case other than to check later on and learn that he had been convicted of rape in the first degree and sentenced to the maximum prison term. But I learned that day, for the first time in my career, that the act that so devastated Eleanor Smith's life, and took twenty-five years of Scott's freedom, was charged in a court of law as one simple, cold statement that I dictated to the typist: rape in the first degree—Penal Law Section 130.35:

> The defendant, Harold Scott (age 30), being a male, engaged in an act of sexual intercourse with Eleanor Smith, a female, by forcible compulsion.

Later that same week, I got a glimpse of my first pattern or serial rapist. A man had been arrested for a series of fifteen rapes, all of which had occurred on the Upper West Side of Manhattan over a period of several weeks. The defendant had devised a clever scheme that successfully gained him access to the homes of many unsuspecting women.

John Miller, an attractive and articulate young man in his mid-twenties, dressed in a khaki outfit that passed for a uniform. He preferred to work the brownstone buildings in the West Seventies and Eighties, presumably because there were no doormen. Miller rang doorbells until he had a response on an intercom from a woman's voice, and then he announced that he was delivering a gift to that woman—

whose name he read off the nameplate strip next to the doorbell. The wariest of his soon-to-be victims asked a few basic questions: "What store is it from?" "Are you with a delivery service?" Of course he had answers, and even when one or two said they had never ordered anything, his polite response was "No, madam, it has a label on it that says 'gift.'" Most of the women were so pleased to be receiving a gift that they buzzed him through the locked vestibule door and waited for him to come upstairs.

When he arrived he either carried with him a brown cardboard box or a clipboard with papers that had to be signed by the recipient—that got him around the women who might direct him to leave it in front of the door—or used his most elaborate ruse, which was to appear with just a tape measure and tell the delighted recipient that she had to open the door so he could measure the frame because the package was so large that he was afraid it might not fit. Once inside, of course, Miller's act became a life-threatening confrontation when he revealed a folding pocketknife and sexually assaulted his victim. It was a dreadful pattern that claimed far too many women and terrorized the neighborhood until his capture that week by an alert group of precinct police officers. Again, I drafted the complaint according to the simple formula printed in the handbook we junior assistants used in our first few months in Room 450—this one was several paragraphs long, one for each victim—and the case was successfully prosecuted by one of my senior colleagues, Jeffrey Rovins.

The last day of the week proved to be the most interesting, although I would not have guessed that at the morning's start. The early part of the day brought the least serious cases; the misdemeanor arrests usually occurred with less police investigation and less corresponding paperwork, so those cops often got to us first. My day began with a thirty-three-year-old defendant, a corporate lawyer, who was charged with criminal mischief (which meant damage to property) and disorderly conduct. The officer explained that the defendant had become intoxicated in one of the popular First Avenue singles bars and ejected by the manager after a loud exchange of words and name-calling. As he left the bar, he grabbed on to and uprooted two slim trees planted in the sidewalk in front of the bar. The cop had stopped him a few blocks away when he saw the defendant staggering up the avenue with a five-foot tree tucked under each arm.

My co-workers and I had almost finished the first round of write-ups when I got a call from one of the lawyers who was in the class ahead of me, and thus working at the next assignment level, the Indictment Bureau. Chuck Heffernan, who later became Mayor Koch's deputy coordinator of the Office of Criminal Justice and then a judge of the Criminal Court, asked if I could try to help him with a case. He arranged to have me relieved in the complaint room and I headed for his office to see what he needed.

We met in the corridor and Chuck described the problem. He was attempting to present a case to the grand jury, but neither he nor the detective nor any of the other male assistants could get the victim to talk. She was six years old, and her mother told Chuck that she seemed to be frightened of all unfamiliar men since she had been sexually assaulted three weeks earlier. Chuck was hopeful that I might be able to make the child more comfortable and ease her into speaking about the crime—without her testimony, the defendant would be freed. Chuck, not only a fine lawyer but also a devoted father, was eager to try any approach that would help the child through this arduous process.

We entered his office, where he introduced me to Mrs. Ruiz and her daughter, Iraida. The first step, as with any witness, was to put the child at ease and attempt to gain her trust. Chuck left the room and I continued to talk with Iraida, asking her what we call background or pedigree questions, eliciting answers about neutral and familiar subjects that she could respond to without emotion. She told me that she had been born in the Dominican Republic and moved to New York City one year before. She was completely bilingual and liked to talk about her new school and her new friends, and how she was helping her mother to learn English.

By the time we had chatted for ten or fifteen minutes, I asked Mrs. Ruiz to go to the soda machine to get Iraida a drink. Chuck had explained to her earlier that it was best if we spoke alone with the child, and that seemed a logical way to have her slip out of the room without objection from Iraida. I learned from my colleagues the critical importance of speaking to every victim alone—for a variety of reasons. Prime among them is that when we repeat some of the details of traumatic crimes in the presence of someone we care about, most of us instinctively alter things—important facts or minor details—to save the other person even more pain.

Children, even very young ones, have the same instincts. They occasionally leave out details or cut the story off abruptly when they see how their parents react. Mrs. Ruiz had been very supportive and loving, but it was still better practice for us to determine that Iraida had neither withheld any of the facts nor been prompted to add anything by her mother.

I asked the child if she knew why she was in our office that day.

"Yes," she replied softly, "it's about the man. Carlos. What he did."

"That's right." And I tried to make her understand that it was important for her to tell us exactly what had happened to her because we, Chuck and I, were going to help her so that the judge would be able to punish Carlos. Iraida knew from her mother's initial response to her that Carlos had done something very bad and that he had to be punished.

She wouldn't look at me at all when she began to tell the story, but slowly and quietly—without a single tear—Iraida described what Carlos had done to her.

On a day when Mrs. Ruiz was late returning to the apartment after work, Iraida had waited for her in the lobby of the building. Carlos, the superintendent, whom the child had known since moving to the apartment, suggested that she visit with him in the basement, his office, so that she would not be alone. He held out his hand and the child took it trustingly, accompanying him as she had on other occasions. But always those other times her brother had been along too. This time, in the silent isolation of the tiny room, Carlos undressed her as she cried and raped her on the cot that stood against the dusty wall. He let her out of the room minutes later, telling her that this was their own "little secret," and that he would hurt her brother and mother if she told anyone what he had done.

Mrs. Ruiz entered the front door of her building to find Iraida whimpering inside the hallway. The story poured out of the child's mouth as soon as her mother began to undress her and saw the bloodstained underpants. They went directly to Columbia Presbyterian Hospital, where the medical team treated the child and called in the local precinct detectives. Carlos was arrested within the hour.

Chuck was able to go to the grand jury, to have Iraida testify in front of twenty-three stunned adults, having won her over during the course of that long summer day. She was a smart child, and there was much physical evidence to support her sad story. By the end of the afternoon she was laughing again—mostly at the sight of her mother, Chuck, and me all smeared with the remains of chocolate bars. We had supplied Iraida with Hershey bars from the candy machine—she preferred them to lunch—and every time she held one of our hands or touched our sleeves, we accumulated more melted chocolate, until even she was amused by the sight.

Iraida's case provided my first experience working with a rape victim, of getting her through a difficult proceeding that was required by law, and learning that with patience, care for her emotional condition, and understanding of her needs it was indeed possible to have her participate in the criminal justice system without inflicting additional harm upon her. I felt tremendous satisfaction that day—perhaps I saw a glimpse of my future.

SEXUAL VIOLENCE

*   *   *

At the completion of our rotation through the Complaint Bureau, my class moved on to the Indictment Bureau in October 1973. There, under the leadership of an outstanding pair of lawyers, Bill Murphy and Sam Yasgur, I began to learn the real skills of questioning witnesses and presenting evidence, as we spent all of our days before the grand juries. Both Bill and Sam had worked their way through the ranks of the office to become bureau chiefs—they were not much older than those of us they taught and supervised, and very knowledgeable and great teachers. Bill, who for more than a decade has served as the district attorney on Staten Island, and Sam, who went on to private practice, contributed significantly to transforming our group into "lawyers."

It is the Constitution of New York State that established the grand jury as the body responsible for the protection of the rights of individuals accused of crimes. It is, as well, the only authority that can decide who should be put to the risk and trial of felony prosecution for criminal matters. Although the grand jury has other functions, its most common duty in our jurisdiction is this charging action.

It is at this stage as assistant district attorneys that we learn some of our most critical responsibilities, since we perform three roles before a grand jury. First, we present the evidence in every felony case, since we are the public prosecutors. Our second role is quasi-judicial, in that we make decisions (later reviewed by a Supreme Court justice) about the competency of witnesses and the sufficiency of evidence, and charge the jurors on matters of law. The third function we have is that of advising the grand jurors—an extremely powerful position—for we must present not only all competent evidence, but exculpatory evidence and witnesses as well (that is, evidence consistent with the defendant's innocence, when it exists).

At the time of our move into the bureau, our class of twelve learned by lecture and demonstration how to inter-

65

view witnesses and how to prepare and present evidence to a grand jury. We also learned by example, as we watched our more senior colleagues in action throughout the first several weeks. When we began our own tentative presentations, it was usually with "simple" cases—cases with a single evidentiary issue, like illegal possession of a weapon, in which the only witness was a police officer. Most of the time, the experienced officers had appeared before grand juries on many occasions, which made the process of witness preparation with them much easier than with civilians.

Our days began, after an hour or so at our desks reviewing case paperwork, by positioning ourselves behind a long counter in one of the grand jury waiting rooms by 9:30 in the morning to meet with and begin interviewing police officers. Adjacent to the actual room in which witnesses would testify, our counters faced rows of benches on which cops and crime victims waited throughout the day for the opportunity to appear and testify. One by one, each officer's name was called out and he or she walked to the counter, where three or four of us stood shoulder to shoulder, interrogating witnesses we were meeting for the first time about the details of their cases. A "good" assistant—one conversant with the law, street-smart, and skilled at efficient questioning—could present between ten and fifteen felony cases a day, as we vied with one another for the highest monthly totals.

Two things slowed the assistants down and cut into the daily output significantly: "paper" cases—frauds, bad checks, banking matters with a lot of complicated record-keeping evidence that inevitably took an entire morning to sort out, comprehend, and fashion into a coherent presentation—and of course, sex offenses, because the problems they presented were like no other cases.

In the first place, the survivors of sexual assaults did not belong packed in a row of benches alongside other prospective witnesses, waiting to be debriefed in the crowded and public roomful of strangers. Even the most aggressive assistants perceived the need to remove those victims from that setting and return down the long corridors to the privacy of their own offices for the interviews. Also, a case involved not only the survivor herself and the police officer, but often medical witnesses and evidence, as well as the person to whom the victim had made the first outcry. It was usually difficult to prepare presentations in less than a few hours. And most important, the overwhelming number of these victims had very special emotional needs unique to this crime. Not all of them could tell their stories to a complete stranger, the assistant district attorney, with ease, much less anticipate facing a room of twenty-three grand jurors to describe such an intimate assault.

Each of us within the bureau recognized the problems presented by these cases. Most of us attempted to handle them with the care and compassion they so obviously required over and above the ordinary legal skills. And it was also clear that not every lawyer liked this particular challenge. I, though, was among the group who looked forward to working on these sensitive cases.

In no other category of crime does the victim approach the criminal justice system with lower expectations of a successful resolution than in the area of sex offenses. Centuries of inequities in the rape laws were responsible for the minuscule number of prosecutions nationwide, until the major legislative changes that occurred in the 1960s and 1970s. That problem created images of what awaited survivors in the courtroom, and brought them to our offices expecting the worst.

During the nine months that I spent in the Indictment Bureau, which was *before* the creation of any Sex Crimes Prosecution Unit, I interviewed more than one hundred victims of sex offenses—children, senior citizens, contemporaries, women who knew their assailants, and those who had been attacked by strangers. In each instance, it was a prosecutor's responsibility to strive for exactly the right balance in a most difficult situation: to gain the trust and confidence of the victim in order to elicit all of the facts of the case and make a valid courtroom presentation, to offer support and understanding that would enable the survivor to get through the impersonal proceedings required by the system, and yet—as with every other crime—to critically evaluate the facts of the case to determine whether the charges were legally sufficient and that the right individual had been charged with the crime. It is a very delicate balance, indeed.

CHAPTER FIVE
THE DETECTIVE AND THE MIDTOWN RAPIST

GEORGE ZITIS did not expect that it would be a quiet evening when he reported to work at six P.M. on July 3, 1985. Detectives in the Manhattan Sex Crimes Squad knew the summer months always brought an increase in rape cases. Warm weather and long hours of daylight kept more people outside more of the time, in parks and playgrounds, on stoops and rooftops, all over the city. More prey available for molesters, with the heat providing an added advantage of allowing them to remove their pants without freezing their genitals during an attack.

There are a handful of detectives in the squad who have exceptional talent in this field, and George was among them. (George died tragically of cancer about three years ago.) Forty years old, he had the intelligence and good instincts of the best street cop, and a warm, gentle manner and easy humor that helped him establish an excellent rapport with the most reticent of victims.

He entered the second-floor squad room of the West Eighty-second Street office and was told by the administrative aide who logged him in that the boss already had an assignment for him.

"What's it about?" George asked, holding out his hand toward the lieutenant for the "scratch," the preliminary report phoned in by the uniformed patrolmen who had first gone to the scene in response to the victim's call to 911.

"Sixty-two-year-old woman—sodomy—knife point—just came in twenty minutes ago, so they're waiting for you at her office. It's in one of those old commercial loft buildings in midtown, Thirty-first Street just west of Fifth Avenue."

The detectives usually worked in teams of two, but manpower was especially low during the summer-vacation period and George had to head out on this one by himself.

"What a dump," he chuckled to himself as he got the first piece of bad news; he would have to walk up the steep flights of stairs to the seventh floor because another group of detectives was at work "processing" the elevator. (The Crime Scene Unit, also a specialty squad, sends its men to crime scenes in very serious felony cases to photograph the location and examine it thoroughly for any forensic evidence.) As George walked up the dim, filthy staircase to the victim's workplace, he knew that the elevator would yield no clues: too many people in it all day, pushing the same few buttons over and over, would leave no clean, liftable fingerprints.

So he kept his head down as he mounted the staircase, hoping that another equally remote possibility had occurred: that the rapist had entered or fled by the staircase and accidentally dropped some identifying paper or document. Hard to believe, George thought, but he knew of many cases that had been solved because the inept defendants had left something in their trails that had led the police right to their doorsteps.

But there was no such luck this time. George reached the top of the stairs and was met by a uniformed cop guarding the entrance to Denman Creations. "She's inside with my partner," he explained as George identified himself with his gold detective shield. "She's in bad shape."

"Tell me something I don't already know," George mumbled as he pushed open the heavy door and entered an enormous workroom which appeared to occupy the entire floor of the old building. George never expected to find anyone in very good shape under these circumstances. He headed back through row after row of tables topped with commercial sewing machines toward the two figures he saw at the rear of the hot, airless factory space.

Sylvia Becker was seated at a desk in the far corner, crying quietly into a handkerchief pressed against her mouth. P.O. Paul Hartman, leaning against an adjacent desk, recognized George from more than a dozen of the cases the two had worked together during the past few years and walked forward to greet him.

Sylvia reminded George of a wounded doe as she started and straightened up at the sound of footsteps in the still room, a look of terror and fear in her eyes at the approach of yet another stranger.

Hartman introduced Sylvia Becker to George, who calmly began to tell her that the investigation would be his responsibility from that point onward, that he would explain everything to her each step of the way, that he would be available to her around the clock, that he was going to accompany her to a hospital very shortly, and that he would do everything in his power—with her assistance—to get the man who had done this to her.

George looked around the grim, impersonal surroundings of the sweatshop. "Is there somewhere more private we can talk?" he asked her as his voice echoed throughout the empty room. He wanted to make her physically comfortable and question her in a setting more conducive to eliciting the information, so intimate in nature, that he would need to begin his investigation.

"There's only my boss's office. But I could never use that without asking him first."

"Don't worry about that, I'll explain it to him."

George sent Hartman downstairs to get the iced tea and aspirin that Sylvia requested and guided her into Jack Denman's office. The office, set off from the rest of the dingy factory space, was air-conditioned and nicely furnished. He settled Sylvia onto the large sofa and began the process of trying to get her to relax.

"I can't believe this happened to me—it's like a bad dream. Thirty-two years I've worked here and never a bad moment. What did I do to deserve this? It's a nightmare."

Let her ventilate, George thought, it's a good sign. He had learned that at the department training seminars he had attended years ago and seen it happen enough times to know that it was a healthy thing for the victim to do. Keep her talking, let her get some of her feelings out of her system and express them to someone. Sylvia went on for several minutes, not with facts about the crime but about the circumstances that had kept her at the office, late and alone, on the eve of the holiday weekend.

"Would you like me to call anyone to be here with you? Anyone you want to meet us at the hospital?" George asked her.

"Only Jack," Sylvia answered. "He's my boss—like my best friend after all this time. But the other officers already called him and he's supposed to be on his way here."

She went on to explain that she lived with her mother, who was eighty-five years old and infirm, and she couldn't possibly upset her by telling her about the attack.

George was ready to start asking questions and was keen to do it before Hartman returned with the tea. He needed to confirm, for example, that the assailant had not ejaculated in Sylvia's mouth or he would not be able to allow her to drink anything before the hospital examination. That was no place to begin, though, so when she finished talking about how eager all the young seamstresses had been to get out of the shop that afternoon, George asked her if she felt up to answering some questions for him.

"But I've already told the other men everything I remember," she said. Sylvia had worked for Jack Denman for three decades, starting as a secretary and now running the factory and showroom as his administrative assistant. He had promised his workers that he would close the place at three on the afternoon before Independence Day, but Sylvia had stayed until five to finish her bookkeeping.

When she had rung for the elevator, the doors opened and a very polite young man smiled at her and held open the door as she locked up the factory and got on with him. As soon as the door closed and before the elevator even reached the sixth floor, the young man pressed the stop button and pulled a knife from his waistband. Sylvia told the officers that her assailant demanded all her money and her jewelry, then forced her back upstairs to the workroom, into a small lavatory near the front door, where he forced her to kneel and to take his penis into her mouth.

She had begun to gag almost immediately and he angrily withdrew. He wanted her to undress and lie down on her back, but the bathroom was too small and he was annoyed because she wouldn't stop crying. Then he left.

George knew that this summary was not "everything."

What he needed were the details—the exact words spoken by the man, every item he had touched, every observation she had made about him, no matter how irrelevant they seemed to her. He had to make her reconstruct the assault, every dreadful second of it, and gently prod her through the ten to twenty minutes she had been compelled to spend with this total stranger.

"I know this is difficult for you, Miss Becker," he said. "But I've got to take you through it again." He explained what he wanted and why it was necessary.

"Yes, yes of course," she said, "sure I'll try to help you. I doubt it will do any good, though. It's like looking for a needle in a haystack."

Maybe so, George admitted to himself. Maybe this was just an isolated strike by a guy who has never done it before and won't do it again. But the more likely reality, as his gut told him, was that this man had some experience, and this would not be his last assault.

Sylvia took a deep breath and started again. She had

walked out of Denman Creations a few minutes before five and rung for the elevator. She explained that it arrived before she had finished locking the door, and she turned to the young man to suggest he go ahead and send it back for her. He told her it was "no problem" and politely held it open. She got on and the doors had no sooner closed than he pulled out the long knife with the black handle that he held against Sylvia's neck.

George knew that he was going to get a good description from Sylvia. The encounter began as a face-to-face meeting—lots of attackers grab their victims from behind and they never get to see more than a profiled glimpse of him; the area on the seventh-floor landing and the interior of the elevator cab were well lighted; and Sylvia was better than she gave herself credit for at providing detail.

"He said, 'Just give me your money and your jewelry. I won't hurt you if you give 'em to me,' " Sylvia continued.

So far, George thought, this was like a million other elevator stick-ups happening every day. The guys from Crime Scene shouldn't have wasted more than ten minutes in that elevator—the only buttons he might even have had a partial tip on were the stop button, and maybe the one for the first floor, if he hadn't run down the steps on his way out.

Now George knew he had to ease her through the more difficult part of the ordeal.

"What's inside?" the man had asked Sylvia.

"Nothing."

"Be quiet—don't yell—you're taking me in."

Sylvia said that her hands had been shaking so badly that she couldn't fit the key into the lock, so he grabbed it from her and got them inside. No lights were on but daylight still streamed through the tall windows.

"Where's the bathroom? I want you to stay inside the bathroom while I look around." But as Sylvia had stepped into the tiny room, in which the toilet and sink barely fit, the man had pushed her down onto the toilet seat.

"You know what I want you to do," he said, the knife pinching the side of her neck.

"No, I don't," Sylvia pleaded. And she hadn't known, she hadn't a clue. "I've given you everything I have—my watch, my necklace, my money. Please leave me alone."

"You want me to hurt you?"

"No."

"You want me to kill you?"

"No."

Then he unzipped his pants with his free hand and told Sylvia to "take it out." What he was going to do became clear to her, and she was shaking and crying and pleading with him not to do it.

Sylvia stopped and looked up at George when she reached that part of the story. "Then, you know, he made me do it, whatever you call it."

George knew that Sylvia wanted *him* to say the words, and to make this be over with. But he knew he couldn't do that, he couldn't assume any of the facts, and he would have to get her to describe just what had occurred, and whether the elements of the crime, in this case sodomy, had been accomplished.

Sylvia went over it again. Yes, the man had been talking a lot. He had asked her if she did this with her "old man," if it was better this time, and even wanted to know what her bra size was when he reached up under her blouse to run his hands over her breasts. He had finally grabbed the back of her head with his left hand and pushed her face against his penis, and had forced it into her mouth. She gagged instantly and actively, and he stepped back from her, telling her, "Shit, you're no good at this."

Then he put the knife down on the sink top, removed a rolled-up newspaper from his rear pants pocket and laid that down too, and started to unbutton his pants, telling Sylvia to get down on the floor. He was still facing her at this point, bracing himself with one hand against the mirror over the sink.

It was clear to both of them that the room just wasn't big enough. The man cursed again and seemed to have decided that Sylvia wasn't worth the aggravation. He pulled up his pants, told Sylvia to stay in that room until she heard the noise of the elevator from the hallway, picked up his knife, and walked out.

Sylvia collapsed into sobs as soon as he walked out. She reached up to bolt the door against the possibility of his return, but remembered that it had been her own idea to remove the lock so the girls didn't stay in there smoking for long periods of time. He was gone, however, and eventually Sylvia let herself out of the tiny room.

George told Sylvia she was terrific—smart and very brave—and let her sip her tea while he went on with questions about the assailant's description.

At first she said, "I'm awful at that kind of thing. I'm no good at guessing heights and weights. That's what I told the other cops."

But George had other ways to get the same information. Sylvia was a big woman—five nine she told George. Yes, she remembered standing face-to-face with him in the elevator, and he was a little taller, no more than an inch or two. She was able to approximate the level of his eyes by comparing it to her own. She remembered that because she had been trying to look him in the eyes, to appeal to him and talk him out of hurting her. But she also remembered that she couldn't actually see his eyes because he had dark sunglasses on, the kind that "you can't see into from the outside."

For the weight estimate, George suggested comparing him to the cops who had responded, if any resembled his build. Yes, Sylvia told him, the young one, Hartman's partner who had remained at the door, had a very similar frame, lean like the attacker, very lean.

Sylvia laughed then—for the first time that afternoon. "After working in the business thirty years, I should be able to tell you not only what he was wearing, but who made it and where he bought it." She gave a detailed description of his clothing—his jeans, including the color and design of the stitching; the style of his underwear; the brand of his sneakers; the kind of windbreaker he wore despite the ninety-degree heat; and the dark blue felt baseball cap with its insignia of the Toronto Blue Jays.

They were just about through with this first phase of interviewing, and George sensed Sylvia needed a break. He was ready to take her over to Bellevue Hospital to be examined by a physician, given antibiotics as a prophylactic measure in the event her assailant had venereal disease, and put in the care of the rape-crisis advocates who would help her deal with the emotional and psychological aftereffects throughout the weeks that would follow.

George stepped out of Jack Denman's office into the main room. He told Hartman to bring the guys from Crime Scene upstairs. The only lucky break in this might come, if at all, in the small bathroom, and he wanted to get them working on it before anyone else went inside.

Fingerprint evidence, a successful device in television and movies, is a luxury in real police work at actual crime scenes. However, bathrooms are often an unusually good place to find prints, having lots of smooth surfaces conducive to retaining the oils that compose a fingerprint, and George was hopeful that the attacker had left some distinctive evidence behind. Sylvia was sure that he had touched the mirror and sink—he had braced himself against them—and the glass and porcelain were good places for the experts to concentrate their efforts.

The last thing to do, before setting the uniformed cops a schedule to canvass the other tenants in the building, was for George to call his office and update the lieutenant. "Hey, boss, we're all done here. I'm taking Miss Becker to Bellevue now, then I'll stop for a sandwich and come back to the office to fill you in."

"Not so fast. Looks like your man hit again."

"What?"

Lieutenant Marcus explained that a call had come in

shortly after George left the squad office at six. "Right around the corner from where you are, one of the big office buildings on Fifth Avenue. Sounds like the same description from the nine-one-one calls, only the second time he got what he wanted—a completed rape. She's still at her office with our men, so you can talk to her there."

Sick bastard, thought George, obviously wasn't satisfied when he couldn't ejaculate with Sylvia, so he just kept stalking till he got off. George hung up the phone and headed back to get Sylvia for the short ride across town to the hospital.

After George Zitis had delivered Sylvia Becker into the care of the Bellevue Hospital medical team, he raced back to Fifth Avenue and Twenty-ninth Street to meet forty-two-year-old Tanya Johnson. The short interview confirmed his hunch—the midtown rapist, who had not gotten everything he wanted from his encounter with Sylvia Becker, had simply walked a couple of blocks and started over again in another building, less than fifteen minutes later.

Once more the same description of the attacker, his clothes, and his weapon. Once more the victim accosted at the elevator by a smiling, seemingly polite stranger who forced her off at a vacant floor, took her jewelry, and then said, "That's not enough." Again into a bathroom, more threats, and a completed sexual assault. Tanya Johnson remained in the deserted toilet area throwing up uncontrollably before going back to the elevator to find someone to help her in the emptied-out tower of offices.

Zitis did not want to hear any more of these stories. A rapist so compulsive he struck twice in the same afternoon in the middle of Manhattan's commercial district, seeming to leave no clues. Tanya Johnson gave Zitis all the details he had come to expect, went to her private physician for her examination, and the next day looked through hundreds of photographs, like all the survivors who preceded her—"With negative results," as George Zitis would type at the bottom of yet one more police report.

CHAPTER SIX
THE SCPU

THE YEAR I joined the District Attorney's Office—1972—was, quite by coincidence, the year that major changes began to take place in sex crimes legislation. One need not be a legal scholar to appreciate the significance of these long-overdue revisions, for it was the archaic mandate of the law that had made rape cases impossible to prosecute for so many decades.

New York changed its laws for adult victims in part by 1972, and further in 1974. Since then, a survivor can testify without corroboration that the assault has involved a sexual act, and that it was without her consent, describing the force or threat employed by the attacker. The jurors can credit her or not, as they listen to the testimony and observe her demeanor—she does have her day in court.

This change was an enormous step toward our ability to convict rapists. It was also a threshold point for changing people's attitudes about sex offenses, making it clear that the victim's word is "enough" and that rape survivors can, at long last, be given the same access to the system as the victims of every other kind of crime. By eliminating the corroboration requirement, the lawmakers eliminated the unjust *codification of the lack of trust in the credibility and honesty of women.*

During this critical period in the evolution of the sexual assault laws, there was a handful of lawyers who had recognized the inequities and who had been battling for the legislative changes. Among them was Leslie Crocker Snyder, now an acting justice of the Supreme Court of the State of New York, who as an assistant district attorney in Manhattan devoted tremendous effort to the cause of rape survivors.

During the late 1960s, the Justice Department created an agency called the Law Enforcement Assistance Administration (LEAA), which was empowered to provide funding to states and cities for projects in the criminal justice field. Snyder drafted a proposal for a special grant based on an innovative plan for the prosecution of sex crimes, establishing a unit within the New York County District Attorney's Office to treat the special needs and unique problems of sex crimes victims.

The Sex Crimes Prosecution Unit, the first of its kind in the country, came into existence in 1974. Snyder, its founder and first bureau chief, was assisted by only one other colleague in the early days of its operation. Since those two lawyers had a steady caseload as a result of the new laws, junior assistants—my classmates and I—were able to work on some sex offenses, under the guidance of the unit, to help handle the overflow. Now, two decades later, the district attorney assigns more than twenty senior prosecutors to the unit to work on these cases.

The credit for the expansion of this unit and the devotion of resources to this critical area of victimization goes entirely to Robert Morgenthau. From the outset, it was clear that he had a special concern for the prosecution of sexual assault cases. Aware that the LEAA grant which had originally made the unit's funding possible had a finite lifetime of just three years, Morgenthau incorporated the unit as a permanent part of the office structure and began the expansion of its staff to meet the demands of the growing reports of sexual assaults. To this day, there is no other prosecutor in the country who has matched Morgenthau's commitment to the investigation and prosecution of these offenses.

There are a number of reasons why the existence of such a specialized unit enhances the ability to better serve the community. First, sex offenses occupy a unique place in the criminal justice system because of the more traumatic nature of the crimes, the most personal invasions an individual can sustain. A key feature of this unit is the recognition that these survivors require treatment that is different from any other crime victims—from very basic practical aspects like removing them from among the large pool of people waiting in the office complaint room every day to have stolen car cases or petit larceny cases drafted by typists, to be able to interview them in more private settings; eliminating for them the "conveyor belt" system which requires that they repeat their stories to four or five different assistant district attorneys during the course of the prosecution; assuring that the cases are handled *only* by lawyers who have an interest in the special needs of these victims; and directing survivors to the appropriate medical and counseling facilities.

Second, sex offenses are more difficult to prosecute than other felony crimes—the intimate nature of the testimony that must be elicited from the complaining witness works a greater hardship on her, and the fact that there is so little understanding of *why* these crimes occur often confounds the jurors in their decision-making process. Although it is not necessary for a prosecutor to prove to a jury the motive for a criminal act—why the crime occurred—jurors almost always struggle with that issue in rape cases because it is so difficult to comprehend that one could force another human being, often a total stranger, to commit sexual acts. We need not only to make the victim more comfortable throughout the entire process, but to understand and anticipate which issues will trouble jurors and present arguments to address those concerns directly.

Third, we have to convict those rapists who are guilty of the crimes charged. Obviously, before the corroboration requirement was eliminated, only a fraction of the assailants had ever been brought to trial. Now we have the momentum of the recent passage of improved legislation and the raising of public consciousness to a new level. Morgenthau's selection of experienced prosecutors and creation of a training program, combined with the close cooperation of the New York Police Department's special units, occasion a swift and dramatic increase in the convictions of these assailants.

The creation of this innovative unit in the District Attorney's Office corresponded with a similar plan undertaken by the New York Police Department. In 1972, the NYPD established two programs to improve services for victims of sexual violence.

One was the Sex Crimes Analysis Unit (SCAU), which has as one of its goals to facilitate and encourage the reporting of sexual assault cases. At that time Federal Bureau of Investigation surveys estimated that only *one* out of every ten women who was the victim of rape reported the crime. The SCAU, which was then staffed entirely by female police officers, maintains a twenty-four-hour hot line service. Victims are encouraged to call at any time, report crimes (remaining anonymous if they wish), receive advice about the criminal justice system, and be directed to medical and legal follow-up.

Although the initial officers wanted to bring survivors into the system, there remains a valid purpose for anonymous or so-called blind reporting of these cases. In such reports, the callers describe the offense but do not identify themselves, at least during the first conversation when they are reluctant to do this. But these calls are important to law enforcement to assist in determining the volume of the crime's occurrence and to detect patterns in locations and modus operandi of serial offenders. With a compassionate officer on the hot line, the blind report is ideally the first step in gaining the victim's trust toward making a formal report.

The SCAU is also vital in amassing data on the behavior patterns of rapists citywide. The officers can compile reports and recognize common perpetrators—sometimes, fortunately, providing leads for other detectives to make arrests. The precinct police are thereby able to link a captured criminal to a series of previously committed crimes, based on SCAU data.

The other program the department created was to have a detective office in each of New York City's five boroughs to specialize only in the investigation of cases of sexual assault. These offices were designated the Sex Crimes Investigation Squads and twenty years later renamed the Special Victims Squads, handling both sexual assault cases and child abuse, both sexual and physical.

The Manhattan squad was originally a team of twenty-five men and women, selected for a combination of investigative talent and experience, as well as sensitivity to the needs of rape survivors. The department developed special training seminars to enhance understanding of the psychological needs of victims and the tools to aid them in regaining control of their lives, since the detectives are often the first people to encounter survivors after the occurrence of the crime.

According to the procedures established by the NYPD when the specialty squads were created, the detective units are to investigate all allegations of first-degree sexual assault. That is, after a crime victim has reported an attack to the police, usually by dialing 911, the first officers on the scene are uniformed police on patrol in the vicinity. Although those cops take the initial report of the crime, they immediately refer it to or bring in the detectives from the Special Victims Squads, who are thereafter responsible for every step of the investigation.

The experience of the public in New York City, from the inception of these squads through their present role today—

although they are severely understaffed because of budget constraints—has been overwhelmingly positive. Time and time again, my colleagues and I have heard survivors compliment the understanding and compassion, and certainly the professional capability, of the police officers who handle these difficult investigations.

CHAPTER SEVEN

A FEW WORDS ON PROCEDURE

T HERE IS a certain standard route that cases take when a defendant is brought into the criminal justice system charged with a crime of sexual violence. Although there are variations in jurisdictions all over the country, the general procedure is quite similar, especially where special prosecution units have been established to handle these offenses.

Once an arrest of a suspect has been completed, a formal complaint is drawn up by an assistant district attorney. The complaint sets forth the facts, which must contain the elements of every crime charged as well as the date, time, and place of its occurrence.

As the prosecutor prepares the complaint, based on his or her conversation with the arresting officer, the defendant is in the custody of the Department of Correction—usually a holding pen in the courthouse—where he is photographed and fingerprinted. Then he is brought into the criminal court and appears before a judge at a proceeding called an arraignment. At this stage, the defendant's lawyer—either privately retained or appointed by the court because the accused is indigent—represents him. The judge informs the defendant of the charges against him, and if the defendant pleads not guilty, then the judge sets bail in the case. In New York, the arraignment must occur within twenty-four hours of the suspect's arrest. The survivor of the crime does *not* need to appear at an arraignment, and most don't.

For the average citizen who has no familiarity with the criminal law until victimized, it often comes as a surprise to learn that the accused is entitled to have the court set bail, in an amount that our Constitution says cannot be "excessive." For recent victims, the setting of a relatively modest bail for a criminal who attacked them hours before is often quite shocking and confusing.

This confusion is entangled in the fundamental premise of our system of justice: that the defendant is "presumed innocent" until convicted, at trial or by a plea of guilty. And because of that presumption, preventive detention is prohibited. Thus when a judge determines the amount of bail in a particular case, he or she is *not* evaluating the credibility of the victim or complaining witness, but rather is considering the likelihood that the accused will remain within the court's jurisdiction and return to face the charges against him in future court appearances. Bail is often granted, even in cases where the evidence against the defendant is substantial, when he meets the criteria used in consideration of his bail status.

The factors that are important in bail considerations include what we colloquially call the defendant's "roots in the community," as Lisa Moreno learned when James Morales was arrested. The judge will begin with the recognition that the offense charged is extremely serious, as for example, any forcible sex offense. The merits or strengths of the prosecutor's case are also at issue (so that, in a rape case involving a stranger, the judge may give more weight to an identification made by a victim two weeks after an attack than he would to an identification made six months thereafter). And finally, the suspect's status or "roots" are considered, including whether or not he lives in the community, with whom he lives and for how long, his employment status, and his criminal history. An accused with no previous arrests who lives with his parents in the same county as the court and has been steadily employed for five years will be eligible for much lower bail than an unemployed ex-convict who lives in a transient hotel—even when charged with exactly the same crime.

Once the judge examines these considerations and bail is determined, the defendant may remain at liberty if he is able to post the amount required to ensure his appearance in court, whether it is five hundred or fifty thousand dollars. Occasionally, in extreme circumstances, such as a defendant charged with a series of rapes who has three earlier felony convictions, the judge may decided to "remand" the suspect, in which case no bail is set at all. On the other hand, in some instances (and most frequently in acquaintance, as opposed to stranger, rapes) in which the defendant seems an unlikely risk to flee the jurisdiction, he will be released on "parole." That term, borrowed from the French, means that he is at liberty on his "word" or promise that he will return to face the charges against him.

The requirements for bail, remand, and parole are the same for crimes of sexual violence as they are for any other charges in the penal law. Naturally, most survivors of violent crimes are upset by the idea of the assailant not being incarcerated and fear it is a reflection upon the merits of their case or upon their credibility. They are also fearful, especially if the defendant knows where they live or work, that he will return to harm them—which is certainly a valid concern. It is essential that a prosecutor explain the purpose of bail and its use to procure the defendant's appearance at future proceedings. It is also critical that the Court issue a protective order, which makes it a new and separate criminal offense for the assailant to have any contact with the victim.

At the arraignment, the judge also sets the next court date for the accused, and the case is "adjourned"—the legal expression for a postponement—until that time.

It is at this point that variations occur in the processing of cases, often depending on local laws and practices.

When I began in the District Attorney's Office, the next

phase for all felony cases was a preliminary hearing, at which the prosecution had to prove to the court that probable cause that a crime had been committed and that there was reason to believe that the accused was the assailant indeed existed. That hearing, held within the same week as the defendant's arraignment, *did* require the presence of the survivor, who was required to testify about the attack in the presence of the defendant, subject to cross-examination by his lawyer. In effect, it was like a mini trial and worked an enormous hardship on the witness because it occurred so shortly after the crime itself in the overwhelming number of cases. The victim was required to face her accuser, often before her recovery process had even commenced.

Fortunately, one of the innovations put into operation by Leslie Snyder when she inaugurated the unit in 1974 was an effort to bypass the preliminary hearing in as many sexual assault cases as possible. For this, the cases had to be presented to a grand jury within the same rapid time frame following arraignment, because the law in New York mandates that no felony can be prosecuted unless there has been an indictment voted and filed by a grand jury.

You might well ask what is the advantage to the survivor if she still must testify so quickly at either a hearing or grand jury. The advantage is, in fact, enormous and this latter route can be made far more comfortable for the witness while still preserving the rights of the accused.

A grand jury, despite its size, has the distinct advantage of being a closed or "secret" proceeding, not held in an open, public courtroom. Of greater significance is that when the survivor testifies, the defendant is *not* present, nor is his attorney. Thus she neither has to appear in the presence of her attacker at this stage nor is she subjected to cross-examination. The only people in the room for the testimony are the victim, the prosecutor who questions each witness, a court stenographer to record the testimony, and the grand jurors themselves.

The defendant has the right to appear and testify before

the grand jury, and if he elects to do so it is not in the presence of his victim. He cannot be required to give any testimony, either at this stage or at the trial, but may do so if he wishes. In fact, defendants rarely appear before the grand jury.

Most witnesses are rather pleasantly surprised to find that their grand jury presentations seldom take more than ten or fifteen minutes. It is never the ordeal that preliminary hearings used to be, often taking hours to complete because of the cross-examination process. This procedural innovation was one of the first ways the needs of sexual assault survivors were creatively met in Manhattan. It required no legislative reform and no additional financial resources, and worked a great benefit to the women who have participated in the prosecution of their attackers.

Following the presentation of the evidence in a case, the grand jurors have three options. They can vote to indict the defendant, which means to charge him formally with a felony sex offense and is referred to as voting a "true bill." They can return the case to the criminal courts with the instruction that it be reduced to a misdemeanor (a less serious crime, with lesser penalties). Or, in some cases, the grand jury can choose the third option, which is to dismiss the charges against the accused, which is the conclusion of the case in the system.

Upon the filing of the indictment in the Supreme Court, which is the court having jurisdiction of felonies in New York State, the defendant again appears before a judge to be arraigned on the indictment. It is a process similar to the arraignment on the underlying complaint, and again, the victim does not have to appear in the courtroom.

From this point on, it falls to the assistant district attorney as well as to the defense counsel to prepare their respective cases for trial. Most of the adjournments are carefully controlled by the judges, since our Constitution also mandates a defendant's right to a speedy trial. The legally sanctioned delays allow a period of "discovery" during which the defense is entitled to make a variety of motions in order to properly gain access to information necessary for the trial of the case. Counsel for the accused may move to suppress evidence gathered by the police—such as a weapon recovered from the suspect or distinctive clothing found in his home—on the grounds that the police action was improper or illegal. The judge may rule on such motions based on the representations made by lawyers on each side, or he or she may require hearings in order to make a determination. Once again, the presence of the witness is very rarely required at such hearings (unless, for example, there is an impropriety involved in her identification of the assailant), but the defendant and his counsel must always be present.

Thus it is that in any large metropolitan jurisdiction, a trial usually occurs in a range of three to six months after a suspect's arrest. When a case is unusually complex because of legal issues, a number of co-defendants (as in gang rapes), or the defendant's lack of mental competence to stand trial, longer delays can and do occur.

On any of the court appearance dates throughout the proceedings, up to and including the time of the trial, the defendant has the option of pleading guilty to the entire indictment. Not to be confused with a "plea bargain" negotiation, which usually involves a plea to a reduced charge or a promise of a lighter sentence, this occurs when a defendant admits his guilt to each and every allegation in the indictment. Although this might sound unlikely, it does occur in many cases, with no compromise on the part of the prosecution—and with surprising frequency in crimes of sexual violence, especially in stranger rape or identification cases.

For example, in many of the serial rape cases, when the defendant has chosen a unique modus operandi, he may be faced with an indictment in which ten victims have identified him and he is unable to supply an alibi in any case. Or in crimes where the identification has been made by forensic methods—such as latent fingerprint matching, or the newer genetic identification by means of DNA analysis—to which the suspect and his counsel have not been able to mount a defense. That is, when the evidence is *overwhelming*, there is a better chance that the defendant will acknowledge his guilt and plead guilty to the indictment. Interestingly enough, this happens with greater frequency in sex offenses than in many other felonies, simply because it is a contact crime and the defendant often links himself to the survivor or to the crime scene—forensically—by his animal greed and the very intimate nature of these violent acts.

When the accused pleads guilty to the indictment and admits to all of the charges against him, he is then sentenced by the judge exactly as though he had been convicted after trial.

In sexual assault cases, like in all other crime cases in cities with overburdened criminal dockets, many of the cases are resolved by the process of "plea bargaining." Unlike the accused just pleading guilty, this resolution occurs when the prosecutor makes a decision to allow the defendant to plead guilty to a less serious crime than the one with which he is charged in the indictment. Thus an individual charged with rape in the first degree, for example, may be offered a plea to the crime of an *attempt* to commit the crime of rape in the first degree. In exchange for that offer, which will carry a lighter penalty, the accused gives up or waives his right to a trial.

While the concept of plea bargaining has a negative connotation to the general public, most responsible prosecutors use plea bargaining selectively and realistically to manage the enormous caseloads that confront them.

In New York County, where more than ten thousand indictments are filed in a given year, every assistant district attorney evaluates every case to decide whether or not there is an appropriate plea offer to be made, no matter what the crime charged. There is no case, no matter how "rock-solid" the evidence appears to be, no matter how credible and cooperative the witness, for which a prosecutor can promise the verdict a jury will deliver. A conviction requires the unanimous vote of twelve jurors, as does an acquittal, but it takes only a single juror to cause a mistrial or "hang" a jury. The victim or witness may be thoroughly convinced of a defendant's guilt, but proving the same to a jury of twelve—beyond a reasonable doubt—can never be guaranteed in advance of a trial.

So each of my colleagues considers the evidentiary strengths and weaknesses of a case as well as the likelihood of obtaining a conviction in deciding whether a plea should be offered. A crime victim is not a necessary party to the negotiation process, which typically goes on between counsel for both sides, subject to the approval of the court. Although many witnesses feel slighted by their lack of participation, it is important for them to understand that these decisions are not made by whim or arbitrary caprice but rather are based on the experience and wisdom of lawyers and their supervisors who have been to trial many times before. In fact, many complainants are pleased to learn that the result of the negotiation is not always such a "bargain" for the accused. In many cases, the plea-bargain process does not greatly diminish the severity of punishment a judge might have meted out after a trial.

One incentive for prosecutors to consider plea bargaining in sex offense cases is the unique trauma often sustained by the survivors and their corresponding anxiety about the trial process.

More than in any other category of crime I have prosecuted, victims in sexual assault cases ask to not go to trial for a host of reasons: to avoid what they anticipate will be the rigors of seeing their assailant and being cross-examined; reliving the terror of their victimization, especially in a public courtroom; the humiliation or embarrassment of describing the intimate acts forced upon them so violently; being questioned about their personal lives. And despite many improvements in the system over the past two decades, specific circumstances still compel prosecutors to negotiate a plea bargain even when their prospects for conviction are very good.

SEXUAL VIOLENCE

Take the case of Jonelle, the thirty-six-year-old woman who was raped at midnight after leaving one of our major hospitals, where she had spent hours in the waiting area of the intensive care unit that evening, allowed only short visits with her mother, who was a terminal cancer patient. When she reached her car and noticed it had a flat tire, she was relieved when a polite passerby offered to help her change it, since there were no open service stations nearby. The "Good Samaritan" turned out to be the man who had intentionally slashed the tire, waited for her return, and forced her into an adjacent hallway, where he tied her hands with electrical cord and raped her.

Not only was Jonelle forced to endure the torment of the sexual assault, but within hours of her release from that ordeal, she was summoned back to the hospital to learn of the death of her mother.

A fine police investigation led to the arrest of the suspect six weeks after the attack. Concerned detectives pleaded with Jonelle to follow through with a prosecution, so she reluctantly agreed to view the lineup and testify before the grand jury. The day the case was brought to the District Attorney's Office, it was my two paralegals who met her first while I was in court on another matter, and who embraced her when she collapsed as she attempted to relive the events for the first time since her mother's funeral.

When we had finished her long day with the afternoon's grand jury presentation, Jonelle sat trembling in my office as she talked about trying to put her shattered life back together. She was a single mother raising a teenage son who was severely handicapped, mentally and physically. She described the strain of the months of caring for her sick mother in addition to managing her son's difficulties and working full-time. This violent assault followed by her mother's death had wrecked her completely and deprived her of what little emotional strength she had maintained.

Jonelle accepted our suggestion that she get counseling to help her through this period, and my paralegals worked through their local social service agencies to find appropriate support near Jonelle's home. Within weeks of that meeting, however, Jonelle stopped returning our calls and retreated from all of our efforts to reach her. When I contacted her therapist, she told me that Jonelle could not deal with the court case, and the prospective trial, at this point in her life. It was her belief that if forced to be a witness, her patient would suffer a complete breakdown. Despite the assurances I offered about the trial process, the therapist explained the complexities of the situation—that Jonelle panicked at the thought of going into New York City, that every conversation about her victimization was intertwined with the deathbed vigil at her mother's side, and that she had been incredibly fragile before the simultaneous blows were struck, because of her circumstances and her lack of any support system.

Through the assistance of the therapist, we reopened our communication, but all of our efforts to encourage Jonelle to come back for the trial failed, and her therapist urged us not to press too much harder. What then became of the case?

This is an example of the positive use of plea negotiation. We had a fairly good case against the defendant, which his lawyer recognized. We had a complaining witness—she wasn't dead, she wasn't missing, she just was extremely reluctant. And if we had had *no* concern about her ultimate well-being we could have found a way to go forward.

The defendant was eligible for a maximum sentence of twelve and a half to twenty-five years—his second felony conviction. When the case was conferenced in court, the judge asked both sides if there was any chance of a plea. The defense attorney suggested a sentence range that he thought was acceptable. I thought it was too low, and the judge agreed. But the defense had given me the signal, by his willingness to discuss a plea, that we might be able to avoid trial and still hope for justice.

Weeks passed and the negotiations continued. My weakness was, of course, the position of Jonelle and her therapist.

The defense attorney's weakness, as he acknowledged it to me, was his awareness that the jury would be completely empathetic to the complaining witness, which would cause them to loathe the defendant, no matter who or what his circumstances were.

The question for any prosecutor then becomes one of balance and principle. There was merit to sparing Jonelle this experience if it would truly be so detrimental to her mental and physical health, but at what price to society if we were to free a culpable defendant? So with a very wise judge mediating the negotiations, they continued over the next few court appearances. When we finished the pretrial discovery process—which included letting the defense understand the evidentiary strengths of our case, from the police reports and the medical evidence—we went back to battling about numbers. The judge suggested that I lower my offer to nine to eighteen years, which I agreed to do if the defendant took the plea that very day.

The case ended ten weeks after the indictment. The defendant stood convicted of rape in the first degree, by his own admission of guilt (the same as a conviction after a trial) and was sentenced to state prison for nine to eighteen years. It was three years less, as a minimum, than the heaviest sentence he might have received at the end of a trial had he been convicted and had the judge chosen to impose the maximum sentence. We were able to negotiate a substantial sentence, which pleased Jonelle enormously, as well as to respect her decisions about her emotional health and recovery.

We try to strike these balances whenever we work at plea negotiations. Often, we must rely on the judgments of the professionals who are assisting the survivors. In many instances of child sexual abuse, especially in familial cases, the psychiatrist or mental health professional working with the child will help us assess what the effect will be on the child when she or he must confront the offender in a courtroom and testify against him in his presence.

The usefulness, indeed the necessity, of these negotiations in the criminal justice system is unquestioned, I think, by anyone who has worked within it. The importance of undertaking the negotiations—the plea bargains—with utmost concern and good judgment is critical. The prosecutor must understand the strengths and weaknesses of the case, the likelihood of conviction at trial (therefore be knowledgeable about the strengths and weaknesses of the defendant's case too), whether the bargained-for sentence is too low to be appropriate for the charges or too disparate from the sentence that might be meted out after a trial, and whether the survivor truly has unique circumstances that would be affected by the trial experience.

Since much of the effort of my colleagues in the last two decades has been in the direction of making sexual assault victims more comfortable in the trial process and effecting substantial increases in the conviction rates of these cases, I am greatly in favor of trials rather than pleas. But there is a valid place in the system for intelligently negotiated resolutions, and sometimes we have no real alternatives.

CHAPTER EIGHT
CAREER CRIMINALS

IN THE FALL of 1974, when my classmates and I had completed our rotation through the Criminal Court Bureau and graduated to the Supreme Court Bureau, which is responsible for the trials of all felony cases, my first assignment was to a subdivision of that bureau known as the Major Felony Project (MFP). Now called the Career Criminal Unit, MFP also started as the result of a federally funded grant, targeting for prosecution the most serious crimes committed by experienced felons—career criminals who were eligible for maximum prison sentences.

The project was headed by Joan Sudolnik, who, along with Leslie Snyder, was one of the two women who had broken the barriers under Mr. Hogan's tenure to become outstanding litigators in the trial division of the office in the couple of years preceding my arrival. Joan is the woman who contributed the most to my training and education once I reached the Supreme Court—as a role model, teacher, and good-humored friend, who was exceedingly generous with her advice, time, and knowledge. She supervised the twelve of us as we struggled with an endless supply of kidnappings, robberies, arsons, and assaults.

The first cases I took to trial were robberies, the kind we call "one-witness identification" cases. In each instance, the complaining witness claimed to have been held up by an armed assailant and was usually the only witness to the event. The basic structure of the trials was a simple one: The testimony of the victim was followed by that of the investigating detective, who explained the identification and arrest procedures. Each of us learned to be comfortable with rules of evidence that governed things like how to link the weapon, if it was recovered by the police, to the defendant, and to lay a proper foundation for its admission into evidence so that the jurors would be allowed to hear about it and view it.

The twelve of us in MFP tried these cases back to back, picking them up one after another the day after an arrest had been made, presenting them directly to the grand jury ourselves, and then moving them to trial. We had holdups in liquor stores and supermarkets, housing projects and elegant town houses, subway stations and taxicabs. And one of the very best resources of our office was, and has always been, the intense camaraderie among the members of the staff. We learned together in seminars and training courses, from supervisors and guest lecturers, and of course from the judges before whom we worked, as they watched us flounder to master techniques, often steering us in the right direction. But just as important as all the formal training was the way we all were helped by each other. Not a day went by nor was a case assigned that we didn't spend a few hours seeking each other's advice, getting a fresh perspective from a friend or a suggestion about how a colleague would approach a legal issue the rest of us had not been confronted with previously. The brainstorming usually continued long into the evening, when we often adjourned to Forlini's—the colorful courthouse restaurant and bar where we relaxed together and spent many long hours waiting for jurors to render verdicts in our cases.

By the summer of 1976, I had prosecuted more than fifteen felony trials to verdict and worked on scores of others.

SEXUAL VIOLENCE

Because the Sex Crimes Unit was too small to be able to handle every sexual assault case that came into the office, many of them fell to us in the MFP. Joan knew of my interest in working on them and had assigned some of them to me. Five of the trials had involved sexual assault charges, like the case against James Morales (Chapter 2). The issues in other felonies seemed fairly static by comparison, with only the facts changing from case to case. But each rape case impressed upon me how complex the underlying societal attitudes are concerning violence, sexuality, and sexual violence.

The practical problem faced by prosecutors is that the issues related to sexual assault are something most of the public—our jurors—have not thought about at all unless the crime has affected their lives or the life of a loved one in some way. So most jurors come to the courtroom with no education about or understanding of sexual assault and impose their own attitudes on the facts that they hear there. And most of them begin with the mistaken assumption that if the facts concern a sexual act, they involve sexuality rather than violence.

So the early trials I handled each presented an opportunity to learn how to anticipate what the impact of these misconceptions are on individual jurors, and how to prevent those complications from becoming obstacles in the way of a conviction.

The second rape case assigned to me, after the Morales trial, is an example of a problem I had certainly not anticipated. The victim, Tanisha Edwards, a nineteen-year-old recent high school graduate, was on her way to a job interview in a huge office building on lower Broadway at 2:30 in the afternoon. As she walked from the subway toward Broadway on one of the side streets, she was grabbed from behind and pulled into an empty truck-loading area adjacent to an old commercial building on the block. Her attacker, Linwood Miller, spun her around and held her by the shoulders, banging her head repeatedly against the brick wall of the building until she was stunned into semiconsciousness. Then he

99

braced her back against the wall by pinning her to it with his
left forearm, lowered her underpants and panty hose with
his right hand, unzipped his pants, and penetrated her vagina with his penis.

After he had raped Tanisha, Miller turned and walked
away, and she slid to the floor of the alleyway, where she
remained until a passerby spotted her and summoned help.

Miller was identified through photographs and a lineup.
Tanisha, who was very timid and soft-spoken, found it especially difficult to discuss the details of the attack and was even
unfamiliar with the language of the events as she had never
experienced sexual intercourse prior to the rape.

I was pleased to be able to tell her, before the trial, that
the defense attorney had made it clear that he was challenging only the identification of his client, not the occurrence of
the crime. He didn't have the advantage, as I did, of getting
to know Tanisha and thereby seeing how credible she was,
but he hinted to me that the reason he would be gentle with
her is that he thought the jury would have such natural sym-
pathy for her—"a teenage virgin on her way to her first job
interview, in broad daylight"—that he would only antagonize
them by giving her a hard time. I didn't care what his reason
was, I was just glad to be able to encourage her that the trial
would not be the ordeal all the made-for-TV movies she had
seen led her to expect.

The case went in like a dream. Tanisha was on the stand
for less than one hour. I took her through the story carefully,
and she was not even cross-examined about the assault. The
thrust of the defense's questions, perfectly appropriate, was
that because Tanisha had been grabbed from behind, and
then even when turned was so badly dazed by the injury to
her head, she did not have an adequate opportunity to see
and describe her assailant. Therefore, her identification of
Miller was not malicious, it was simply a mistake.

It was a good attempt at a defense in this case, and has
worked successfully in many like it. Our summations were
both "clean" in the sense that we agreed that the case had but

a single issue for the consideration of the jury: Was Linwood Miller the man who attacked Tanisha? We both talked about the occurrence of the rape, and even Miller's attorney conceded what a dreadful crime it was to which Tanisha had been subjected.

The jury got the case late on a Wednesday morning. I went back to my office and tried to keep myself busy while they deliberated. My concern grew when they had not reached a verdict by the dinner hour, so some of my colleagues kept me company at Forlini's, our local eating place, and then I returned to the courtroom at 8:00 P.M. We all knew identification cases could go either way and we assumed that the jurors were carefully poring through all the details of Tanisha's description and matching them to characteristics of the defendant.

As my adversary and I sat in the courtroom after supper, we both heard the occasional outbursts of raised voices from the jury room, which was just off a corridor outside. Usually, lawyers rely on friendly court officers for unofficial hints about the "tone" of deliberations, but we didn't need any help to figure out that tempers were flaring among the group. Not a good sign.

We felt the judge was sure to sequester the jury and send them off to a local hotel by 11:00 P.M., but with only a half hour to go until then, the buzzer by which they communicate with the courtroom rang loudly. They were back with a verdict, and they found Linwood Miller guilty of rape in the first degree and sodomy in the first degree.

After the judge thanked the jurors for their service and dismissed them, the young foreman raised his hand and asked if it was permissible for those among them who wished to speak with either of the lawyers to do so. Since the case was over, the judge said it would be fine.

The jurors were led back into their room to gather their coats and books and belongings, and I remained at counsel table packing up my exhibits and files. The foreman and a middle-aged woman who had been on the jury came up and shook hands with me, asked me how Tanisha was doing, and wanted me to relay to her their respect for her courage in confronting Miller and being a witness.

They were eager to talk to me because they wanted me to know what problem had arisen and almost hung the jury. Deliberations had begun with a round-table discussion of the facts. From the very first vote, less than one hour after they had been in the jury room, every single one of them agreed that Linwood Miller was the man described and later identified by Tanisha Edwards.

Then came trouble. One of the jurors, a sixty-three-year-old man, married and the father of four children, who worked for the telephone company, announced that something was wrong with Tanisha's story. "What she said is impossible—two people can't have sexual intercourse *standing up*! You can't do it that way."

For ten hours, eleven human beings had fought like cats and dogs with a man whose only sexual experience had been in the missionary position, and who refused to believe that any other kind of intercourse was physically possible. No matter that the defense conceded the manner in which the crime had occurred, this juror had his own perspective on things. He brought his own view of sexuality to the trial and didn't listen to any other arguments until the foreman and the woman beside him threatened to prove it to him by standing up, undressing, and having intercourse in the jury room! He didn't call their bluff but accepted the collective wisdom and experience of his peers after a long battle, and the real issue went quickly and finally to a vote.

From that near disaster I learned never to assume a single fact, or ever to think that because *I* know that rape has to do with sexual violence—not sexuality—that anyone without exposure to this crime or education about it can separate it from his or her personal sexual experience. I realized that every summation must address the kind of sexual acts performed directly and graphically. That lesson has served me well over many years, and especially in those cases with more bizarre sexual conduct.

During my stint in the MFP, Robert Morgenthau was elected district attorney of New York County after the death of Frank Hogan. Although most of my colleagues and I had not known Mr. Morgenthau before the election, we were excited by the prospect of his leadership because of his reputation as the nation's premier federal prosecutor established a decade earlier. Mr. Morgenthau, brought up in a family tradition of public service, had been appointed by President Kennedy to be the United States Attorney for the Southern District of New York in 1961. He ran that prestigious office throughout both the Kennedy and Johnson administrations and was widely respected for his integrity and investigative ability. The lawyers who trained and worked with him there are the giants of New York's legal community today.

Upon his arrival in the District Attorney's Office, Robert Morgenthau—"the Boss" as he is known to his staff—brought with him creative ideas for modernizing the methods by which cases were processed, one of which was so-called vertical prosecution—assigning senior assistants to felony cases from the intake stage, as we were beginning to do with sex offenses. He also attracted some brilliant additions to the legal staff, such as Pierre Leval, now a distinguished federal judge in the Southern District of New York, and Peter Zimroth, now a senior partner at the firm of Arnold and Porter.

Among the most significant changes in the office was Mr. Morgenthau's respect for the role of women in the criminal justice system. All positions were open to us, and before very long, almost half of the attorneys on the staff were women. I am sure that the young women lawyers who join our office today, waiting to be assigned to murder and rape prosecutions, have no idea that as recently as twenty years ago, Joan Sudolnik, Leslie Snyder, and I had to fight to be allowed to handle cases such as these. The Boss, who is married to an extremely talented Pulitzer Prize–winning journalist and novelist, Lucinda Franks, has always recognized the ability of the professional women with whom he has worked.

Mr. Morgenthau remains today an innovative and aggressive prosecutor, accorded international respect for his stunning investigation of the scandal at the Bank of Credit and Commerce International and widely credited for his pursuit of white-collar criminals and organized-crime figures. I think, however, two of his most overlooked accomplishments are his professional mentoring of women in the law, and his determined commitment to the issue of sexual violence.

As a junior assistant when Mr. Morgenthau came to the office in 1976, I had very little contact with him throughout the first year. But as I have joked with him many times since—knowing that Mr. Hogan thought the job would be too tawdry for me—I think it is one measure of his genius that he recognized in me the qualities that would thrive on that tawdriness.

Soon after Leslie Snyder tendered her resignation in 1976, I was summoned to the office of the Chief Assistant District Attorney, John Keenan. Mr. Keenan, now a federal judge in the Southern District of New York, had long before earned a reputation as one of the foremost prosecutors in the country. He was a Hogan assistant and had headed the prestigious Homicide Bureau under him, trying some of the most notorious and difficult murder cases in the city. He was liked and admired by all the young lawyers, not only for his skill but also for his easygoing manner, approachability, and great wisdom.

Mr. Keenan told me that Mr. Morgenthau would like me to take over the leadership of the Sex Crimes Prosecution Unit. As pleased and flattered as I was, I was hesitant about the offer for a number of reasons. I had been in the office less than four years and was still learning things from my colleagues and superiors every day. How was I going to be able to teach and advise other assistants about rape cases?

Mr. Keenan reminded me that my experience with hundreds of rape victims in the Indictment Bureau, added to my recent trial matters, placed me second to Leslie Snyder in terms of my familiarity with the field. No one else in the office had handled the volume of sexual assault cases that we two had.

My other reluctance was my happiness with the work being assigned to me in the Major Felony Project, where I thought I had the best of both worlds. The variety of interesting felonies was quite unusual, and I still had a generous proportion of sex offenses, so why give up the former for a steady diet of the latter? Mr. Keenan assured me that Mr. Morgenthau wanted me to try the position for a year, and if I was unhappy there, he would move me out to whichever bureau attracted me. That seemed more than fair and I accepted immediately. In fact, as Mr. Morgenthau has offered me other positions over the years, I have steadfastly refused to give up my work with the SCPU—it is the most richly rewarding job, to my view, in law enforcement, and yet my vision was so narrow that I had to be prodded to take it.

I spent the next three months after accepting the position cleaning out my caseload of everything except rape cases, which I would, of course, take with me when I started the new job in September. Among the last cases I tried in MFP were two of the most interesting. The first involved a series of thefts in an elegant midtown hotel, managed by a smart woman—incidentally, the only female manager of a major New York City hotel at that time—who had the suspicion that one of her employees was responsible for the thefts. With the help of an energetic NYPD detective and our office, she set up a sting operation to try to catch him in action. A beautiful young woman checked into the hotel on a Friday afternoon with so much fanfare that it would have been impossible for anyone on the staff not to notice her—with her several Vuitton trunks, a fur over her arm, and lots of jewelry dripping from her wrists, ears, and fingers. As she registered, she told the desk clerk she would be going out of the city for the day on Saturday and arranged a limo for that purpose.

It worked like a charm. After she left the next morning, the video camera the police had concealed in her cosmetics bag was activated. When we watched the playback many hours later, the first thing we saw was the chambermaid—and the hotel manager had a rude awakening. She started to make the bed, and when she reached the room service tray, she sat down and began to pick at the leftover cold toast and eggs! She finished her work, and then took some of the pretty dresses out of the closet and held them up against herself in front of the mirror, just to see how they looked. She replaced everything, though, and went on to the next room empty-handed.

An hour later in came the prime suspect: the bell captain. He had no business being in the room at that time, so we already had the misdemeanor crime of trespass established. Then he got to work. He opened all the drawers and sorted through the jewelry, picking out some of the pieces he liked and placing them on the bed. Next he found the stack of traveler's checks, and he carefully unpinned the clasp in the wallet and removed several of the bills from the middle of the pile (so the woman might not notice right away that any had been taken). Then, much to our surprise, he walked right to the case holding the concealed camera and picked up the bag to open it. As soon as he realized what it held, he dropped the bag and scrambled around the room frantically trying to replace all the items and get out of there. He didn't get far before he bumped into the arresting officers, who took him away in cuffs. That was probably the last case I tried that was at all amusing—no traumatized victim, no emotional content, and a lot less satisfaction than the major undertaking coming to me in the form of the SCPU.

The other MFP case that was most fascinating did help prepare me, unexpectedly, for my new position in two important ways: dealing with victims at the crime scene—having contact with them moments after their release by their captors—not in a clinical office setting a week later—and interviewing a defendant immediately upon his apprehension.

At five o'clock one Tuesday afternoon, Joan Sudolnik called me into her office. She asked if I was free to go directly to a crime scene, an unusual hostage situation that was still under way in a bank in Greenwich Village. We didn't know much more than that, but I grabbed a yellow pad, ran downstairs and got into a taxi, and headed to Sixth Avenue and Thirteenth Street to meet the detectives and be briefed on the events. As the cab crossed Eleventh Street, we were stopped by police barricades, so I got out and squeezed past row upon row of passersby and homebound pedestrians, displaying my blue-and-gold D.A.'s badge like a cop in a B movie in order to get through the solid line of blue uniforms and up to the plainclothes detectives.

The entire block of Sixth in front of the bank was empty of people. I was led into a corner bar, which had been turned into a temporary police operations office and was full of police brass and detectives as well as members of the extraordinary Hostage Negotiations Squad. They told me what they had learned so far, which was that shortly before the bank's three o'clock closing time, a young man had walked in, pulled a gun out of a gym bag, and threatened to kill everyone unless they complied with his demands. He locked the doors and thereby had as his hostages four bank employees and the six customers who had happened to be inside at that unfortunate moment.

All the police knew about the kid was that his name was Ray Olsen, that he called himself "the Cat," and that he had just come into Manhattan from Long Island and spent the weekend in a hotel room, venturing out only to see the newly released film *Dog Day Afternoon—eighteen* times!

I asked the cops what he wanted.

As he had herded his hostages toward the rear of the bank, the Cat had heard noises, which he assumed to be the police, and he had fired a shot from his pistol as he told them

107

to back off—he was "not fooling around." He had then announced that he was a member of the Symbionese Liberation Army and that all he wanted was the release of Patty Hearst. In addition to his pistol, he had a 30.30 Marlin rifle with fifty rounds of ammunition and an apparatus resembling a radio with two glass vials attached, which he told his captives was a bomb capable of destroying four city blocks.

Just minutes before I arrived at the scene, one of the young male bank customers had tried to jump the Cat and overpower him. But the defendant came out on top in the brief tussle and decided to release the troublemaker and his girlfriend because they were too difficult to handle.

I had met and interviewed hundreds of crime victims by that point in time, but always hours or days later in the calm surroundings of my office. Never before had I been present at a crime scene, in the eye of the storm, while a defendant held the lives of his hostages in his hands, and not a single one of us could know the outcome of the situation or the ultimate fate of any of the women and men still held inside the bank.

I watched and listened in horror as the young couple described to the detectives how their nightmare had started, just because they had entered the bank to get fifty dollars. It was especially terrifying, they said, because the Cat seemed so irrational and so volatile. He hadn't made any effort to get the bank's money; in fact, he said he didn't want any of it. It soon became obvious that his demands to free Patty Hearst were nonsense; he was not a member of the SLA, knew nothing at all about the organization or its members and goals, and seemed more interested in insisting that the disc jockey on the local radio station he was listening to in the bank play Grateful Dead songs for him.

What, then, was his motive? He kept repeating to his hostages—between the threats to their lives—"I just want a few more hours in the spotlight."

As the police concentrated on the crucial task of negotiating with the Cat for the safe release of his hostages, they assigned to me the task of debriefing and comforting the individuals we prayed would be let out over the course of the early evening.

This experience drove home for me as never before that the police have a far more difficult first encounter with crime victims than do prosecutors. They are often the first people to whom an outcry is made, and they meet victims fresh from the grasp of the offenders. I, on the other hand, see them at a remove of time and place, after the police—and often medical personnel and counselors—have helped give some comfort and care.

Between six and ten o'clock that evening, trading human lives for sandwiches and cold beer, the Cat released his hostages one at a time. I watched as hostages emerged from the bank—some trembling, some sobbing, and others without any apparent emotional reaction except relief—and dealt with the entire gamut of victim responses that included disbelief, anger, fear for the lives of the remaining hostages, and concern for the loved ones waiting at home and in nearby police stations for news.

The police officers were incredible. Captain Frank Bolz, who commanded the Hostage Negotiation Squad, for hours patiently bargained for the lives of the victims with someone who had no articulable goal and not much to lose by hurting anyone. Other cops gave support, physically, to those "lucky" ones released without injury. We listened to them, answered their questions, and slowly tried to convince them that control could be restored to *them*—that it would be their decision about who they wanted to see and where they wanted to be talked to and whether they wanted medical attention.

Finally, at eleven o'clock the Cat held only the bank manager and two customers. The youngest hostage, a sixteen-year-old kid, began to cry as the Cat cocked his pistol, sat on the floor with his gun pointed at the three exhausted victims, and began to meditate. The police had cut his telephone lines, so his access to the media, the local radio stations that had been broadcasting his hours in the spotlight, was over.

He was stationary for fifteen minutes, absolutely silent, until he looked up at the crying youth and said, "You can all leave now." He handed his guns to the hostages and let them walk out of the bank.

He had had his "hours in the spotlight." I was later to see this motive over and over again in sexual assault cases—a defendant committing a crime that made no sense to any objective onlooker but that gave him during its occurrence complete control over his victims and anyone else within range. It was clear to each one of us who were twenty feet away from the Cat, on the far side of a brick wall, that we were absolutely powerless to stop his victimization of the ten human beings he held at gunpoint. He could take their lives at any moment, or let them go, but that choice was entirely his own. Many countless times rape victims have asked me *why* the crime occurred, and still it is impossible to describe to someone that for many assailants it is this need to control, to dominate, and in their own perverse world to be at the center of the universe, briefly in the spotlight.

In the aftermath of those nine hours of torment, one contrast struck me more powerfully than anything else. Those hostages were all heroes. They had been powerless, as had an entire police force, to do anything to stop the domination of an irrational human being who controlled their lives. Everyone involved, from the bank manager who was the group spokesman, to the negotiators, to the passersby praying for the safety of ten souls unknown to them, everyone knew that the deal that had to be cut was simple: Tell us what you want, we'll give it to you—just *don't hurt anyone*. And what did I find so ironic? That that response works with every crime except sexual assault. The rape laws in New York at that time required that the victim of a sexual assault *resist* the attacker—an absurdity not mandated for any other kind of crime. The law still read that unless the victim offered "earnest resistance" to the defendant's force, the crime could not be proved. Why couldn't a rape victim, like any other kind of hostage, say, "I'll do anything you want, just don't hurt me?" I knew she could not, and that those of us working to change those laws would have to go on with that effort with renewed vigor.

Again, the rare opportunity to experience the trauma of victims firsthand impacted on me tremendously and helped me to understand the seriousness of their loss of control, powerlessness, and the threat to their lives. The defendant, who wasn't out to take money or avenge an old grievance by shooting or stabbing someone—that is, a defendant who wanted only to control other lives for a period of time—was a character I would be seeing a great deal more of in the SCPU.

CHAPTER NINE

ANOTHER STRIKE IN MIDTOWN

SHORTLY AFTER 5:30 on July 9, 1985, the several hundred members of the legal and support staffs of a prestigious Manhattan law firm began to empty their thirtieth-floor offices and head for the steamy summer street from their landmark building on Park Avenue. Only a handful of partners and the associates assigned to work with them planned to remain throughout the evening to complete a project for a corporate client who was about to make a tender offer for a world-famous conglomerate.

Marina Lamb, a sixth-year associate in the securities department, got the word from a senior partner late in the day. She called her husband to tell him not to expect her until well after midnight and then she walked out of the suite of elegantly appointed offices to freshen up in the ladies' room before heading into a meeting in the conference room.

On her way down the long hallway, Marina was passed by a young man moving in the opposite direction. He was casually dressed and smiled at her from beneath the visor of his baseball cap, an envelope in hand, and she assumed he was one of the hundreds of messengers who moved around the enormous building throughout the day on his way to the firm with a missive from a client.

Security in the building was good, and Marina opened the ladies' room door with her key. Within minutes, yellow pad in hand, she pulled the door open and was about to step back into the hallway.

To her shock, the door was blocked by the same young man she had just passed minutes earlier, who held a knife up to her face as he pushed her back into the ladies' room. He took her beyond the large mirrored anteroom back into one of the cramped toilet stalls, where he demanded her money. Marina had eighty dollars in her purse, which she retrieved and handed over. Strangely, then, he wanted her subway tokens too.

"I'll give you everything," she pleaded. "Just don't hurt me." She dumped out the contents of her purse and her trembling hands tried to pick up anything of value to give to the robber.

"I won't hurt you . . . *if* you do exactly what I want," he told her.

What he wanted next was Marina's watch. Of course she complied. She removed her pearl necklace and was startled when he asked her, "Is it real?" When she told him they were simulated pearls, he gave the strand back to her. Then he asked her how much her slim gold wedding band had cost, and when she responded fifty dollars he lost interest in that too. Marina thought her ordeal was almost over.

"Now give me what I want," the man said, no longer smiling. He pushed Marina down onto the toilet seat, unzipped his pants, and grabbed her by the neck as he thrust his penis toward her mouth.

He stood straight as they both heard the sound of a key turning in the locked door. Like a cat, the man stepped up on the thick pipe behind the toilet seat, crouching with his knife against Marina's neck. Only one pair of feet was visible in the stall, and the unidentifiable woman used a toilet several stalls away and was gone without a word.

SEXUAL VIOLENCE

During those three long minutes Marina had weighed her opportunity to scream for help. She was stopped by her memory of news stories of the young Harvard graduate whose life had recently been ended on a rooftop on Manhattan's West Side when she resisted an armed assailant by screaming as he attempted a sexual assault. The six-inch blade was on Marina's skin, and she tried to reassure herself that her assailant might actually "honor" his words and let her live if she obeyed all his commands.

Marina was the first to speak when the woman left the room. "You see, I'm not trying to get you in trouble. I didn't say anything. But I'm due at a meeting at five-thirty and people will come looking for me when I don't show up."

It was a good strategy and one that should have worked, but the man still didn't have what he wanted. He recognized the danger of his discovery that the ladies' room seemed to pose, so he again threatened Marina to keep her mouth shut and dragged her to the door. He checked to make sure the hallway was empty, then took his captive several feet to the heavy fire door with the EXIT sign, leading to the stairwell.

Marina balked, paralyzed with fear of being isolated in the unused stairwell of a large commercial building. She knew there would be no traffic, and that not a sound could be heard once the steel door slammed behind them.

Now she couldn't think at all, but the man was smart enough to tear a sheet of paper from the young lawyer's pad to stick over the door lock so he could regain entry to the corridor if he chose.

Then he focused again on his quarry. He pushed the slight woman onto her knees, exposed his penis, and forced it into her mouth. He started to undress her and became angry when he found a gold necklace inside her blouse. "Why didn't you tell me about this?" he fumed.

Marina reached for the clasp and urged it on her assailant. Ironically, she had worn it only because her apartment had been broken into recently and it was one of the few things of value she still had, so she had forgotten it was under the collar of her shirt, rather than on her night table at home.

Once that final distraction had been resolved, the man got back to his business. "Take off your shoes, your stockings, your underwear. Get down on the floor—you'd better know what to do."

Marina obeyed. She was certain her life was going to end in that stairwell. She couldn't control the tears at the thought of not seeing her husband, her parents again. The stranger climbed on top of her and penetrated her vagina with his penis—he raped her—and her mind struggled to pretend that she wasn't there, that this was happening to some other person.

The man then removed himself from her body and was wiping himself with her underwear. Marina turned to run down the endless flights of stairs, but her attacker grabbed her by the time she had taken three steps, warning, "I told you not to do that."

He directed her to sit down on the steps and to stay there for at least ten minutes. He seemed calmer now, talking quietly and sheathing his knife inside his jacket pocket. At the end of this twenty-minute ordeal—an interminable twenty minutes—the rapist slipped the wad of yellow paper out of the doorjamb and re-entered the corridor, letting the weight of the steel door slam as it locked Marina in the soundproof stairwell.

She sat at the top of the staircase for several minutes, giving her assailant time to wait at the elevator bank for his escape. Knowing her reentry to the thirtieth floor was impossible, she tried the door anyway before she began the dizzying descent down the double-height stairwell. Every few flights Marina banged on the massive doors, but at each level the doors were tightly locked—a security measure. It was not until she reached the thirteenth floor, seventeen flights below her own floor, that the distraught young woman, banging against the metal door, was heard by another lawyer at yet another firm in that vast building. The curious litigator opened the fire door to see a tearful and disheveled woman who asked to come inside, saying, "I've been attacked. Could you take me to a telephone?"

Marina called upstairs to her own office and reached one of her partners. Immediately he came to accompany her back to their firm, where she called her husband, the police, and an ambulance to take her to Bellevue Hospital, where detectives from the Sex Crimes Squad told her they would meet with her to begin the investigation of her case.

CHAPTER TEN

LEGAL PROGRESS FOR RAPE VICTIMS

In September 1976, at the same time my commitment to remain in the District Attorney's Office was about to expire, I assumed the title of Bureau Chief of the Sex Crimes Prosecution Unit. Taking that position at this time was especially exciting because of the important changes that began in this decade in the perception of these unique violent crimes both by the justice system and by society.

Because of the new laws and specialized police squads resulting in an increase in reported cases and corresponding arrests, the SCPU had just been expanded to four lawyers, including me, and one paralegal. The secretary, John Dalton, has remained as my assistant until this day and is a fiercely loyal friend as well as a great resource for the office attorneys, with his wealth of historical knowledge of almost two decades of sex offenders. He is a model of sensitivity in his treatment of survivors, since he is often their first contact with the prosecutor's office. Mr. Morgenthau also had the foresight to arrange with the NYPD to assign a female detective to the unit, to serve as a permanent liaison with the Special Victims Squad, so that there would be a regular and open line of communication between the two departments.

The woman who has held that position for almost ten years, Detective Maureen Spencer, is an extremely intelligent and experienced investigator who conducts victim interviews and coordinates field investigations on many of our cases with the police teams who originally catch them in the squads.

My new duties were detailed in the job description Leslie Snyder had created for LEAA's grant review. It would be my responsibility to examine every arrest report for a felony sex offense in Manhattan and then assign the screening of cases to unit members, keeping some of the caseload for myself to try. Each of us was to handle a case every step of the way, according to the "vertical" process I mentioned in Chapter 4, from the intake evaluation through trial or disposition by plea—for the primary purpose of providing the survivor with a single contact throughout the system. Our tasks included interviewing witnesses, conducting identification procedures like lineups, responding to police precinct station houses on a twenty-four-hour-call basis to take statements or admissions from defendants in custody, appearing at speaking engagements to continue to educate the public about changes in the legal system, and of course, trying felony cases to verdict. It was to be my responsibility to maintain daily contact with the Manhattan Sex Crimes and Special Victims squads to keep current on arrests and investigations, and to offer legal advice for the purpose of assuring the propriety of police procedures for their eventual use at trial (that is, for example, if a lineup is not conducted properly, the victim will not thereafter be able to tell the jury how and when she identified her attacker).

In addition, the four of us continued to assist drafting proposals for still-needed legislative reform. And to this day, as from the unit's inception, we are called upon and consulted by police and prosecutorial agencies across the country and abroad—in Alaska and Japan and Oklahoma and war-torn Bosnia—for guidance in investigating and prosecuting their difficult and unusual cases.

SEXUAL VIOLENCE

There has rarely ever been a "slow day" in the SCPU, and we all quickly became accustomed to the heavy volume of complaints that come in on a steady basis, day and night. Unlike in the earlier days when many of the survivors were terrified during their first meetings, barely able to articulate details of their assaults and apprehensive about participating in the criminal justice system, there began to be a change in the response of many of the women we encountered. The attention directed to the crime of rape by the feminist movement, which I believe prompted *responsible* media attention (as opposed to the usual tabloid coverage) to this crime, urged survivors not to be silent about their victimization and demanded reform of the system. At last, this combination of feminist and journalistic involvement sparked the legislative efforts that succeeded throughout the next decade to eliminate corroboration for adult victims, to remove the "earnest resistance" requirement, and to impose rape shield laws.

We more frequently met survivors who were assertive and eager to fight back through the courts at their assailants, to be informed about their cases and to follow the progress closely. Many wanted to participate in the legal process and were pleased to work with the new, pioneering unit. They wanted their cases prosecuted vigorously and were willing to cooperate in whatever manner necessary.

All of us in the unit went on trying cases and teaching ourselves with every courtroom experience, often surprising ourselves as the conviction rate improved with successive court terms.

The daily tragedies we witnessed—a five-year-old incest survivor or a thirty-five-year-old patient who had been "seduced" by her therapist in the course of treatment or a foreign tourist who had been raped by a gun-wielding gang of teens in a deserted subway station when she asked for directions or a junkie who was stabbed and sodomized when her drug deal turned sour—were horrifying. We had two goals in confronting every tragedy: to convict those assailants who were guilty of the crimes charged and to bring the survivor through her experience intact. Only when both goals were met did we feel we had done our job.

After the elimination of the corroboration requirement in New York, which was accomplished shortly before I joined the SCPU—there remained two critical issues that resulted in more legislative change between 1975 and 1983. Together, the new laws had a dramatic effect on our prosecutions and continued in the direction of making a survivor's courtroom experience less of another victimization after the crime itself.

As most people are aware, and as Susan Brownmiller's history describes in exquisite detail, the most common defense in sexual assault cases—and one that had worked well for *centuries*—was an incorporation of details or innuendos about the sexual history of the victim. The idea was to convince the jury that the complaining witness was not a chaste woman and therefore the legitimacy of her claim was suspect—on the theory that if she had consented to sex with other men at other times, she probably had consented this time.

Allowing unlimited questioning about a victim's proper sexual history worked against her in at least two ways. At trial in the courtroom, it diverted the jury from the issue of the defendant's guilt by trying the witness for her "promiscuity." And even worse, it worked to keep many survivors from participating in the legal process and subjecting themselves to debasing and humiliating treatment. Before the introduction of the so-called rape shield laws, then, many witnesses simply refused to expose themselves to such mistreatment.

The New York legislation, which Leslie Snyder and several other lawyers drafted before I had even begun in the field, began with a specific declaration that "evidence of a victim's sexual conduct shall *not* be admissible in a prosecution" for a consummated or attempted sex offense. It thus forbade the introduction of information about a complaining witness's past sexual activity, with the exception of five narrowly defined areas that were specified in the same legislation. Considered as a whole, this legislation was a tremendous effort to strike a fair balance between protecting the rights of victims and the rights of defendants in the rare circumstance when such evidence might indeed be relevant. The five areas of exception are an important part of the great achievement this legislation has been for survivors, providing solid assurance for them that they cannot and will not be harassed in the courtroom.

First, the victim can be asked about "specific instances" of her prior sexual conduct *if* they have occurred with the man who is the accused in the case on trial. That is, while a survivor of an assault committed by a stranger cannot be questioned about her prior unrelated involvements, a woman who has charged with rape someone with whom she has had a sexual relationship may be questioned about it. In fairness to both parties, it is an exception that makes a great deal of sense. The rape did not occur in a vacuum—rather, whatever circumstances brought together the victim and assailant will have had a basis in their prior social, and possibly sexual, history. So it is altogether logical for this exception to exist, since the issue may be directly relevant to the jury's consideration.

Second, the defense is permitted to prove that the complainant has been convicted of prostitution within three years of the occurrence of the crime at trial.

This is *not* to bar prostitutes from the justice process or to say that a prostitute cannot be the victim of a rape. In fact, because the very nature of their occupation makes them so vulnerable to abuse, these women are frequently victimized and are often afraid to seek help from within the system. But many prostitutes do come forward and press charges and—as you will read in Chapter 14—many of the cases are successfully prosecuted.

What this exception does accomplish is limit the questions the defense may ask the victim. It was previously common for attorneys to ask witnesses whether they had ever worked as prostitutes without *any* specific evidence to support the inquiry—the idea was merely to sully the woman's image before the jury by planting that notion. Now, only if she has been *convicted* of prostitution can the victim be questioned about it, and only if that conviction is within the three years preceding the crime. Again, if such evidence does exist, and if it is relevant to the circumstances of the complaint at trial, the jury may be entitled to hear it.

The third exception addresses a reverse strategy that is sometimes adopted by the prosecution. That is, there are occasionally cases in which we may wish to prove that the complaining witness never had sexual intercourse before the assault. It happens frequently in attacks on teenagers, for example, when a survivor may explain during a hospital examination—in response to a battery of questions from nurses and doctors—that she doesn't know if the assailant ejaculated because she has never had intercourse before. If *we* want to introduce that evidence of her prior "chastity," and if the defense has specific evidence to rebut our claim, this section entitles the defense to use it.

Similarly, the fourth exception relates to cases in which the prosecution attempts to prove that the survivor contracted venereal disease or became pregnant as a result of the criminal act with which the accused is charged. The defense, again, is allowed to rebut that claim by specific testimony—not random, unfounded allegations—about a different source of the pregnancy or disease.

The final exception, and the one that created the greatest furor in the passage of the legislation, is a "catchall" exception that reads that the court may allow such questioning about a complainant's prior sexual history that it determines "relevant and admissible in the interests of justice."

Not unwisely, most concerned prosecutors feared that the judges would fall back on this general exception and regularly permit fishing expeditions by the defense concerning a victim's reputation, and thereby void all the gains accomplished by the rest of the legislative package. In actual practice, though, after trials of hundreds of sex crimes cases, we have never had a judge in New York County rely on the fifth exception in abuse of the discretion that is so broadly given. Although prosecutors across the country report varying degrees of success with similar statutes, I think it speaks to the quality of the judiciary in New York that the rape shield laws have been applied so fairly in the interest of survivors who have testified at trials.

It is still rare to encounter a survivor who does not ask a prosecutor, usually early on, "How much of my personal life will they bring up in the courtroom?" "Can the defense attorney ask me about everyone I've ever slept with?" "Will they try to make me look promiscuous?" "My mother doesn't know my boyfriend was living with me when the rapist broke into the apartment—does she have to find out about it at the trial?" All of the concerns and fears that women have about the privacy of their relationships have received enhanced protection with this legislation, and it is a great relief to be able to assure victims that *before* they ever reach the witness stand, we will know exactly what questions of this nature—and in most instances there will be none—they will be asked. In the overwhelming number of assaults by strangers, not a single inquiry about a complainant's sexual history should enter the case at all. That is a remarkable change from two decades ago.

Ironically, for me, the importance of the rape shield laws haunted me throughout the trial of a well-known murder case. In the *People* v. *Robert Chambers,* the killing of Jennifer Levin in Manhattan's Central Park in 1986, the defense devoted enormous time and energy both before and during the trial to feeding rumors to the press and irrelevancies to the jury about the sexual activities of the vibrant eighteen-year-old Chambers killed. Because it was a murder case—*not* a sex offense—the innocent victim was denied the protection that the rape shield law provides to living witnesses. In large measure as a result of the defense's ugly and offensive tactics, there followed an effort to extend the legislation to protect victims in homicide cases, which was endorsed by many victims rights groups, with the support and encouragement of the Levin family who were subjected to the cruel and completely irrelevant slander of their child's reputation.

The lobbying efforts were successful, and in September 1990, the legislature extended the protection of the rape shield law to homicide victims. The new law prohibits the introduction of evidence about the past sexual conduct of the deceased in murder cases unless the court has determined that it is relevant and admissible in the interests of justice.

An even more fundamental and important change in the law of sexual assault resulted from a combination of case law and legislative reform in the period between 1977 and 1983. It concerned the inequitable requirement that the victim of a rape *resist* her assailant.

This condition was every bit as offensive and archaic as the corroboration requirement which had been eliminated by 1974. As I mentioned in Chapter 8, *only* sexual assault survivors had to prove that they had resisted their attackers—it was not expected of the victim of any other category of crime in the penal law.

In that statute rape is defined as sexual intercourse that occurs by forcible compulsion. The same statute went on to define that last phrase as "physical force *that overcomes earnest resistance,* or a threat, express or implied, that places a person in fear of immediate death or serious physical injury to himself or another person. . . ."

Then, in 1977, the Appellate Division, in considering the appeal of a case that had been tried in New York County several years earlier, overruled the jury's verdict of guilty and interpreted the language of the penal law to be that "earnest resistance" meant "*utmost* resistance." The case that brought the issue to a boil is an interesting focus for the attitudes represented on both sides. The trial was originally won by an experienced prosecutor, Bob Seawald, another of my former colleagues who has gone on to serve on the Supreme Court of the State of New York.

The victim in the case was a twenty-two-year-old woman

from Alabama who was newly arrived in New York City in the fall of 1973 and was living in the YWHA. She met the defendant, David Yanik, shortly thereafter. She attended church services with him and agreed to go on to his apartment for coffee and more conversation. Once there, he attempted to kiss her and made other sexual advances, but she broke away and began to cry. The defendant apologized for his behavior and walked her to the subway.

When her friends told her that she had been silly and unsophisticated, the woman called Yanik and apologized for *her* reaction, and the two agreed to meet again. After a dinner together, she returned to Yanik's apartment, where this time when he made similar advances, she claimed that he struck her in the face, ripped her dress, and struggled with her in an attempt to force her to have intercourse. Finally, to avoid further harm, she submitted to his force and threats . . . and then reported the rape.

Yanik admitted that they had had intercourse but denied any force or threats, and ascribed the marks on the victim's nose to "overemotional excitement accompanying the sex act."

The issue for the jury was, as it often is, whether or not the complainant was a voluntary participant in the encounter or the victim of an attacker's forcible acts. And since the jury had convicted the defendant of rape—believing the woman's version of the events—the issue for the appellate court was whether the trial judge had explained the definition of "forcible compulsion" to the jury with proper and sufficient detail.

It does not seem too difficult to understand the definition, does it? Well, the judges who heard the appeal agreed with the defense attorney's argument. They concluded that in order for the defendant to be guilty of rape in the first degree, the jury had to believe that the victim opposed her attacker—not just by saying no, but by resisting to *"the utmost limit of her power"*—and that the resistance must be "genuine and active," not "feigned, or passive or perfunctory."

Not surprisingly, there was quite an uproar over this

decision and the even greater burden it placed uniquely on sexual assault victims—not to mention the greater risk of increased physical harm to which it exposed them. The New York State Legislature moved swiftly to overrule the absurd "utmost resistance" requirement, and so the statute was amended in 1977 to redefine forcible compulsion as "physical force which is *capable* of overcoming earnest resistance." The law also went on to state, specifically, that "earnest resistance does not mean utmost resistance."

The lawmakers finally acknowledged that in a great many circumstances during an assault, the likelihood of sustaining physical injuries increases when the victim offers resistance to her assailant. And most significant, they stated that *unwilling submission* to a rapist may be the victim's only alternative to save her life. (The Court of Appeals, New York's highest court, later rejected the interpretation that the Appellate Division had applied to the *Yanik* case.)

The 1977 revision was marked progress, but obviously still had retained the "earnest resistance" language in the statute. It was not until 1983 that the definition was finally amended so that the focus was taken off the conduct of the survivor and placed squarely where it belonged: on the actions of the offender. The new language declared that forcible compulsion could be established from the defendant's use of "physical force"—not on any subjective view of the victim—or from a threat, express or implied, that placed the victim in fear of immediate death or physical injury to herself, himself, or another person.

After a very long battle, the law came to reflect that submission to a sexual assault—for survival, to preserve one's life or well-being—is *not* consent to a sexual act. It is an argument prosecutors have been able to use thereafter on many occasions in their statements to jurors, and it has been a critical factor in countless cases of rape.

CHAPTER ELEVEN
DATE AND ACQUAINTANCE RAPE

WITH THE CREATION of our specialized unit, my colleagues and I embarked on an effort to inform ourselves about the subject of sexual assault. We were all rather surprised to learn how little data exists. There were statistics, though none terribly accurate since everyone acknowledges how underreported this category of victimization is. We also had Brownmiller's comprehensive historical treatise; recent media coverage; lots of fiction, usually romanticized; and some scholarly law review articles. But for whatever reason, the psychiatric, psychological, and sociological communities, until the last two decades, had never elected to invest a great deal of interest in the study of this subject.

The public has for a very long time been willing to express outrage about stranger rapes, and the legislative changes of the 1970s made prosecution of those crimes far easier than ever before. But the information that probably surprised most of us as much as anything we learned was that *more* than 50 percent of reported rapes were—and continue to be—assaults by men who were *known* to their victims (and a much higher proportion of what comes to a prosecutor's office, since known assailants are easier to apprehend than strangers). The survivors of these crimes, whether raped by casual acquaintances, dates, former lovers, or family members, have vastly different experiences in the courtroom than survivors of stranger rape.

In my experience, the most misunderstood area of criminality is what we call acquaintance or date rape. Except its victims, most people tend to distinguish it from sexual assault by strangers—thus the label "date rape"—with the implication that it is different from, and therefore less serious than, "real rape."

It *is* real rape. And to the many millions of women who have been victimized by a known, trusted assailant, it is every bit as traumatic as an attack by a stranger. Yet rarely is the support offered to survivors, even by family and friends, the equivalent of that in other rapes, and, sadly, the criminal justice system has only recently begun to address many of the difficult aspects of this crime.

The single common denominator in the range of rapes and sexual assaults committed by acquaintances, for those of us in law enforcement, is that the assailant is, indeed, known to her—whether through a brief meeting at an office, a party or a public place, or because of a prior relationship, sexual or not. The significance of this description is simply for investigative purposes. That is, in cases in which the victim had never seen or met her attacker previously, the issue for the investigator is one of *identification*, of finding out who the perpetrator of the crime was in order to apprehend and prosecute him. On the other hand, if the two individuals had any prior contact, the assailant's identity is known to his victim, or can be determined more readily by the police.

Acquaintance or date rape encompasses an extraordinarily broad range of relationships. By definition, all cases of domestic violence and incest occur between people with marital or blood relationships, often living under the same roof; many other cases are reported by women who admit a previous sexual involvement with the defendant but did not consent to the act they reported; millions of cases have taken place on dates, where there has been a social connection between the parties but never a sexual one; and in just as many cases, the survivor and offender are acquainted but just barely that—for example, the attacker may work in a local supermarket and his victim knows him only by his first name, or he may sell drugs in the neighborhood and she occasionally purchases them from him.

The nature of the problems in these situations is extremely diverse, as are the needs of the survivors. And the most pressing among those needs is for all of us—as family members, friends, law enforcement officials, and jurors—to recognize that being sexually assaulted by an acquaintance *is* rape, and is every bit as traumatic as being similarly assaulted by a stranger.

While stranger and acquaintance rape are legally equal in terms of the seriousness of their criminality, there are many important distinctions between them that lead to problems in the courtroom.

One of the earliest and most significant works on the psychosocial impact of sexual assault was the study of the clinical presentation of rape victims at Beth Israel Hospital in Boston, Massachusetts, by Ann Burgess and Lynda Holmstrom, which resulted in the 1974 paper describing and defining Rape Trauma Syndrome. Their landmark work also differentiated the two kinds of attacks, which they called "blitz" and "confidence" rapes. The former—which police and prosecutors refer to as stranger rape—is the sudden surprise assault by an unknown offender, and the latter—acquaintance rape—is characterized by some nonviolent interaction between the victim and her attacker before his intention to commit the crime materializes.

In all of the similar research that has followed that study, the distinctions between the two types of attacks and their effects on the victims have been corroborated. Blitz victims have more frequently reported, for example, fear for their lives during the attack. They have more likely experienced actual threats to their lives and were twice as likely to have been threatened with weapons or the implied use of a weapon.

In confidence rape, the rapist has gained control over the victim by winning her trust to at least some degree before the crime occurs. Studies confirm that these victims are more likely than blitz victims to have consumed alcohol or drugs; that they report feeling more anger (rather than fear for their lives) than blitz victims during the assault; and that they generally wait longer before seeking medical or legal intervention after the occurrence of the assault.

Thus in a report published in the *American Journal of Psychotherapy* in 1990 by a medical team, again at Beth Israel Hospital (Sally Bowie, Daniel Silverman, S. Michael Kalick, and Susan Edbril), researchers interviewing one thousand survivors confirmed earlier accounts finding that "the psychological impact on the victim will differ according to the type of rape." Therefore they should not be thought of as a homogeneous population with uniform needs for legal, medical, and counseling intervention.

Blitz victims most often have as their immediate concerns, according to the Bowie study, "their sense of safety and their fear that the rapist may return." For survivors of confidence attacks, the primary concerns are "guilt and self-blame . . . (they) will have strong doubts about their ability to discern who is truly trustworthy . . . (and) they tend to isolate themselves socially."

The nature of the distinctions between the two types of rape serves a valid purpose in determining the clinical needs of victims and in guiding law enforcement efforts to apprehend an assailant. Tragically, an acquaintance rape victim's self-blame all too frequently is mirrored by a public perception that the woman has done something to occasion the attack—with the odious result being the tendency of others to *blame the victim* for the occurrence of the crime—something that rarely occurs with stranger assault.

It is my belief that most sexual assaults occur when there

is a combination of two critical conditions: opportunity and vulnerability. The rapist needs the *opportunity* to commit the crime, and he succeeds when a victim is *vulnerable* at the moment of his opportunity. When a burglar breaks into a dwelling at nighttime for the purpose of stealing jewelry and furs, he has created for himself the opportunity to commit a crime. If at that moment he encounters a woman alone in her home, sound asleep in her bed, and he awakens her to rape her as well as take her material possessions, no one would ever dream of "blaming" her for her victimization, which occurred at a point in time when she was especially vulnerable. But when an office worker invites a co-employee she has seen and talked with every day for the last six months at their office to her home for dinner, and then reports the next day that he raped her, many people, including close friends, will inevitably question the event itself and who was at fault. "Why did you invite him to your home, unless you wanted to be intimate with him?" "Face it, you've had a crush on him for months, haven't you?" or "He's such a nice guy, such a gentleman—I can't believe he would do something like *that*."

The fact remains that during that evening, the defendant found his opportunity—whether something that he had pre-planned, or on the spur of the moment—and the victim was vulnerable. She was vulnerable precisely because she *did* know her assailant; she was vulnerable because she *trusted* him. And we rarely speak with a survivor attacked by a co-worker, date, friend, or relative who doesn't tell us that the reason they were together (and usually together alone) was because she knew him and trusted him.

A major obstacle in the path of both the complaining witness and the prosecutor, then, is the archaic societal attitude, which remains so disturbingly pervasive, that sexual assaults are victim-precipitated crimes. This is the only category of criminal conduct that is perceived to have happened because of the victim's actions, not the assailant's. "What was she wearing?" "How much did she have to drink?" "What was she doing there at that hour of the night?" Any one of those factors may have facilitated the rapist's goal, but it was *his* criminal conduct that was solely responsible for the assault.

This is clearly an area in which the laws have changed faster than public attitudes (truly a sad commentary, in view of how long it took to effect the legislative changes). The legal reforms I described in earlier chapters—elimination of the corroboration requirement, introduction of rape shield laws, repeal of the "earnest resistance" rule—make it possible to litigate acquaintance and date rapes in our courtrooms as we never could before, but every case is tried to a jury of twelve human beings, each of whom brings to that forum his or her own biases and beliefs.

What are these biases that can prove so lethal to the witnesses in rape trials? A decade ago, the National Center for Prevention and Control of Rape, a division of the National Institute of Mental Health, financed a research project to study the attitudes of jurors in sex offense cases. The sociology professor who conducted the study, Barbara Reskin of the University of Michigan, summed up the least surprising finding, which evidenced the sharp contrast in attitudes between stranger and acquaintance rape. It was, she said, that a survivor was most likely to be taken seriously by a jury if she was a married woman who was "assaulted by a stranger in her own home when the door was locked!"

Reskin found that jurors admitted that they knew they were not supposed to be judgmental about the victims but went right on to state that, indeed, that is exactly what most of them were. The behavior traits judged most harshly by jurors, which are consistent with my colleagues' experience, were alcohol consumption, use of drugs, keeping late hours, and frequenting bars. And most significant, *despite the direction the laws have taken,* victims who had been sexually active were often viewed as being of "questionable moral character."

Our experience with juries in acquaintance rape cases has taught us a number of other lessons about juror biases. When most of us read about a stranger rape in our local newspapers, we tend to form a mental image of the assailant as a criminal type who looks unsavory—the kind of guy you wouldn't want to run into late at night in a dark alley. Date rapists, on the other hand, look like part of the community— they often present an "attractive" package, in that they are usually employed, often married with children, rarely with any documented criminal history (although there may well have been other *unreported* incidents of sexual assault). The stranger rapist may look as though he stepped out of a wanted poster or a mug shot, but the acquaintance assailant is likely to make a very presentable appearance before a jury.

What difference does the defendant's physical appearance make when he is charged with a violent felony?—a question an intelligent individual might ask. The sad response is, a world of difference. One of the most tragic facts about the trials of sex offenders—and one confirmed by most jury studies in this field—is that jurors in acquaintance rape cases are inordinately swayed by the physical appearance of the man on trial. Although this anomaly never occurred to me in my first several trial experiences, my colleagues and I have now heard hundreds of times—especially when middle-class, professional defendants stand up in the courtroom—the murmurs of prospective jurors or public onlookers saying, "I can't believe it—he doesn't *look* like a rapist." or "He doesn't look like he'd have to *force* someone to have sex with him."

Unfortunately, this dangerous perception is more widespread than imaginable. During the long months of the Robert Chambers "preppy murder case" trial, much of the public conversation, including comments from among the more than four hundred prospective jurors who were interviewed, concerned whether someone with Chambers's looks and middle-class breeding could commit the kind of violent murder with which he was charged. Whatever became of the adage that you can't judge a book by its cover? Rapists come in every size, shape, color, and physical description—from every ethnic, religious, and economic background—and there is absolutely no question, in my experience, that it is

135

more difficult to convict a man of the forcible sexual assault of an acquaintance if he is "attractive" to the jury.

Closely linked to the appearance factor is whether or not the defendant is married or involved in a steady sexual relationship. Jurors often make the mistaken assumption that the defendant would not have had to resort to raping the victim if he had another source of available sexual gratification. Again, this reflects the widespread ignorance of the nature of rape—an act of violence, power, humiliation, and control, rather than sexual coupling. Defendants may have perfectly "normal" sexual relationships with spouses or lovers (or, in fact, equally abusive relationships), but when they assault their victims, it is to fulfill their other needs, whether to exercise power and control or to express anger and hatred. Not infrequently, those rapists who attack strangers or friends are involved in violent domestic relationships—but much of that spousal battering and abuse goes unreported and undocumented.

These are some of the myths, then, that persist in making it so difficult for prosecutors to succeed with acquaintance rape cases in the criminal justice system. Although our laws now permit us to prosecute them, not until we are able to inform and educate the public—the men and women who serve on our juries—will we be able to convict more of the men who are guilty of acquaintance rape.

Some of the cases we have tried in Manhattan illustrate the practical problems and unusual features of this type of victimization, and how the courtroom experience with it differs from that of the stranger rape victims you will see thereafter.

CHAPTER TWELVE
ACQUAINTANCE RAPE: THREE CASES

In any rape trial in which the accused is a stranger, the defense counsel can treat a victim very gently on the witness stand by conceding that she is telling the truth, that she was subjected to a dreadful ordeal during the assault—that is, that she indeed *was raped*—while arguing to the jury that the traumatic nature of that ordeal renders her confused, incapable of making a proper identification. The crime occurred as she claims, but his client is mistakenly identified, the wrong man.

A woman who has been raped by an acquaintance faces an additional burden in the courtroom. *Never* will the defense concede the victim's version of the events. The identification of her assailant is not the issue at all, so the defense is inevitably an offensive launched at her entire story. Jurors in an acquaintance rape case will be urged to see the victim as a liar—she was not raped, they will be told, she was a willing participant in a sexual act with the defendant, and now she is fabricating a crime. The most common defense in acquaintance rape cases today, as it has been for centuries, is that the victim consented to have sex with the accused—she asked for it.

It is no wonder that women are so often reluctant to report acquaintance rapes. Perhaps the biggest myth about the prosecution of rape cases is that district attorneys' offices do not take such cases to trial because they are more difficult to win. There is no question that these trials present problems to survivors and prosecutors, but in large urban offices like ours, acquaintance rapes constitute a much higher percentage of the rape cases that go to trial. The experience of lawyers in specialized units like ours enables them to anticipate the defense with a view to overcoming it, prepare the witness for the nature of her cross-examination, enhance the case by doing a more thorough investigation, and attempt to prove to the jury the absurdity of the defendant's claim.

Let us look at three actual trials and see that even though the relationships between the victims and defendants in each are quite different—acquaintances on a first date; acquaintances who work together and plan to socialize in a group after work; and acquaintances who have absolutely no social connection to each other—the defense in each is the same basic accusation that the woman is a liar who had consented to a sexual encounter and later cried "Rape!"

The first of the cases involved two young people, Cindy and Nick, who were both trained as classical ballet dancers. Each of them was twenty-five years old, and they saw each other often at the reputable studio where they both took classes several times a week. Over a period of several months they introduced themselves to each other and had casual discussions until Cindy gave Nick her telephone number when he suggested he would like to take her to dinner the following weekend.

Nick arranged a Friday evening dinner date and arrived at Cindy's apartment to pick her up. She invited him in for a drink and they sat in the living room talking about their mutual interests in dance and theater. Nick had brought some marijuana with him, and together they shared a joint before heading out to a nearby restaurant.

The couple enjoyed a leisurely dinner at a casual neighborhood bistro and shared a bottle of wine as they talked on for a couple of hours. They walked back to Cindy's apartment holding hands, and she thought nothing about Nick coming upstairs to collect his bag of dance clothes and shoes, since he had come to meet her directly from the studio. She liked him, she was getting to know him better, and she thought this date had been the start of a new aspect of their relationship.

But once inside the apartment, Nick refused to say goodnight and leave. He grabbed Cindy to hug her, and as she tried to push him away after several seconds, he threw her onto the floor and straddled her body with his. She began to yell for help immediately, but Nick covered her mouth, telling her to be quiet and obey him if she didn't want to get hurt. He told her to take off all her clothes, and when she refused, he slapped her across the face, telling her, "The pretty ones always say no."

The struggle continued, and although Cindy was able to get to her feet, Nick took her by the neck and pulled her into the bathroom. She bravely fought against him as he kept ripping at her clothes, saying that he wanted her "now," until he finally overpowered her. Although she had screamed at first in hopes of alerting neighbors to her attack, no one had responded and it was clear to Cindy that her screams just made Nick angrier and more determined to subdue her forcibly. Finally, he penetrated the terrified young woman, both vaginally and anally, telling her throughout that he was doing this because his girlfriend had walked out on him. And after he had completed the attack, Nick rolled off Cindy onto the floor, where he fell asleep.

Then, afraid to wake him for fear of more violence, Cindy fled from her apartment at three o'clock that frigid December morning, dressed only in a shirt, and hailed a cab to go to the apartment of her best friends. For all the traditional reasons—"No one will believe me." "What was he doing in my apartment?" "Wasn't I attracted to him?" "Would I eventually have gotten into bed with him?"—Cindy resisted calling the police. It was the calm reasoning and good sense of her friends who talked her into making a police report and who reminded her that she had done nothing to be ashamed of—she had been raped.

Police officers responded immediately, and when they returned with Cindy to her apartment, Nick was still sound asleep. He awakened to find himself under arrest.

I first met with Cindy the following day, after she had been examined at St. Vincent's Hospital and introduced there to an advocate who specializes in counseling survivors of sexual assault. During the interview, I explained to Cindy the importance of her being very candid. I would need to ask a lot of questions that were personal and probing, but the only way we could attempt to protect her in the courtroom would be for me to know absolutely every detail of conversation and of what occurred between her and Nick throughout the entire evening. I reminded her, as I do every witness, that Nick would also have a version of the events that he would tell to *his* lawyer, so it was critical that she try to reconstruct things as accurately as possible. It would be her details that would lend credibility to her story and would ideally make the jury see the untruths in the defendant's tale.

Cindy went through her story with me, acknowledging that she had deliberately omitted the part about smoking marijuana with Nick when she made the police report. She had feared that the police would have been less sympathetic to her if they knew she had smoked pot with him, so she just left it out. I thanked her for being open with me and explained that if Nick were to testify to that fact at the trial, and Cindy had never mentioned it or had denied it when questioned, it is exactly the type of collateral issue that has no direct bearing on the rape but can give the jury just enough reason to distrust her. And once they distrust her on a minor issue, their faith in her entire story is undermined.

She understood completely and accepted our need to know "everything." When that mutual trust *is* established, the team of witness and prosecutor are off to a good start on building a solid case.

We sent the police officers back to Cindy's building to canvass the neighbors, on the chance that someone had heard her screams. They found two men who lived in adjacent apartments. Each of them described hearing noise—one called it "a yelp" and the other "a loud cry"—at exactly the time Cindy said the struggle had commenced. Both men said it surprised them because she was usually a very quiet neighbor, and yet neither man had undertaken to call the police.

The case was assigned to my colleague and deputy chief of the unit, Steve Saracco, who has an outstanding track record with trying difficult date rape cases—he has probably tried more of them than any prosecutor I know, with his fifteen years of experience in the office. Nick's story at trial was the familiar one, of course. He and Cindy were getting along so famously at dinner that she invited him up to the apartment to get him to make love to her. He complied and everything was beautiful until he told her afterward that he had another girlfriend. She was so upset by that news, since she liked him so much, that she "flipped out" and began screaming at him. He calmed her down and fell asleep, since she had invited him to spend the night. But she obviously decided to frame him on a rape charge because of her jealousy about the other woman.

The jury was hung when they tried to reach a verdict. Although eleven jurors voted to convict Nick of rape in the first degree, there was a single holdout. The case had to be tried a second time, and after again being exposed to the same process of direct and cross-examination, Cindy got the verdict for which she had prayed: Nick was guilty of rape and sodomy. The jury had believed her. The defendant was later sentenced to four to twelve years in state prison.

Cindy's case is typical of many date rape situations. She was with Nick and had allowed him to come to her home precisely because she liked him and trusted him. She had relied on her judgment about character, as we all do in our daily lives, and thought that she had had plenty of opportunity to get to know him over the months they had had casual encounters in a professional setting at the dance studio. Nick had seized on Cindy's vulnerability at the same time, relying on the fact that she trusted him to get her to the position in which he wanted her. Clearly, he thought he "deserved" to have intercourse with her that night, and neither her verbal nor her physical resistance was any bar to what force he was willing to use to accomplish his goal. It was only by her eventual submission to Nick's threats and physical abuse that Cindy was spared a further beating at his hands.

Like most survivors, Cindy came to us saying, "But the only evidence is my word, my testimony." Thank goodness, that testimony—when it is credible—is all that is needed to convict a rapist, as it is any other criminal. Cindy's case was made even easier than many date rape situations by her prompt outcry to her friends, her complete candor with us, and the extra boost from the neighbors who had heard her screams. We would probably have been unable to prosecute the case a decade earlier, before the corroboration requirement was eliminated, but we now try many cases like it every year.

While Cindy's case is typical of many date rape stories, there is another category of relationship that exposes women to the same ugly attacks in the courtroom even though they were not "dating" the men who became their assailants.

Thousands of cases a year, all over this country, occur of individuals who meet at their workplaces and socialize with their colleagues and co-workers. And occasionally a case comes along that reveals so much depravity within the human spirit that it is difficult to think about the perpetrator without becoming enraged at his actions and at the powerlessness of his victim.

The case of the *People* v. *Ashe, Howard, Kearney and Allison* began in the benign setting of the New York Public Library at Forty-second Street and Fifth Avenue. In the bowels of that enormous building work many shipping clerks, restorers of damaged books, file assistants, and messengers.

Among the hundreds of employees were two young women who worked in the catalogue department and had become friendly during the year they had been employed there. Both of them were twenty-two years old and single, and they relied on each other's good sense of humor to get them through their long and tedious hours underground every day.

These women, Carla and Karen, worked adjacent to the shipping department, where they regularly encountered forty-four-year-old Johnny Ashe, one of the shipping clerks.

For several weeks in the early winter, Ashe had papered the employees' bulletin board with flyers advertising the Johnny Ashe Revue, which the personable clerk explained was his real love: a collection of amateur singers and dancers he was organizing to appear in a stage show which would be videotaped with a view to selling it to cable television.

Ashe encouraged many of his acquaintances to buy tickets for the February performance. Both Carla and Karen were as interested as many of their co-workers and were flattered when Ashe offered to take them uptown on Friday afternoon to see one of the rehearsals, gratis. When their shift finished at four o'clock, they met Ashe and another clerk, Tony Howard, to go to the auditorium, and Ashe promised to return them to the front of the library so they could catch their respective buses home by the early evening.

Once they reached the neighborhood of the theater, Ashe said he had to make a brief stop at his apartment to pick up some of the sound equipment for the revue. The women, having known and worked alongside Johnny for the better part of a year, didn't think twice about accompanying him upstairs to help carry the things he needed. They entered through the kitchen door, and he suggested they sit at the table and help themselves to a soda while he and Tony disappeared inside to pick up the items they had come for. Then the men joined the two women, opened several cans of beer, and sat down to talk about their tastes in music.

When Karen said that they had better get on to the theater or she would miss her bus home, Tony Howard stood up in front of the apartment door while Ashe dragged his chair over and hooked it in place under the doorknob. He told the anxious young women that they had better follow orders if they didn't want to get hurt and threatened that he had a gun in one of his drawers that he wouldn't hesitate to use if they made any noise.

Carla ran to the door anyway, screaming for help, but Ashe grabbed her as Howard blocked Karen's exit route. Then, still holding on to Carla's arm, Ashe picked up a wire hanger and proceeded to heat it by holding it over an open flame on the gas stove. He pulled her toward the bedroom, lifted her skirt and lowered her underwear, and branded her on her buttocks as she screamed in pain.

Karen ran to her friend's aid and recoiled in horror at the sight and odor of the burned flesh. Ashe and Howard assured her that unless she cooperated they would do exactly the same thing to her.

What followed was several hours of literal torture, as Ashe and Howard took turns repeatedly raping and sodomizing both of the women. Ashe ran a bathtub full of scalding hot water and forced the pair to get into it, telling them they were too "dirty" to have sex with him. And although the two victims screamed and cried, no one either heard or attempted to rescue them.

Sometime after midnight, Howard made a phone call and summoned to the apartment two other fellow clerks, William Allison and Charles Kearney. One might think the newcomers would have been shocked by the scene they had entered, but Allison and Kearney joined in the assault quite readily, continuing the threats of the heated wire hangers as they watched Ashe reapply the brands from time to time.

This unspeakable horror went on throughout the night

until seven o'clock the following morning. By that time, Karen was desperate enough to get out that she was willing to risk being shot in the back—Ashe's constant threat—as she tried to escape. While the men were concentrating their attention on Carla, she ran to the door, unlocked the three locks and bolts that secured it, and ran on to the street half-naked screaming for help. People looked at her as though she were crazy, and no one offered to help.

Karen jumped the turnstile on the subway and took the train to its farthest destination—the last stop in lower Manhattan. There she approached the first uniformed policeman she spotted and sobbed the story of her sexual torture and fear for her friend, who had been unable to follow her out of the apartment. The officer calmed Karen and took her to Beekman Downtown Hospital. The examination revealed that she had suffered a severely bruised and inflamed vaginal area, lacerations in her anus, major burns on her buttocks and thighs, and trauma to her face and throat.

The police who were ensuring that Karen was in safe hands at the hospital had radioed the news to their counterparts in Ashe's neighborhood. Backup teams broke in to save Carla and arrest Ashe, who was the only one left there by that time. The other three assailants were arrested at their library posts when business resumed on Monday morning.

It must be hard to imagine at this point that there would even have to be a trial for this. What defense could these men seriously mount? That Karen and Carla *wanted* such treatment, that they "asked for it"? A sane person wouldn't think it possible, but of course, the defense of the library clerks would be exactly that: a vicious character assassination of the two complaining witnesses.

According to the defendants, who took the stand to testify, and through the bold cross-examinations and arguments of the four lawyers, Karen and Carla had been pursuing Ashe and Howard for months, begging to go out with them and to begin sexual relationships. The picture of the two women that the defense painted was that they were so sexually voracious the defendants themselves came close to crying rape. And the sado-masochistic aspect of the occurrence was completely the design and wish of the women—the "rough sex" defense was not invented by Robert Chambers's attorney.

It was not enough that the flesh, faith, and spirits of Karen and Carla had already been shredded by the savagery of their "friends'" attack, now the men were off to destroy their characters at a public trial. And the victims' families were shocked that the defendants could make any counterclaims against the shattered women.

One of the peculiarities of criminal trials is that a defendant may call people to the witness stand to attest to his good traits and qualities—so-called character witnesses. Even if Jack the Ripper were in the dock, family and friends could tell the jury about his wonderful reputation in the community for truth and decency. The first thing many victims ask about a trial—in this instance, it was the girls' parents who asked—is why we cannot call character witnesses on behalf of the *victims*. It is terribly frustrating to answer that it is not the victim who is on trial, when in fact that is exactly what comes to pass in many acquaintance rape cases.

Outraged at the defendants' allegations, Carla's mother begged me to let her testify, saying, "I want the jury to know that my daughter is a good girl, that except for being with relatives she has never even spent a night away from home, that she isn't sexually active." Though logic would suggest that it would be useful for the jury to know those things about Carla in deciding whose story made the most sense, the good character of the victims cannot be proved by supporting witnesses—a luxury enjoyed only by the defense.

First I had to explain to the jurors that the fact or occurrence of the sexual acts was not in question. The two women and four men all claimed repeated acts of intercourse in a variety of ways, and the physical evidence supported that testimony. That meant that the sole question was whether the acts were committed with or without the consent of the women. The jury had to understand that there is a world of difference—not only morally and ethically, but legally as well—between submitting under fear of torture and death, and consenting freely.

Ashe and his co-defendants portrayed a very different image of Karen and Carla. In vivid detail, they described weeks of conversation with the women concerning their sexual habits and appetites. They built this into the evening of the "party" which had been organized at the direction of the young women.

The only part of the story that the defense could not make too much sense out of was the fact that Karen escaped and went directly to the police while Carla was still at Ashe's apartment. If she were not telling the truth and the police soon after found Carla, how could Karen count on her friend telling the very same story? Instead, she might have said, "Karen, I don't know what you are talking about. You're just upset because you stayed too late and you're going to be in trouble when you get home." If the situation had indeed been an orgy, why would only one of the witnesses have been certain that the other would back her up as to every single detail? If the jury couldn't know enough about either of the women to know how absurd the defense was, they couldn't ignore that argument.

The jury convicted all four of the defendants. The case was tried before Supreme Court Justice Edwin Torres—a former prosecutor and a tough and eloquent jurist (and novelist who has written, among other things, *Q&A*)—who described the crime at the time of sentence as one of "almost unspeakable barbarity." He added that the branding of the women like cattle and other acts of depravity "would have raised the eyebrows of the Marquis de Sade." He then went on to sentence Ashe to the maximum term of imprisonment of twelve and one half to twenty-five years in state prison, as a repeat offender. He had, in fact, previously served time for an earlier sexual assault.

It is hard to focus on the fact that Karen and Carla had

only the most casual acquaintance with Ashe and Howard. They had never dated, they had no interest in developing a more intense social relationship, and they left the library together only for the purpose of going to see a musical performance for an hour before going home. Subjected to sexual and physical torture, they were also victims again of the basic acquaintance date defense: We (the defendants) only gave them what they wanted. Fortunately, the jury rejected that argument . . . but at no small emotional cost to the young witnesses who had to sit before an open courtroom and be smeared by their attackers.

The third case illustrating yet another kind of acquaintance rape is one I tried involving a defendant named Vaughn Lee. It is different from the other two cases in that the pair were neither dating nor even as well acquainted as co-workers—they had once been in each other's presence for less than fifteen minutes on a single occasion. And yet again, the old familiar defense was thrown back at this victim throughout the trial.

Janey was a twenty-four-year-old college graduate who had come to New York City to enroll in one of the country's premier acting schools. Friends introduced her to Lynn, who had a two-bedroom apartment on the Upper West Side that she wanted to share with a roommate. Janey went to the apartment to discuss the arrangement and learned that the room was going to be available because its current occupant, Robin, had moved her boyfriend into the apartment unexpectedly, and Lynn didn't want him there. Lynn and Janey hit it off well, and before she left that evening she was introduced to Robin and Vaughn, the couple whose room she was to move into. That brief introduction was the entire extent of her "relationship" with Vaughn Lee.

That is, until two weeks later, on a Wednesday morning, when Janey had taken advantage of a day without classes to sleep late. She was awakened by a noise at ten o'clock to see Vaughn standing in the doorway of her bedroom. As he walked into the room and sat down on her bed, she asked him to leave, reminding him that he didn't live there anymore.

Vaughn laughed and responded that he wasn't going anywhere: "I'm here for one reason—lie down." Janey clutched the blanket cover up around her chest and continued to plead with him for almost fifteen minutes, offering him her jewelry and money if he would leave her alone. She hadn't even realized she had begun to cry until he picked up the clock radio next to her bed, held it up against her face, and told her he would "bash in her skull" unless she shut up and gave him what he wanted.

She did shut up, and she also did exactly what he told her to do. After she had undressed, Lee made her stand up, saying, "I want to look at this meat." Then he assaulted her anally and vaginally. After it was over, Lee refused to leave Janey alone in the apartment, afraid she would call the police before he could get a good distance away, so he demanded that she put her clothes on and walk out of the building with him. They went together to the corner of Columbus Avenue where he finally left her. The next thing Janey was aware of was that an elderly woman, a complete stranger, had approached and put her arms around her, urging her to stop crying and asking how she could help. The woman took her to a nearby phone booth and called her roommate's office. Lynn rushed to meet Janey and took her to St. Luke's Hospital for an examination.

Janey was also reluctant to make a police report, fearing reprisal from Lee and aware that her submission to his threats left her with no visible injuries. She also knew that if her family in North Carolina heard about this, it would confirm their worst nightmares about New York and they would probably insist that she return home. Lynn was adamant, and encouraged by the supportive rape crisis advocates at the hospital—one of the best programs of its kind in the country—Janey called the police.

By this time, you all know what the defense was at the

149

trial. Janey, on the basis of a fifteen-minute introduction to the defendant two weeks earlier, seduced him when he came to the apartment on the morning in question to pick up the rest of his belongings (none of which, in fact, were even there).

The woman who defended Lee mounted an aggressive attack on Janey, starting with the fact that she was studying for a "theatrical career," hence her ease at simulating hysterics for the courtroom audience. The truth is that most survivors get through the trials without crying, but that is not something that can easily be anticipated or controlled. I warned Janey that no matter how she was baited by the defense on the stand, she should try to keep her composure, since it was clear that the lawyer was out to ascribe all her conduct to acting lessons. She was tremendous.

Lee, a twenty-nine-year-old pimp with a conviction for promoting prostitution (no, the jury was *not* allowed to know that fact), testified in the same manipulative manner that he had been so successful with in his career. He admitted letting himself into the apartment that morning with the key he had kept in order to look for some of his belongings. He said that Janey came out of her bedroom with a blanket wrapped around her, and he "knew what she wanted—it was just a matter of time." He "patted her on the butt, she smiled," and then she led the way into her bedroom for the same sexual acts that she had described, minus the threats of violence.

How does a jury make a decision in such a case? They never get to see or know as much about Janey as her friends and family do, or even as much as we prosecutors learn. They observe her and listen to her for perhaps a few hours on the witness stand, with testimony limited to the account of her attack. The defendant has the same opportunity to testify, and also (unlike the victim) to sit in the presence of the jury day after day. In this case, that the counsel sitting beside him was a woman—vigorously arguing his innocence—may have sent a subliminal message to some jurors that he couldn't be too dangerous or that woman wouldn't be representing him. What a fallacy!

I urged the jurors to examine all the circumstances of the testimony; to look for inconsistencies; to use their common sense; and to consider who had the stronger motive to lie. Lee, of course, had expressed his anger at being forced to move out of the apartment, and admittedly had no business being there on the morning of the attack. Janey was forthright and direct in her testimony, and the defense was unable to suggest any motive for her having to concoct this story—particularly when the allegation exposed her to such a difficult process. The jury saw Lee for exactly what he was: a manipulative liar. They rejected his story of seduction and convicted him of rape. He, too, received the maximum sentence of imprisonment.

One minor follow-up to this case occurred two years later, when I had a call from my secretary informing me that Janey was in the office to see me. She was there because she had received a summons to appear for jury duty. It is very common for victims of violent crimes to ask to not serve on juries in criminal cases because of the emotional strain of reliving their own experiences. Often they come to our office for documentation of their cases to provide to the court clerk, and I was certainly ready to do that for Janey. "No, that's not why I'm here," she said. "I would never refuse to serve on a jury. If there hadn't been twelve men and women willing to serve on *my* case, I would never have seen Lee brought to justice. The system works." She had come to say hello and tell me that she had recovered well, had a terrific job, and was about to be married. She was still pleased that she had had the courage to go through the court process. It had been very cathartic for her—she had been able to put the rape behind her and get on with her life.

Unfortunately, not every date and acquaintance rape case ends with a conviction in the courtroom. In many jurisdictions throughout the country, a lot of these cases do not even get to trial. Prosecutors weigh the likelihood of conviction, which is often slim, and they do not have the ability to try every case. However, this is another area in which Robert Morgenthau has set an outstanding example by providing our unit with the resources to take to trial every case in which a credible victim is willing to participate.

These cases, for the most part, are made entirely (that is, convictions depend) on the testimony of the complaining witness. Rarely, unlike stranger rape cases, is the police investigation a critical factor. Fingerprints might identify an assailant in a stranger rape case, but identification is not the issue in an acquaintance rape case. Physical injury, which is not a necessary element of the crime of rape, is rarely present since the victims are smart enough to submit to clear threats of force in order to survive the attack.

For these among many other reasons, the survivor's actions *after* the crime may be very useful in the prosecution of the case. While a victim is often reluctant to report the incident to a law enforcement agency, it is very helpful that she tell *someone* what has occurred. Whether she confides in a family member, friend, counselor, or hot line staffer, we are able to present evidence of an immediate or prompt outcry, no matter to whom it is made. It is easy to explain to a jury why the victim avoided police or prosecutors, since she is able to articulate that fear or reservation, which usually makes good sense.

And it is crucial to her own physical and emotional well-being that every survivor seek some kind of medical attention after a sexual assault. Unless the victim is a child, physicians are not required to make police reports when they treat rape victims. And whether or not a victim is aware of this, her reluctance to have the crime reported should not stop her from going to a hospital to seek treatment. Also, the medical costs can be absorbed by crime victims' compensation organizations in most jurisdictions, if not by prosecutors' offices or local rape crisis intervention programs.

Medical treatment is essential for a victim, whether or

not she ever chooses to prosecute. Many assailants are in-
fected with venereal diseases to which the victim may have
been exposed during the attack, and for which she should be
tested and treated. While most of those diseases are curable,
many assailants—especially intravenous drug abusers and repeat offenders who have spent time in the prison system,
where HIV infection rates are inordinately high—are in-
fected with the incurable HIV virus, so prompt examination
and baseline testing is recommended for all victims put at
risk.

In addition more than two thirds of reported rapes occur without any external physical injury being caused to the
survivor. Those who are grateful to have no "apparent" or
demonstrable cuts and bruises should not assume that there
is no internal damage, something only a physician or nurse
can ascertain by examining the vaginal vault. Forced intercourse, even in a sexually active adult, may result in lacerations or abrasions because the sensitive area may not have
been lubricated as it would be in a consensual act. Some
women may require follow-up medical care. Certainly, in the
event a victim later decides to prosecute, even minor abrasions are enough to make the point to a jury that she was not
a willing sexual partner of the accused.

In one instance, I prosecuted a case in which a woman
had been attacked in an elevator in a housing project. Neighbors heard her screams and came to her aid by breaking
open the small window in the elevator in order to pry open
the door. The crowd was able to pull off her attacker before
he had penetrated her. He was arrested and charged with
attempted rape (because he had not completed the act of
intercourse), and the grateful woman refused police offers to
take her to a hospital because she knew the defendant had
not accomplished what he set out to do. When she got home
and went immediately into the shower, she realized for the
first time that hundreds of small particles of glass were em-
bedded in the rear of her thighs because she had been rolling
on the elevator floor on top of the glass from the broken

window. Her whole body ached so much she had been unaware of the fragments. The officers returned to her home
and escorted her to Metropolitan Hospital for doctors to
treat her and document her wounds.

The volume of data on acquaintance rape is growing
steadily and the crimes are serious, sometimes deadly so. We
all need to respond to survivors with compassion and concern, to encourage them to report and to prosecute the offenses when possible, and to place the blame where it
belongs: on the rapist.

CHAPTER THIRTEEN
"BUT HE DOESN'T LOOK LIKE
A RAPIST"

"**B**UT HE DOESN'T *look* like a rapist!"

Hundreds of times I have had women repeat to me this response they have received from family and friends when they have described a sexual assault by a mutual acquaintance. As I have mentioned, one of the most persistent myths about rapists is that they are physically unattractive, uneducated, and from the lower socioeconomic class. Since so many intelligent people make their preliminary judgments about guilt based on a man's appearance and station in life, imagine the response women get when they report assaults by professional men they have consulted for treatment or business purposes. They are universally disbelieved. Doctors, dentists, lawyers, accountants, religious leaders, teachers—educated, articulate, charming, sometimes married professional men— are often the toughest target of law enforcement officials precisely because they do not fit the public's stereotypical portrait of a rapist.

One of the most clever breakthroughs in the prosecution of sex offenses committed by professionals resulted from an investigation undertaken initially, with great creativity, by Leslie Snyder, which I took to trial after she left the office. It

involved several allegations of abuse reported against a fifty-
three-year-old dentist named Marvin Teicher, who had practiced in the Chelsea neighborhood of Manhattan for nearly
thirty years. He was married, had three grown sons, and
lived with his family in Westchester County.

In August 1975, an eighteen-year-old woman named
Alice went to Teicher's office for her first appointment. Before he began the dental work, Teicher sedated her with a
combination of drugs for painkilling purposes—to which she
readily agreed—and she was put in a state of "twilight sedation," conscious (but just barely so) and unaware of her surroundings. As the effects of the drugs wore off but while
Alice was still subdued by their action, she realized that
Teicher was kissing her face. He proceeded to lift her blouse,
kiss her breast, then pick up her hand, placing it on his penis,
which she realized he had exposed. The strength of the anesthesia made it impossible for Alice to act to stop Teicher.
The fondling continued, then he coolly completed the dental
work and left the room, allowing Alice to recover from the
effects of the drug before she left the office.

The shaken young woman told a friend immediately,
and although skeptical, he accompanied her to report the
abuse to the local police station house, where an experienced
detective listened to the story. Instead of making a summary
arrest, the detective decided to investigate by going to the
office and confronting the well-respected dentist—an opportunity not offered to most street criminals.

Teicher received the detective quite cordially. He acknowledged that he had treated Alice using his regular
method of anesthesia, a technique called "conscious sedation" which is a combination of the drugs Seconal and Valium. Under this the patient remains conscious in the strictest
sense but is rendered unaware of the dental procedure. In
support of his claim that Alice had obviously been *hallucinat-
ing* about the sexual overtures she had alleged, Teicher gave
the detective a pamphlet from the manufacturer of one of

the drugs, which suggested that a possible adverse side effect was hallucinations.

It is not very surprising that the detective closed the case at that point. After all, the word of a teenager, who had admittedly been drugged during the occurrence she described, against the statement of a mature medical professional, supported by scientific literature, would undoubtedly give Marvin Teicher the first round.

With such a direct warning signal as a criminal complaint, one would think that the dentist would have considered himself lucky to have gotten away with his conduct—if he were in fact guilty—and altered his behavior. Instead, he must have thought he had beaten the system since he brazenly continued on the same path.

The following month, a twenty-five-year-old woman named Barbara was in Teicher's office for the second phase of a treatment. She, too, was injected with a painkiller which she assumed would make her unconscious. Her only recollection after the needle was opening her eyes to see that the dentist had exposed himself, then feeling him kissing her as he fondled her breasts and vaginal area with his hands.

Unlike Alice, Barbara was reluctant to report her experience, since even her closest friends expressed disbelief when she told them what had happened. After some delay, she took herself to the same station house, and even though Barbara and Alice had never met, the officers made the connection with the recently dismissed complaint. When the precinct detectives called in the Sex Crimes Squad, the decision was made to present the matter to Leslie and enlist her help in conducting an investigation.

Everyone involved knew it would be impossible to go to trial with only the bare complaints. The testimony of Alice and Barbara could be easily attacked because of the very nature of Teicher's "weapon": drugs. Both women admitted that they had drifted in and out of awareness before and after the abuse, neither could estimate the duration of the episodes with any certainty, and the obvious defense argument—good enough to raise reasonable doubts among the jurors—would be that the women's sexual fantasies were drug-induced. The prosecution needed more stable evidence to be able to take the case to trial.

Barbara gamely agreed to return to Teicher's office for the purpose of gathering proof of his actions. The investigators would not allow her to take the risk of being abused again, so she was not going to consent to be sedated. She carried a recording device, concealed in her pocketbook, that transmitted her conversation simultaneously to the backup team, who monitored it from a nearby position outside the office. But because of the noise of the dental equipment and the piped-in music system, most of the conversation Barbara was able to conduct about her last appointment, trying to get Teicher to make admissions about his conduct, was inaudible. He finally, clearly, admitted that he had kissed her—and enjoyed it "very much. Very very much, very much!"

Wisely, the prosecution team wanted more. Once they realized that the dentist's office was not conducive to a quiet confrontational conversation, they directed Barbara to ask Teicher for a date, which she agreed to do—for investigational purposes. Again she concealed a recording device and again the police monitored the meeting. This time, the restaurant he selected for the rendezvous also proved too noisy a background, and the suave dentist's comments were mostly self-serving and wary. Again he admitted the kisses, but described Barbara as the aggressor and attributed all her other recollections to the effects of the drugs. The investigation seemed stalled.

In May of the following spring, twenty-three-year-old Cathy, yet another patient, had her first meeting with the ever-tactile Teicher. Awakening from her sedation, Cathy found her hand was being held by Teicher as he rubbed it against his penis. Then he asked her for a "head job," which she thought meant an act of oral intercourse. She lost consciousness again as he tried to talk to her about going to her apartment and making love. When she recovered, her vaginal area was irritated and raw, as though it had been rubbed or abraded.

Cathy told only her boyfriend, but he insisted that she go to the police. Again, when the squad was informed, they enlisted Cathy's assistance to reactivate the investigation. This time, Teicher called *her* to ask to visit her apartment. For several calls she refused his entreaties to meet with her—until the police were able to set up the necessary recording devices. He called again and offered to make a "house call," bringing with him his "bag of goodies." None of the detectives wanted Cathy to be alone with Teicher in her apartment, so she again refused.

By that point the futility of eliciting admissions from Teicher, now ten months after the first complaints, was apparent, and the police-prosecutorial team came up with a daring and innovative approach. They decided to send an undercover policewoman into Teicher's office to pose as a patient—and to surreptitiously make a video recording of his efforts to molest her!

How would it be possible?

An undercover police agent, like each of the other victims, would be rendered unconscious or unaware of the dentist's actions because of the sedation. Thus she would be in no better position to testify than the other three women. Also, an audio tape recorder or transmitter was of very little value since the sexual abuse could obviously occur without any words being spoken. The only solution would be a videotape or film of the action—but nowhere in the country was there a legal precedent to permit the secret installation of a recording device like this, nor was there a simple practical means of obtaining one.

The investigative team then commenced a legal strategy to get the court's permission to install a hidden camera in Teicher's office. In order to make the necessary analogy to cases in which the courts have allowed electronic eavesdropping—what we know as wiretapping—Snyder argued that despite the three separate victim complaints and ten months of dogged police work, all their techniques had been exhausted. The only way to ensure the safety of the undercover agent in the only location where the crime would occur was to film the crime's occurrence, and to monitor it at the same time so it could be interrupted as soon as any kind of illegal touching began and did not escalate to rape or sodomy.

On July 15, 1976, a Supreme Court Justice granted the application to allow a legal "break-in" to place the surveillance camera in the dental office to record *only* the appointment with the undercover police agent, not with any unknowing patients. Obviously, the privacy rights of other patients could not be violated.

The next step was to find a willing decoy. The New York Police Department refused to expose any of its members to the potential of sexual abuse. But there was a volunteer at the Westchester County Sheriff's Office, a bright young woman named Debbie—who also happened to have an abscessed tooth which made her a perfect candidate for the dental chair. Would she be his "type"? The only prerequisites seemed to be that she was young and female.

The introductory appointment was made and Debbie was examined by Teicher. He told her that she needed to have her wisdom tooth pulled and she agreed to be sedated for that occasion, which they scheduled for Teicher's first session of the morning for July 28.

During the preceding night, the District Attorney's Office's squad detectives, experts in electronic surveillance who were armed with their authorization to surreptitiously enter Teicher's office, committed their "burglary" to conceal the camera. With a bit of good luck, there was an air-conditioning duct positioned almost directly above the reclining treatment chair, so the detectives removed it and placed the camera within that recess. It was the dentist himself who activated the recording when he entered the room in the morning to set up for Debbie's procedure.

The nervous undercover cop, dressed in a sleeveless

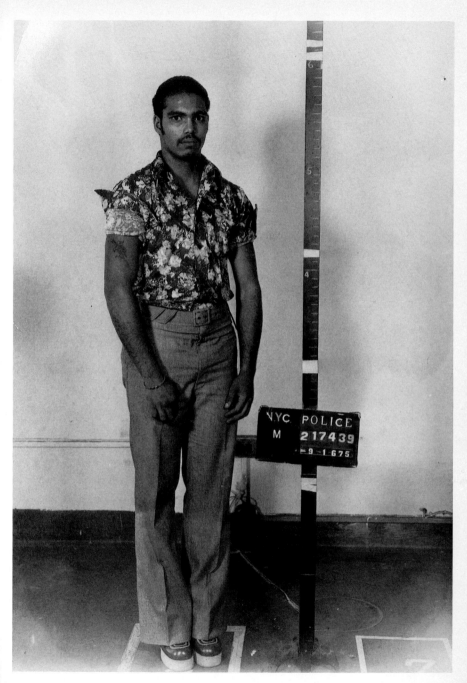

James Morales, after his arrest for rape—the second time—in 1975. The New York Police Department takes a "standing photo" of defendants arrested for violent felony charges.

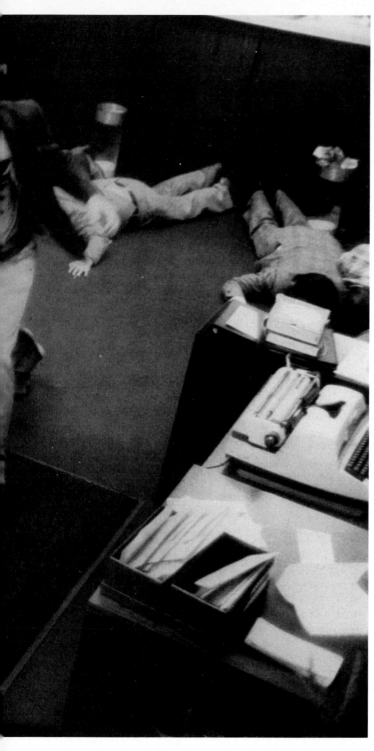

A surveillance camera caught Ray "the Cat" Olsen moments after he pulled a gun out of his gym bag and took ten hostages inside a Greenwich Village bank.

Sex Dentist Must Fill 4 Months

Dr. Marvin Teicher leaves court with wife, Betty, after sentencing.

By MIKE PEARL and THOMAS COLLINS

Dr. Marvin Teicher, the dashing dentist, videotaped while fondling a sedated female patient in his dentist's chair, was sentenced to four months in jail yesterday for sexual abuse.

The tall, gray-haired Teicher stood expressionless in Manhattan Supreme Court as Justice Dorothy Cropper told the hushed courtroom that the 53-year-old dentist had "betrayed a professional and public trust."

Teicher's wife, Betty, trembled and their 23-year-old son, Tom, choked back tears as they listened to the judge.

"His victims were vulnerable," Justice Cropper continued, "because they had no reason to suspect him."

Given Week's Delay

Cropper then sentenced Teicher to four months in jail. She permitted a week's delay in Teicher's surrender to give his attorney time to gain a stay of the jay term while an appeal of the sex abuse convictions is under way.

Teicher was found guilty last June of two counts of sexual abuse after an 11-day non-jury trial before Justice Cropper.

In pleading for a jail sentence, prosecutor Linda Fairstein, assistant Manhattan district attorney, said Teicher deserved to go to jail because "he grossly misused his position." She also said that although only four official complaints were lodged, "these women are only the tip of the iceberg.

Teicher's attorney, Jacob Heller, pleaded for mercy. "He tries to hold his head up high because he believes he is innocent," Heller said. "Let Dr. Teicher do some good instead of wasting away in jail."

Although the State Board of Dentistry yesterday refused a summary suspension of Teicher's license, Heller said the dentist may be prohibited from practicing again.

Marvin Teicher, a dentist charged with molesting three patients and an undercover policewoman, as he left the Manhattan courthouse during the trial of his case.

Man arrested in college film fraud

NYU students spur inquiry resulting in felony charges

By JANET ROSEN

After a three-month investigation by the Manhattan District Attorney's office sparked by complaints from several NYU students, an Internal Revenue Service employee was arrested yesterday for allegedly operating a fraudulent film-casting scheme.

Stephen Davidson, 42, of Glen Rock, N.J., was arrested yesterday morning by detectives as he exited a Chambers Street PATH station. He was charged with forgery, criminal impersonation and scheming to defraud.

Davidson had been allegedly operating the scheme for more than three years through Columbia University, City College of New York, Hofstra University, and, in recent months, at NYU, according to sources in the district attorney's office.

The sources said Davidson tricked young women he had contacted through the colleges into entering into acting contracts with a fictitious California movie company. Davidson arranged screen tests for the women in which he persuaded them to partially undress and, in some cases, allow him to spank them, the sources said.

Police said at least 10 to 20 of these young women were prepared to testify against Davidson, but one source added that "hundreds" of women who have not yet come forward may be involved in the alleged scheme.

The district attorney's office first learned of the case from a worker in NYU's Student Employment Service who

suspected that Davidson was not actually a film producer. Detectives said that the worker, Karen Carreras, was instrumental in the case since without her original tip and her steering young women who doubted Davidson's veracity to the detectives, there would have been no investigation.

Detectives said a total of six NYU students were part of the investigation, in which a telephone at the employment service was equipped to tape record conversations with Davidson. In addition, sources close to the case said detectives videotaped one of Davidson's alleged screen tests with an NYU student.

Davidson's contact with NYU, the sources said, began last Aug. 6, when, posing as Steve King, a producer for D.C. Productions, he telephoned in a job order to the Student Employment Service.

The service, located at 21 Washington Place, receives job listings from NYU and outside employers and posts them on bulletin boards for students to pursue.

Carreras said she received Davidson's call and posted the listing—which asked for actresses, both bit players and extras, for an upcoming film—on the arts section of

the bulletin boards.

Carreras said she took Davidson's order "without question" since employment offers received by the office are never checked for veracity.

Carreras, who graduated from the School of the Arts last June, said the office was quiet that day and "on a whim," she and three friends set up an interview with Davidson for the following Monday.

Davidson met with the girls in the employees' cafeteria at Two World Trade Center, claiming he could not meet with them in his office because he had a high-level security job at the Center, according to Carreras.

Carreras said that Davidson told them the film was titled "School Days, School Days" and would star Nancy Walker and Paul Lynde. She added that he gave them a

(continued on page 5)

sheet describing the film thusly: "Imagine a mostly all girls college in New York State filled with rich spoiled coeds...A place where the dean spends all his time chasing girls around the office..."

He explained that the girls, upon completion of a screen test, could play extra parts at $50 per day and could earn an additional $2000 by appearing topless in a crowded beach scene to be shot in Bermuda, Carreras said. The girls were told that upon their acceptance of the part, they would be contacted by the film's producer in California with further details.

The group, Carreras said, returned to the student employment service where a student had called with some questions about "King" and his project. Carreras said the student said she had already met

WSN Photo by William F. Biasiore

Suspect Stephen Davidson (center) being escorted by detectives from the district attorney's office yesterday.

The Internal Revenue Service investigator turned fraudulent movie producer —spanker Stephen Davidson in tabloid headlines

Police Department mug shots of Park Avenue dentist Benjamin Koplik after his arrest in 1984. Koplik had lost his license to practice dentistry for the same offense fifteen years earlier, but had it reinstated after a year of therapy.

Michael Koplik—Benjamin's twin brother and dental partner—upon his arrest, five years after Benjamin's case for the sexual abuse of a patient

Ballet student Nicholas Kabir's arrest photograph, following the rape of a classmate on the first date

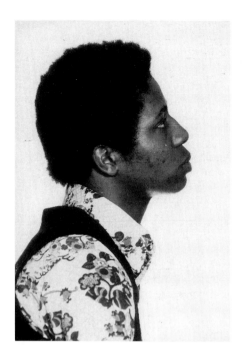

Twenty-year-old Russell West, arrested and charged with a series of rapes in midtown Manhattan . . . the *first* time, in 1974. This black-and-white photo had been removed from the files of the Sex Crimes Squad shortly before the second series of attacks began.

Russell West's 1985 mug shots, taken after his arrest which ended the second reign of terror caused by the Midtown Rapist

WANTED

FOR SODOMY AND ROBBERY

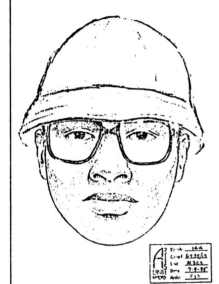 

THE ABOVE IS A SKETCH OF A SUSPECT SOUGHT FOR SODOMY/ROBBERY IN OFFICE BUILDINGS IN THE MIDTOWN SOUTH AND 17TH PRECINCTS.

DESCRIPTION: MALE/BLACK, 20-30 YEARS, 5'8"-5'10", MEDIUM BUILD.

WEAPON: STEAK KNIFE

CLOTHING WORN: BLACK BASEBALL CAP, WHITE FLOPPY HAT, SUNGLASSES, (RECTANGULAR FRAMES), VARIOUS COLORED SHIRTS AND SLACKS.

FACIAL HAIR: PRESENTLY STARTING TO GROW A BEARD BUT IS SOMETIMES CLEAN SHAVEN.

M.O.:   PERP WANDERS ABOUT VARIOUS BUILDINGS IN MIDTOWN AREA ABOUT 1700-1800 HOURS. WHEN VICTIM GETS ONTO ELEVATOR HE ROBS THEM AT KNIFEPOINT THEN BRINGS THEM TO A SECLUDED AREA, EITHER A BATHROOM OR STAIRWELL AND FORCES THEM TO COMMIT ORAL SODOMY.

ANY INFORMATION PLEASE CALL MANHATTAN SEX CRIMES SQUAD TEL# 580-6436 OR LOCAL PDU.

INFORMATION TO BE KEPT CONFIDENTIAL.

A New York Police Department artist created this composite sketch of the Midtown Rapist, based on the victims' descriptions, and detectives circulated it throughout Manhattan office buildings in search of the assailant.

Two photographs taken by the Crime Scene Unit experts in the Midtown Rapist case, at the scene of Marina Lamb's attack in the ladies' room on her law firm's floor. The black powder on the toilet seat—on which a footprint is visible—and on the door of the stall—on which fingerprints are visible—is the "dusting powder" applied by detectives to visualize and lift latent prints.

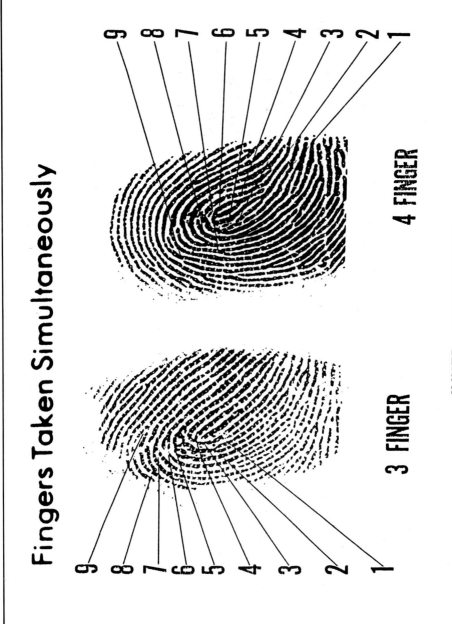

Fingers Taken Simultaneously

3 FINGER   4 FINGER

INKED FINGERPRINT

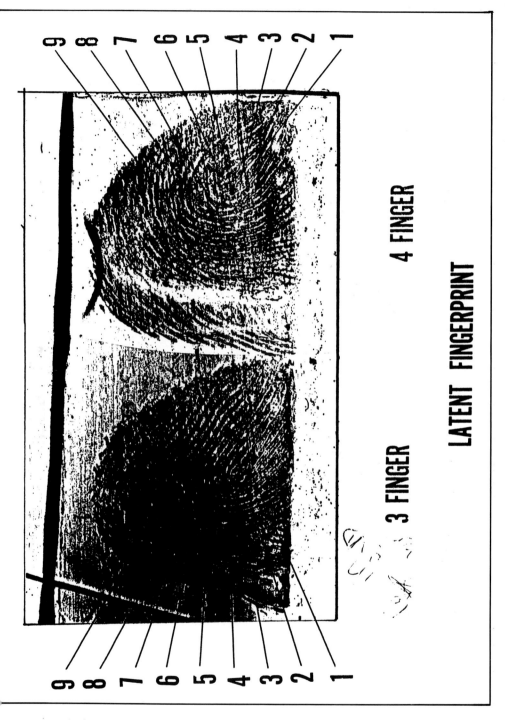

A chart prepared by the NYPD fingerprint expert Detective Jose Vasquez, to explain his findings to the jurors in West's case. The top half shows two inked prints of West's taken after his 1974 arrest; at the bottom are fingerprints found at the crime scene. The numbers represent the points of comparison—loops and ridges—used for identification of West's distinctive prints.

★★★★
Sports
Final

DAILY ⊚ NEWS

30¢ Saturday. July 27, 1985   **NEW YORK'S PICTURE NEWSPAPER**   Cloudy, damp High 80 to 85 Details p 2

Plutonium in reservoirs

WATER THREAT

HARMLESS—KOCH

Warning bared in free-Goetz letter

Story on page 3

Ex-con held as Midtown Rapist

Suspected Midtown Rapist Russell West (center) is taken from E. 51st St. police station for booking yesterday. West, who is held in attacks on seven women in Manhattan office buildings, previously was convicted of similar assaults in 1974, had served 10 years and had been released on good behavior. **Page 5**

Newspaper headlines showing the arrest of Russell West by Sex Crimes Squad detectives Paul Lizio (*left*) and the late George Zitis (*right*) in 1985

Polaroid photographs taken at the Sex Crimes Squad office of the lineup viewed by West's victims on the day of his arrest

An artist's rendering of my four-hour summation to the jury at the conclusion of the trial of Robert Chambers for the murder of Jennifer Levin, whose photograph appears on the easel to the right.

T-shirt and short denim skirt, was accompanied to the office by her "boyfriend" Joey, who was actually one of the other detectives assigned to back her up and interrupt Teicher when and if the abuse began. Others on the team were linked to him by a hidden earpiece as they prepared to watch the action on a monitor screen in the basement of the same building.

Debbie walked into the room and was seated in the chair. Teicher, sitting beside her on a stool with wheels, scooted between her chair and the table laid out with tools as he made small talk with her, finally injecting her with the anesthetic. His dental assistant appeared briefly, remaining only for the few minutes it took for the drugs to take effect and for Teicher to yank out the problem tooth. Debbie lay helplessly out on her back—apparently feeling no pain—as Teicher completed the extraction and the hygienist walked out. Then, his work over, Teicher wheeled himself back to Debbie's inert body. Since Teicher was not one for a traditional white uniform, all the viewers could see at that point was the back of his Hawaiian shirt—the flamingos, palm trees, and hula dancers—as he reached over to put his arms around the young woman's torso.

Video technology was not as advanced as it is today, and the camera was a stationary one. No one had anticipated that Teicher would *lift* the patients out of the chair while they were drugged and remove them from camera range, but that is precisely what occurred. The stunned detectives doing Debbie's backup watched incredulously as he tried to prop her limp figure between his legs, pressing her body against his own and lifting her shirt to reach beneath it with both of his hands. As he rubbed her breasts and then reached down to caress her buttocks, moving out of the limited range of the camera—the only sound on the audio was the lilting Muzak version of "Raindrops Keep Falling on My Head."

The surveillance team immediately transmitted the orders to Debbie's partner to stop Teicher, so Joey raced from the waiting area down the hallway and burst open the closed door to the treatment room. As he did, Teicher still had his sleeping patient on her feet, supported between his thighs, with his arms around her chest.

He gently placed her back into the chair and told the timely intruder, "She's in respiratory distress—I was just trying to help her breathe and ventilate."

The detective's response was direct: "You're under arrest."

Leslie Snyder indicted Teicher for the sexual abuse of the four women. The legal theory of the prosecution was not that of a forcible offense, as most of the cases I have described have been. Rather, these crimes occurred while the victims were "physically helpless," and thus, by law, incapable of consenting—drugged by the dentist and therefore unable to communicate their unwillingness to submit to his actions.

It was several months later, after Leslie Snyder had completed this innovative investigation and left the D.A.'s office for private practice, that I inherited the Teicher case for trial. How could there be a trial in this case when one of the episodes of abuse was filmed? you might ask. The first problem for the prosecution was that Teicher had moved Debbie out of camera range when he lifted her from the chair, so the crime with which the defendant was charged never fully appeared on the camera as the investigators had planned. Second, Teicher still intended to rely on the argument that the first three women had fantasized the sexual events as a result of the medication he had administered to them. Third, of course, would be the tried-and-true attack that would be launched on the character of those women (after all, what kind of women would have sexual fantasies. . . ?). And fourth, unlike street criminals, Teicher had the impeccable credentials of a successful professional and a happily married family man, whose wife supported him throughout the trial and sat in the front row of the courtroom with him every day. Teicher hired a well-respected criminal trial attorney to represent him, and both sides prepared for trial.

For a reason that was never explained to me, Teicher

and his lawyers elected to waive a jury—a choice that was his, as the defendant in a criminal case, to make. The case was tried, then, before Justice Dorothy Cropper of the Supreme Court of the State of New York.

By the time the trial started, we were down to three complaining witnesses. Alice had disappeared from town, leaving no forwarding address, and all our efforts to locate her failed. It was not until that time that we found out that she had been supporting herself by prostitution, and she was afraid that her lifestyle would be revealed because of all the media attention to the case. (Although it certainly would have given my adversary an easy target on which to base his character assassination, it would not have made any difference in the case—Teicher certainly was not aware of the fact at the time he treated Alice.)

Barbara, who worked as an assistant in a doctor's office, and Cathy, who was taking graduate courses, were eager to go ahead with their charges, and Debbie, the decoy, was set to be our first witness.

Her testimony described in detail her first appointment with Teicher, and how he recommended sedating her during the extraction that would occur on the subsequent visit. He promised that she would be completely unconscious, feel "very high," and have—in the dental chair—"an erogenous experience." Debbie went on to talk about her second appointment, which consisted of a brief conversation before she was injected and lost awareness of her surroundings.

She actually remembered coming to after the surgery and being told by Teicher to stand up and hold on to him. She was unable to stand by herself, so he lifted her against himself and began grinding his lower body against hers. She was so frightened—"scared to death"—that she began shaking uncontrollably and crying, but she was so weighted by the drugs that she could not even move her arms to push away from the dentist's grasp. Debbie also remembered the relief at her partner's rescue of her, when she was slumped back into the chair and her head stopped spinning.

Barbara and Cathy followed her to the stand with their stories. The detectives also testified and the videotape was introduced into evidence and played for the Court.

After we rested our case, the defense presentation began. Unlike in every other sex offense case with which I had been involved up until that time, the defense was neither identification nor consent. This was tried as a complex scientific defense, relying on expert medical testimony about Teicher's method of anesthesia. Both sides had educated ourselves by reading complicated texts and questioning knowledgeable physicians, since his British technique of "conscious sedation" was less well known and little used in this country. And that had, of course, made it difficult to find experts to evaluate and interpret the technique Teicher used.

Teicher's first witness was a specialist in dental anesthesiology. Although he tried to concentrate on the propriety of his colleague's dental technique, that is, the patient's sedation for the extraction, he admitted to being a bit baffled by the particular method of "resuscitation" that Teicher had employed with Debbie. The best he could offer was that it seemed to be a combination of two practices, neither of which had been used in more than fifty years. The reason Teicher's claim was so outrageous medically was because any attempts to resuscitate (if, in fact, the patient is in respiratory distress) *must* place the patient in a prone position. By standing Debbie on her feet, the oxygen supply was not going in the direction of her brain, as it would have needed to do—so lifting her from the chair actually endangered Debbie's physical condition while allowing Teicher to sexually abuse her.

Notwithstanding their inability to evaluate Teicher's technique, there was no shortage of dentists willing to testify on his behalf.

And they were topped only by his parade of character witnesses, including a nun who reported that she had been treated by him for years—always in the presence of another nun when she had been anesthetized—and had never been molested.

The defendant himself also testified. Since one of his major hobbies was amateur theatrics—he appeared regularly in community stage productions, playing leading roles in musicals like *South Pacific* and *The Music Man*—I knew that he would be self-assured and eloquent as he asserted his innocence.

Teicher followed his personal background and training information with a history of dentistry. Then he explained how he described his sedation method to his patients: "I tell them that they will have a feeling of euphoria, and the patients will look at me and it is totally Greek, and so I will tell them . . . they will space out a little and have good vibrations. I will tell them that they will have no recollection of the experience and basically they will have amnesia. I will tell them they should not be alarmed if they should have any other type of dreams; they can have a melancholia, they can come out depressed, they can wake up crying. They can have confusion, hyperexcitability, they can hallucinate."

Even the judge seemed incredulous, asking him if he told all his patients "all that?" He told her that he did. The tape was very clear, however, in Debbie's case, that the only thing he told her was that her episode would be *"erogenous and erotic."*

And although Teicher reiterated his claim that Valium was a hallucinogen, he was unable to identify for us any patients, other than the three who appeared in court, who had ever experienced hallucinations in the more than five hundred times he had administered the very same drugs he used in these cases.

We then presented a rebuttal case, calling a brilliant practitioner and professor of anesthesiology at the University of Pittsburgh, who had written the definitive text on the conscious sedation procedure. His name was Richard Bennett. As a proponent of this technique, he was offended by Teicher's ridiculous defense and outrageous conduct.

Bennett explained that between his own practice and his instruction of dental students over the years, he had supervised the use of these drugs more than thirty thousand times. Never had a patient developed respiratory problems, because the patient is not actually rendered unconscious (hence the name of the technique). Further, never had a patient experienced hallucinations when given Valium in any of the work that he had supervised. (The only reason the Valium literature listed that possible adverse side effect is that during the drug's testing phase, before its release to the medical profession, three patients being treated for the alcoholic condition of delirium tremens, which are themselves frequently accompanied by hallucinations, had reported them. They were *not* erotic.)

We made our closing arguments to the judge, and the trial was over. Teicher was convicted of two counts of sexual abuse. The judge obviously believed that a dentist's hands belonged in his patient's mouth—not on her breasts and buttocks. She pronounced his testimony "contrived, self-serving, completely unconvincing, and not worthy of belief." Although his sentence was only four months in jail, the more important result was that he lost his license to practice dentistry—which had been *his* weapon to molest unsuspecting victims.

While it is not permissible to speculate about such things in a courtroom, it is hard not to wonder how many other women, conveniently anesthetized to the extent that they had amnesia about the experience, were taken advantage of before Teicher was stripped of his license. From watching the videotape and observing Debbie's condition while in his care, it appears that the only thing distinguishing the dentist's one-sided sexual overtures from necrophilia was that Debbie was still breathing.

An individual like Teicher, and the many others like him, is really a conundrum to most of us. He is an educated man with a professional degree. He had practiced dentistry successfully for more than two decades. He had a fine family, a fancy suburban house, and many friends in the community. In short, he had a tremendous amount to lose by what he did. Nevertheless, the compulsion to feel a woman's breasts, to rub his body against the seemingly lifeless, unresponsive body of a complete stranger he had just drugged, was so overwhelming that it overpowered all of his rational impulses about self-preservation.

You may think, at this point, that this type of case is unique. However, the following story should convince you otherwise.

In July 1984, Joann, a twenty-four-year-old woman who had recently moved to Manhattan, sought a new dentist for a toothache she had. She wound up in the office of Benjamin Koplik, a sixty-three-year-old dentist who shared space with his twin brother on Park Avenue. When he started to work on her, Koplik offered her nitrous oxide, which many dental patients know as "laughing gas." Although Joann readily accepted the gas to relax herself, she was shocked and horrified to discover, as her dreamlike state faded, that Koplik had unzipped his pants and had placed his penis in her mouth as she reclined in the chair, helpless to react.

Joann could not bring herself to tell anyone about this for days, fearing ridicule and disbelief. When her tooth pain persisted, along with her sleeplessness and loss of appetite, she called me for an appointment, having read about our unit in a magazine and hoping that we might be able to help her.

Maureen Spencer and I listened to her story together. Joann asked if she had a case. We certainly believed her and told her she would have a *better* case if she could summon the emotional strength to attempt a taped telephone conversation with Koplik to try to get him to make admissions. That was the first step if we were to go further—as in the Teicher investigation—and even through Maureen and I did not expect this initial attempt to be successful, it was the starting point for what we expected might have to be video surveillance.

Joann accompanied us upstairs to the detectives' squad room that same morning. Maureen attached a recording device to the phone and she and I scripted the conversation we recommended Joann to follow to elicit the information we needed from her molester.

A receptionist answered, but once he heard who was on the line, Koplik took the call immediately.

At our instruction, Joann told Koplik that she still had a toothache, three weeks after his treatment. He urged her to come back and see him as soon as possible. She told him that she wanted to but that she was upset about what he had done—and she described exactly what she remembered as the effects of the gas had worn off. She said that she would not return until she had an assurance from him that it would not happen again.

We assumed he would deny the accusation and lay the foundation for the next step, as in Teicher's case. Instead, to our amazement, he admitted that he had sodomized Joann, just as calmly and routinely as if he admitted having stepped on her toe, and apologized for it as though it were just that insignificant: "I'm sorry. I'm really sorry. I don't know what came over me. It was just so hot in that room—I just unzipped my pants. I've never done anything like that before." He was so eager to see her again that he offered to do all of her dental work for no charge.

Not only was Koplik arrested, but much to Joann's delight he pleaded guilty—because of the irrefutable taped admission—and she never had to testify at a trial. He also lost his license. We were all surprised to learn that he had been convicted of *exactly* the same charge fifteen years earlier. At the time of that case, his license had been suspended. After a brief period of psychiatric treatment, Koplik was pronounced "cured" by his therapist, and his licence to practice had been restored. That would not happen again after Joann's case.

Incredibly, the story goes on. In 1989, a young artist named Rose called and asked for an appointment with me. She, too, had been given nitrous oxide by a dentist and, regaining her awareness, found him fondling her breasts. She, too, was met by disbelief when she told questioning friends and family and decided against a police report. She wanted action taken and was unable to forget about the molestation that had occurred.

At the end of her short summary of the facts, I asked for the name of the dentist. My jaw dropped, literally, when she said that it was Michael Koplik—the *twin brother* of the man we had prosecuted five years earlier. Rose did not know about Benjamin—Michael had simply told her that he had retired a few years before.

Again we thought of an attempt at an audiotape, but this time Maureen and I were certain it would fail. After all, Michael Koplik knew all the details of his brother's case, and had even been in the office the day we had taped the fatal phone call. He had watched detectives take his brother into custody and arrest him for abusing a patient. But we still had to try it before we could move on with any other kind of investigation.

Back to the phone with Rose, and a familiar script. Much to our surprise and Rose's delight, Michael Koplik admitted his misconduct and apologized for it. He, too, was arrested and pleaded guilty without a trial. Rose was also able to get a substantial settlement from Koplik as a result of a civil law suit she filed, again without ever having to testify at a trial.

Our success in getting admissions from sex offenders on tape never ceases to amaze me. It is a technique we employ as frequently as possible in cases like I've just described and with many other acquaintance and date rape situations, when the survivor has the fortitude to confront the offender for the purpose of securing evidence and building a stronger case. This method is legal in New York State, where taping phone conversations is permitted by the courts as long as one party to the call (in our case it is obviously the victim) consents to the recording being made. It also strikes me that most street criminals are far too savvy to succumb to this ploy, but the colossal arrogance of the better-educated offenders—the professional men, especially—frequently lets them play right into our hands. They always seem to be so certain that they can explain their conduct satisfactorily or assuage the aggrieved woman with an excuse or apology, and they often end up incriminating themselves instead.

For these offenders, the words "involuntary" and "without consent" seem to have no meaning at all. They are not the criminally insane who do not understand the laws, nor are they the culturally deprived who have no access to things they might desire unless they take them by force. In what most people regard as the most cosmopolitan, sophisticated city in America, these are simply people who put their own needs and desires ahead of the personal dignity of other human beings. These offenders *know* that what they are doing is wrong and not in conformity with the rules of society. The tragedy is that they just do not care.

CHAPTER FOURTEEN

"NO HUMAN INVOLVED"—
PROSTITUTION AND RAPE

IT IS UNLIKELY that any occupation or lifestyle exposes a woman to the threat of assault and gratuitous violence as constantly and completely as prostitution. Every year we see scores of "working girls" who have been victimized by assailants who are confident that these women will be unable to go to the police for help since they live outside the law.

The questions most often posed in this regard are: "Can a prostitute be raped?" "Isn't she assuming that risk by the very nature of her work?" "Isn't it impossible to convict a rapist of forcing a prostitute to have sex with him? That's what she was going to do anyway."

There are jurisdictions in this country in which these women are denied protection of the law, which is a rather shocking commentary on societal views of both women and rape. In 1991, for example, a journalist published a report that the police in Oakland, California, had closed more than two hundred reports of sexual assault—those made by prostitutes and drug addicts—without a single interview or follow-up investigation. The cases were simply "unfounded"—police jargon for saying that no crime ever occurred. It was only when the news story about their failure to examine the complaints appeared that the police were forced to re-open the many cases.

Similarly, in a Southern California community the same year, police closed all rape reports made by prostitutes and addicts by placing them in a file stamped "NHI"—No Human Involved. It is astounding to see in how many towns and cities this travesty is tolerated. In New York, and in other urban areas where prostitution flourishes despite its illegal status and accompanying risks, the police know full well the reality of the situation and generally are responsive to such complaints.

Are there ever false reports, and don't these cases cause serious credibility problems for juries? The answer to both questions is sometimes.

The most obvious kind of problem in complaints made by prostitutes is what police call "fare beat" cases. This is somewhat analogous to the individuals who jump a turnstile in a subway station to avoid buying a token and paying the fare. They are guilty of a crime called theft of services. They have cheated the system by not paying the fare as the rest of us must—hence they are "fare beaters."

Many of the street prostitutes, working alone on corners in midtown Manhattan or near the tunnels and bridges that lead to suburban areas in Westchester, Long Island, or New Jersey, do most of their business by responding to propositions of passing motorists. They negotiate a price—say, fifteen dollars for an act of oral intercourse—and once the offer is accepted, they get into the john's car and complete the transaction in a matter of minutes. The average exchange ends as the prostitute gets out of the car and the john drives through the tunnel on his way to his home.

Every now and then, an inexperienced prostitute will make the mistake of not demanding her money up front, before even entering the car. Once she has completed her end of the deal and requests payment, an occasional customer will tell her she's not getting a nickel and throw her out of the car before he drives off.

Ages ago, some understandably angry young woman thought of an appropriate "payback." She picked up the phone and dialed 911, reporting a rape and giving the plate number and description of the car, and the direction in which it was headed. She had figured that the best way to aggravate the john who had stiffed her was to have him locked up—especially if he had to call his wife from the station house and explain why he would be detained overnight.

In "fare beat" cases no rape has occurred; there has been no force, no threat, no violence—as the woman usually admits . . . the next morning. There has, instead, been a theft of her services. The sexual act was consensual but the woman was defrauded of her fee. It is obviously critical to identify these cases and get them out of the system—they *do* jaundice law enforcement workers who have much more important things to do than chase down false reports.

That issue aside, the rape and sexual assault of prostitutes illustrate better than any other kind of victimization that these crimes are *not* about sex. The availability of commercial sexual partners in a place like Manhattan is, sadly, limitless. The prices are correspondingly very low—almost every kind of act is for sale for less than the price of a meal at McDonald's. But as everyone who understands the history of this behavior recognizes, prostitutes are victims of rapists whose motives are degradation and humiliation, control and possession, anger and hatred, intimidation and terrorization. These women desperately need the protection of the law and yet are too frequently denied access to the system of justice.

Danny Minella, by the age of twenty-eight, appeared to be a model citizen in the small Westchester village in which he had been raised. He had achieved the rank of Life Scout during his high school days, gone on to a prestigious college before returning home to help his immigrant parents run their thriving retail clothing business, and served in the community as an auxiliary police officer.

In September 1983, a prostitute working on West Forty-third Street was propositioned by a handsome young man driving a Lincoln Continental. Her pimp, several doorways down the sidewalk, nodded his approval and Ginger, the prostitute, negotiated a price and tucked the thirty dollars the driver handed her into her boot before she got into the front passenger seat. They drove around the corner to Tenth Avenue, which Ginger expected, but she did not expect to see the gun that her "date," as she called the driver, removed from beneath his seat and held against her head.

From his back pocket, the driver then produced a pair of handcuffs, attaching one circle to Ginger's wrist and the other to the steering wheel. Holding the gun directly to the side of the anguished woman's head, he told her he was going to play Russian roulette with her and commanded her to suck his penis. When he had ejaculated, he calmly lowered the gun, unzipped Ginger's knee-high boots to remove the several hundred dollars she had made that evening, uncuffed her, and let her out by the side of the car in her bare feet. He told her there was no point in reporting to anyone what had happened since he himself was a police officer.

By the time Ginger walked back to her usual corner, she was determined to go to the Midtown South Precinct and make a formal complaint. She knew her pimp had recorded the plate number as she entered the car, and she knew the fancy Continental even had a small brass plate on the dashboard that said "Danny." She knew that some of the cops who had locked her up in the past would believe her this time since she had never cried wolf before. But her pimp disagreed. He saw no need to call police attention to either of them, and said that if the same driver came back, he'd take care of the guy himself.

During a period of five weeks, Danny made repeated forays into the midtown strip. He became bolder and bolder, cocking his gun and actually pulling the trigger as he sodomized and raped his cuffed victims on the front seat of his car. On one occasion, after blindfolding the young woman he had lured in, he drove her to a storefront in Westchester, took her down to the basement stockroom, and attacked her there, before driving her halfway back to Manhattan and throwing her out on the side of the parkway.

He had claimed four victims by this time, two of whom had gone to the police, described their plight, and given the partial license plate they had remembered. The midtown cops, well aware of the vulnerability of these women, were looking for the Lincoln every night between midnight and four A.M. And so were the pimps, because word had spread on the street. On October 11, 1983, at one in the morning, Ginger spotted the car and Danny cruising the Deuce (as Forty-second Street is known in the trade). She ran to a pay phone to call 911, fearful that her pimp would attempt to take Danny on himself and be shot to death.

Two patrol cars were on the scene immediately and one group of cops recognized Ginger. She repeated her story and the officers confronted Danny, whom she identified face-to-face. When the cops searched him, they found a switchblade in his pocket and a loaded semiautomatic gun under the car seat, next to a pair of handcuffs and a magazine clip with seven more live rounds.

The following morning, after all of his victims had identified him in a lineup, he was placed in a police car for the ride downtown to central booking. One of the detectives leaned his head in the front window to tell the cop, "Take the paperwork to Fairstein's office—she'll write up the case." Minella groaned, "You can't take me there." Nobody paid any attention to him, but when the cop walked into my office with the arrest report, the problem was immediately apparent. I had known Danny Minella and his family all of my life. His parents were fine, decent people who had worked a lifetime to establish a successful retail business and raise a family. I had gone to school with their sons and shopped in their store. I didn't want to see Danny any more than he wanted to see me.

I assigned the case to one of my senior colleagues, Peggy Finerty. She indicted Minella for the series of rapes and robberies. Months later, the case actually went to trial—I think Minella and his lawyer both believed that the women would never show up, or in the alternative, that jurors would neither care about them nor believe their testimony. He was convicted on all counts and sentenced to a term of nine to eighteen years in state prison. The morning after the verdict, when Peggy called to tell the women that the rapist had been found guilty, one of them said to her, "God bless America! Where else could a prostitute be raped and be believed in a court of law. Thank you."

Not long thereafter, a working girl named Julie was picked up on Eleventh Avenue at 2:30 on a freezing winter morning. She and her "date" agreed on twenty dollars for oral sex, and she drove around the corner with him and parked on a deserted strip on Forty-first Street. Then, William Crest pulled a gun from beneath his jacket and announced that he was going to take care of this "the easy way." Julie urged him to put the gun away and assured him that she would willingly cooperate. He refused—he wanted to keep the gun in his hand, to display his control throughout, and to heighten Julie's fear every moment of the encounter. Crest told her that if any police cars drove by and she made any noise, he would shoot her as well as the cops.

Crest grabbed Julie by her ponytail and pulled her head to his penis. After several minutes of oral contact, he told her, "This ain't gonna do." Still holding the gun against her body, he lowered his pants and made her sit on his penis. Then he turned her onto her stomach across the front seat, slit her skirt off by running a sharp knife down its length, and penetrated her anus, with the gun against the nape of her neck. When she was finally allowed to sit up, Julie saw a patrol car half a block away. Thinking that she was likely to die anyway, the half-naked woman opened the door and ran screaming down the middle of the street. Crest floored the car and headed southbound on Twelfth Avenue.

Two uniformed cops pulled Julie into their car, took chase after Crest as she told her story, and radioed ahead for assistance. Crest ran all the lights until he reached an impasse of stopped cars at Twenty-ninth Street. He made a U-turn but headed straight for a police roadblock, and actually collided with a patrol car before he got out and ran the short distance to and climbed a metal fence into the area of the heliport on the edge of the Hudson River. The cops moved in and surrounded him, and watched in disbelief as Crest removed his sneakers and eased himself over the side of the ramp into the biting cold water of the Hudson!

None of the officers followed. In fact, they assumed he would be swept away by the current and waited shoreside as the men from the Emergency Services Squad responded with their searchlights and rescue equipment. Half an hour after he had slid into the freezing water, the cops found Crest clinging to the pilings near the very spot at which he had entered and pulled him out. He was treated at St. Vincent's Hospital for hypothermia—his body temperature had dipped to eighty degrees—on his way to his arraignment. The police soon discovered that the car in which Crest had been cruising had been stolen twelve hours earlier. And unlike the "model citizen" that Minella was, Crest had recently been released to parole after serving a sentence for manslaughter. His guilty plea on the rape case earned him fifteen years consecutive to the many years he now owed on the earlier sentence because he had violated parole.

The vulnerability to violence of the women who live on the street—whether they are prostitutes or drug addicts, or merely homeless or mentally ill—is extraordinarily greater than that of those with a more sheltered lifestyle. The criminal justice system must be made accessible to every woman who is victimized, no matter how unsavory or unappealing the circumstances under which the attack occurs.

CHAPTER FIFTEEN

DNA IDENTIFICATION

IN ADDITION to the procedural techniques that have improved the likelihood of success in rape cases, there has been an exciting scientific breakthrough in the past decade that promises to be a superb method of identifying and convicting sex offenders. The science of DNA analysis, still new and controversial, is continuing to be refined and perfected, and to gain acceptance in courts across the nation.

DNA analysis, like the theory of fingerprint evidence, is based on the unique nature of each human being's DNA. The substance, present in most of our cells, is structured in the shape of a double helix—and the billions of "base pairs" within one DNA molecule define a person's genetic code, which is different from all others.

Each of our cells, no matter what body material is examined, contains the identical DNA. The importance of this is obvious in the investigation of a rape case. If, for example, a stranger assailant has completed an act of rape or sodomy, the victim's body or physical evidence at the crime scene may contain some of his seminal fluid. When DNA technology is available,* if evidence of the seminal fluid is properly collected and preserved by the investigating officer, it can be extracted from the evidentiary or forensic sample that has been submitted to a crime lab and then developed on a photographic print. Each print or "autorad" produces a banding pattern, exhibiting the different DNA sequences of each chromosome.

Eventually, when a suspect is caught, the prosecutor can apply for a court order to obtain a sample of the suspect's blood, since the DNA sequencing in his blood is the same as in his seminal fluid. If the court finds there is probable cause to grant this request, often based on a photo or lineup identification, then the suspect's blood is drawn and submitted to the lab for DNA analysis. If the banding pattern from the original crime scene evidence matches the pattern from the blood of the suspect, the analysts prepare a statistical method of computing the frequency of the particular banding pattern within an appropriate population.

When a match is declared between the crime scene evidence and the suspect's blood, and the technique in the laboratory has met all of the quality-control standards, this identification of the rapist through DNA analysis becomes an extraordinarily powerful tool for the prosecutor to present to a jury.

Many trial courts throughout the country have ruled that DNA evidence *is* acceptable at trial because of its reliability and general acceptance within the scientific community. Because it is such a new science, and laboratory procedures as well as population control studies have varied widely in their accuracy, many successful challenges have been asserted since the attempt to use this evidence in courtrooms in the late 1980s. But great attention has been devoted to correcting the methodology, for it is as valuable a device for exonerating individuals who have been mistakenly iden-

* Before the introduction of DNA technology, and still in most jurisdictions where DNA is too expensive a method to be used regularly, more established serological tests may be performed by laboratories to determine the presence of seminal fluid.

tified as it is for confirming the guilt of those identified by more fallible means.

Recent cases illustrate the successful use of DNA technology in the resolution of sexual assault cases. This is an example. In the late summer of 1991, a twenty-five-year-old ballerina with a touring national dance company of Germany was visiting New York City. Shortly after midnight one evening, she descended the steps of an entrance to the Fourteenth Street subway station on her way back to her hotel and was surprised to find a closed gate at the foot of the stairway, so she turned to walk up to find another entrance. As she began to climb, a man pushed open the closed gate and grabbed the woman by the neck from behind, covering her mouth with his other hand and dragging her back down the stairs into a dark and deserted section of the train platform. The attacker continued to choke the slim dancer until she fell to the floor, almost unconscious. Her brief opportunity to see the man occurred when he demanded all of her money and she reached up to give him the paper bills as well as the German coins still in her pocket. The man then made her stand up and face against the wall of the station and remove her pants and shoes—telling her that she would die if she refused—then he bent her over a railing so that she still faced away from him and raped her vaginally while standing behind her.

When the sexual assault had been completed and the man stepped back, the young dancer seized the moment to break away and run down the subway corridor, screaming for help. The rapist fled up the staircase but was chased by a police officer and passersby who had heard the loud screams of the ballerina. Almost ten minutes later, while other officers were tending the victim, the first officer to have heard her outcry returned to the station with a suspect in custody. The dancer looked at the man and was able to say that he looked *like* the man who had raped her, but she could not be 100 percent certain. She had been grabbed from behind and assaulted from behind, and she had had only a brief look at the face of the rapist, in a dark tunnel, when she looked up to give him her money. The witnesses who had participated in the chase were not eyewitnesses to the occurrence of the crime. They could add that they had chased this character from the top of the subway steps to a distance a few blocks away, but that did not make the suspect guilty of rape. A search of his pockets revealed a small amount of currency, the most damning part of which were the German coins he was carrying—which the dancer *was* able to describe and identify.

The suspect, Roland Stephenson, was a twenty-year-old cemetery grounds keeper with a previous record for robbery. There was enough circumstantial evidence to charge him with the attack on the dancer, but a good attorney would be able to mount a vigorous defense based on the identification issue at a trial. The Sex Crimes Unit assistant working on the case was Patti Prezioso, who called me to get authorization to attempt DNA analysis. We both realized that if the hospital examination had resulted in findings of evidentiary material in or on the victim's body—seminal fluid—then the potential existed to make a positive identification of Stephenson or to exclude him as the dancer's assailant. Patti prepared the necessary paperwork for the approval of the DNA testing, an expensive process that had to be performed by a private laboratory.

Patti also met with the dancer before she left the city for her home in Europe. The procedure was explained to her, and she agreed to submit a sample of her blood for analysis, which is a routine part of the process. Then, a court order was obtained from the judge before whom the case was calendared, based on Prezioso's showing that we had probable cause to request the defendant's body fluids, blood and saliva, for testing and comparison.

At the end of January 1992, the case detective delivered blood samples from both the dancer and the defendant to the laboratory at the Lifecodes Corporation in nearby Westchester County. The development of the DNA pattern takes weeks to complete, so it was not until March 25 that Patti Prezioso received the news in a Lifecodes summary of results: The DNA print pattern from the vaginal swabs (taken from the ballerina) matched the DNA print pattern from the blood of Roland Stephenson.

Further, Prezioso was told, the occurrence of the pattern obtained from Stephenson's sample would have an approximate frequency of 1 in 426,000,000 in the population of black males in North America, based on the population control studies of DNA testing.

These results were next presented to Stephenson's lawyer and to the trial judge. In this case, as in most others, the lawyer had the detailed report analyzed by his experts to see if there was anything to challenge in the methodology of the process. Since there was not, there was also no defense to this dramatic and conclusive form of scientific identification, which would be supported by the circumstantial evidence already on record.

The benefit for the survivor of the crime and for the system? Roland Stephenson pleaded guilty to the crime of rape in the first degree, the crime with which he was charged, with no bargaining and no trial. He was sentenced to a term of ten to twenty years, which he probably would have received had a trial been conducted, since the maximum for which he was eligible was twelve and one half to twenty-five years. The dancer was spared the ordeal of returning here to relive her experience in the courtroom. The outcome was final; there would be no opportunity for an appeal by the defendant.

While the larger number of sexual assault cases occur under circumstances that afford the victim a good opportunity to identify the attacker, there are many rapes—like this case of the German ballerina—in which the assailant remains behind his prey or blindfolds her or covers her head with bed linens or clothing. And of course, tragically, in murders of sexually assaulted women, circumstantial evidence has often been the only link to a suspect. With DNA testing, though, we have a means of using the rapist's own body fluids, the best evidence of his sexual violence, to prove his guilt with greater certainty than most critics accord the testimony of eyewitness identification.

One of the uses to which we hope to be able to put DNA analysis in the future is the creation of genetic data banks for the purpose of criminal investigations. For example, upon the conviction and sentencing of a sex offender, the law would mandate the drawing of his blood for the purpose of permanently recording his genetic code information. In the same manner that fingerprint comparisons are now used by police agencies to help solve major crime investigations, the DNA print records retained in data banks would be used to solve sexual assaults, serial rapes, and murder cases in which the victim was sexually assaulted before or after her death—in short, any kind of offense in which seminal fluid or blood evidence can be evaluated to link an offender to the crime scene. The discovery and introduction of the use of DNA technology in rape cases is a phenomenal tool that promises more satisfactory outcomes in cases that might have been difficult or impossible to prosecute in the past.

CHAPTER SIXTEEN
SEXUAL SCAMS

Sexual scams—fraudulent intercourse but not forcible intercourse—represent another form of victimization in which thousands of women are targeted and taken in every year by men who have designed ingenious plans to satisfy their sexual impulses. As you will see from the stories that follow, the victims involved have been "violated" physically and emotionally, yet there is nothing the criminal justice system can do to punish the offender. In many of these situations, although the abuser's behavior has been abominable, he has committed no crime. Even in our jurisdiction, where women are often more wary and mistrustful because of the crime stories associated with New York City, that these scams are as successful and numerous as they are leaves me no doubt that women everywhere are preyed upon by these carnal con artists.

Let me begin with a man called Paul Hannon. Although recently deceased, in his lifetime he was well known throughout the country as an acting teacher and coach, many of whose former students are legends of the American stage and screen. His prominence in the theatrical community brought him many students by word of mouth, and his classes were also filled with aspiring young actors and actresses who responded to ads he placed in local newspapers.

Hannon's introductory classes were composed of large groups of men and women who gathered in an enormous studio to learn and practice his particular technique. His early efforts were directed at convincing the students of the need to "feel loose" and "open up." (As much as those phrases alarm me whenever a victim of a date rape has described them as her escort's exhortation to an excess of alcohol or drugs, they seemed to be perfectly appropriate to a class of actors.)

To make his point Hannon had a number of methods designed to encourage his students to free themselves of their inhibitions. One of the first was called the "beach exercise." Hannon told the class members to lie on their backs on the floor of the studio, close their eyes, and pretend to be alone on a magnificent stretch of deserted beach, waiting for their lovers to appear. He proceeded to walk in and around the fifty bodies, reminding them that the sun's intensity was relentless and urging them to do whatever they thought necessary to make themselves more comfortable as they anticipated the arrival of their lovers. Slowly but surely, men unbuttoned and removed their shirts, women pulled off their jeans, and the more adventurous thespians unhooked bras or removed Jockey shorts to "sunbathe" nude. Those pupils, Hannon remarked to the class, were "doing beautifully."

At the second or third session, in the course of the beach exercise, Hannon would approach several of the women, kneel beside them, and tell each to imagine that he was the long-awaited lover. "Here is my hand," he would say to a woman whose eyes were closed, placing it within hers. "Put it where you would like it to be." Most—as they told us later—guided his hand to their foreheads or cheeks, to wipe the imagined perspiration. Hannon would then often move his hand to cover an exposed breast, saying, "Doesn't it feel better there?"

From that starting point, he would move to another favorite technique called the "one action, one objective" method. The distinguished sage would lecture to the class that "objectives are the things that you want, and actions are the things that you do in order to get the things you want." Hannon explained to them that sex was the strongest objective that human beings had, and that only sex could stimulate the power and intensity he wanted to see in his students when they were acting. "You have to want something so badly that you would kill for it—whether it is sexual fulfillment or a piece of candy."

Have I neglected to mention that the students were paying Hannon for the mastery of this technique, and paying quite dearly? What led to our involvement was that the professor would occasionally select students from the large class—presumably those he thought had great promise but had not yet "loosened up" sufficiently—and recommend that they might benefit from several private sessions with the master. His usual fee for a private lesson was more than one hundred dollars, but he would waive that fee ("in just this instance only, young lady") because of the talent he perceived beneath the surface.

After a number of private sessions over a period of several months in the early 1980s, one very distraught student began to discuss Hannon's method with some of her acquaintances in the class. Once five of them discovered their common experience, one of them called me to schedule an appointment for the group to see whether any crime had been committed or any action could be taken against the revered Hannon.

The women arrived and one named Alison was the spokeswoman for her companions. She had graduated from college the previous spring and moved to SoHo, supporting herself as a waitress while she tried to break into commercials and soaps to start her acting career. Like the others, she had heard great things about Hannon and registered for his classes. The beach exercise neither surprised nor shocked her, until the third class, when Hannon lifted her hand to

187

rub it against his clothed penis as he whispered to her to relax. Alison sat bolt upright amid the bodies surrounding her on the beach and eyeballed Hannon, saying, "I don't get it. What does *that* have to do with acting?"

He replied that it had everything to do with her ability to learn to free herself from her inhibitions and to trust him as a teacher. She had to learn to be submissive, and he could help her master the craft, as he had done for so many others. As usual, he threw in the names of many of the women— major stars and accomplished actresses all—who had been nurtured in his studio.

Several weeks passed without incident, until the afternoon Hannon complimented Alison on her progress but reminded her that she still seemed to have a few inhibitions that were holding her back. He offered her the gift of a few private sessions, and she didn't think twice about accepting them from this distinguished sixty-year-old genius.

Alison appeared at the studio on a Sunday morning. Hannon was reading in his small office adjacent to the large classroom when she arrived and showed Alison correspondence he had from directors and casting offices across the country. He could place her, undoubtedly, if she continued to progress. She had grown to trust him and certainly believed in his ability to help her succeed, and—just as he probably assumed—she was eager to please him.

For half an hour the lesson was straightforward, with several readings and routine improvisations. Then Hannon, littering his promptings with the names of famous stage temptresses, asked Alison to start to remove her clothes. She hesitated. "I want to help you," Hannon repeated. "You are the only one in the class I can do this for, I can help you be free. Do it very slowly, as though you are capable of seducing every man in this world." And slowly she began to undress, to follow his directions, to move as he told her to move—as though on a stage and not confined to a small office in a silent building.

Alison followed every sentence as though it were a command, yet she was the first to say Hannon never forced her to do a thing. "I was mesmerized, I guess," she tried to explain, so that when Hannon snapped his fingers, pointed to his crotch, and told her that he wanted her to unzip his pants and perform fellatio, she did that too. It was part of the "one action, one objective" technique and he told her it was crucial to her growth and freedom as an artist.

She did perform fellatio on him. Then she turned from him as she became sick to her stomach and started to cry, curled up at his feet.

Alison never returned to the Hannon studios. She had lost all sense of her dignity, her self-respect, her prospects for a future onstage, and more than a thousand dollars in fees for acting lessons . . . or whatever those classes had been.

Unable to understand why she had succumbed to these commands, Alison called another woman from the class a few months later and revealed her story in a midtown coffee shop. This woman had also been singled out for individual treatment, also the "only" one in the class with a future, and had continued to submit to the professor for weeks after Alison had left. He had persuaded her that it was essential to take off her clothes, perform fellatio on him in his office, masturbate in front of him while alone in the studio, and tell him over and over again that she was his "sex slave." She, too, wanted to believe—as Hannon told her—that all this was liberating!

These two women then took it upon themselves to try to get in touch with all of the other women they could remember and identify from the class. It was a rather unusual "reunion."

There had been only one professional actress in the group who had a steady role in a soap opera. She told Alison that the first time Hannon had laid a finger on her she knew she was in the wrong place, told him to get lost, and found another coach. One of the saddest episodes involved a nineteen-year-old woman who was recovering from cancer surgery and chemotherapy and had enrolled in the course simply as a diversion and an opportunity to overcome her shyness. Hannon had convinced her that her "modesty" was the result of the fear caused by her serious illness. Although he had never gotten her to "open up" by putting his penis in her mouth, he did make her believe that it would enhance her self-esteem if she undressed in front of him and pretended to pose for him like a centerfold in a men's magazine. She did and he photographed her.

The group laid out their complaints about Hannon in detail to me. It was their contention that he had sexually abused and sodomized them. Each conceded that she had not been "forced" to submit to him with a weapon or verbal threats, but that his presence was in itself overpowering. He was in a position of responsibility and authority, and obviously aware that he was, at least psychologically, coercing his students into this behavior.

It was a difficult and fascinating situation. As the women told their stories, it was easy to feel and to understand their outrage. They had trusted Hannon and relied on his distinguished professional reputation, and therefore assumed he was putting them through this sexual routine for some legitimate purpose. When they learned that he was in fact taking advantage of them purely for his own gratification, they felt thoroughly violated.

We knew from day one that we had an unlikely case on our hands, however, at least in a criminal court. In order to charge the crime of sodomy or sexual abuse, we had to be able to prove the element of lack of consent. Each of the students Hannon had engaged in this manner had followed his directions as though it were a stage performance—some expressed an initial reluctance, but each of the complainants had submitted voluntarily, according to the law.

My very experienced and able colleague, Steve Saracco, agreed to present the women to a grand jury in an effort to have the jurors determine whether any criminal act had been committed. The women testified credibly but the jury simply could not find any appropriate charge, and no true bill or indictment was voted.

When people are deprived of their property illegally, there are several recourses available to them. For example, the forcible taking of property or money, as in a gunpoint stickup, satisfies the elements of the crime of robbery. And in many instances when people are victimized by con artists or surrender their hard-earned cash to someone who misrepresents his purpose to them and then absconds with their money, those thefts are illegal and establish the crime of larceny—larceny by trickery or deceit. Clearly, legislatures have always considered it a serious matter for a person to deprive another person of money or property by dishonest means, by scams. But sexual abuse by deceit—which forcibly takes away dignity and self-respect—these scams have never been legislated. Paul Hannon and men like him, in many professions, have behaved in exploitive ways, painful and harmful to their victims—in this instance, to women who had entrusted him with their hopes and their futures—who for this have no legal recourses available to them.

Lest you think that this phenomenon is extremely unusual, let me assure you that my colleagues and I encounter it with alarming frequency. The victims of Paul Hannon cannot simply be dismissed as starstruck young women who went along with a casting couch ploy, as other examples will make clear.

One of the most pernicious schemes we encountered involved a man who advertised his services in the yellow pages as a "therapist." It came as quite a surprise to me to learn that this is not a title of a *licensed* profession in New York. Any one is permitted to hang out a shingle and be a therapist, without fulfilling any requirements of educational training, degrees, or state regulation.

Hugh Richards, a man who first came to our attention several years ago, described himself to our complainant as a therapist who specialized in holistic healing. His office was in a "wellness center," and he explained on her first visit that his method of helping her overcome her problems included a change in diet that he would monitor closely. By the second visit, at sixty dollars per hour, Richards convinced the very intelligent graduate student of the importance of before-and-after photographs to prove the effectiveness of the change in diet. She undressed and allowed Richards ("Call me 'Doctor Hugh' ") to photograph her.

As the therapy progressed, Richards explained that the only way to test whether his patient's system was purging itself of unhealthy chemicals and accepting the new diet was an examination of her bodily fluids. It didn't seem unreasonable, and so our complainant allowed him to press his mouth against the back of her hand, as though tasting the surface of the skin. Several appointments later, Richards announced that he thought he was tasting too much salt in the fluid, and the only way to get a more accurate reading was for him to taste the secretions that came directly from more sensitive ducts, not through the exposed skin. So the patient removed her clothes and allowed Richards to place his mouth on her body and suck on her breasts. She continued to pay him for each visit, although the depression for which she had originally sought treatment seemed to be deepening. Finally, suffering from a toothache one evening at home, the woman called Richards's number to see if he could give her medication until she reached her dentist the next morning. His holistic approach, he responded, made medication unnecessary (not to mention that he was not a physician and could *not* prescribe it!), so he told the woman to make herself comfortable on her bed, think of her favorite sexual fantasy, and stay on the phone with him detailing the fantasy while she masturbated.

After four months of not questioning Richards's treatment, the patient wanted to know how his recommendation would alleviate the dreadful pain in her mouth. He told her that by "pleasuring herself" she had the power to alter the sensation she was experiencing from pain to pleasure. The woman hung up on Richards, spent an excruciating night before she had her root canal work done the next day, and then called our unit to report what had been going on.

Our first shock came when we contacted the New York State Department of Education, the division that licenses medical and dental professionals, and learned that no state agency had any regulatory power over therapists. Wasn't Richards practicing medicine without a license, I inquired. No, not as long as he was not holding himself out as a *medical* doctor. I told the agent that he had called himself "doctor," but since his office sign and advertisements described him as a therapist, we were legally unable to touch him in a criminal court.

That complaint came to us in 1987. In the years that followed, Richards became bolder. By 1991, a new series of complaints came in to us. Although he still billed himself as a therapist, he had added the title "N.D." for Doctor of Natural Medicine. His office walls were covered with phony degrees and certificates, he wore a white lab coat and a stethoscope around his neck during appointments, and he had expanded his advertising with the telephone company in their "medical reference" directory, accepting referrals for everything from skin cancer to baldness. His treatment of female patients now included breast and vaginal examinations, and his unwitting victims submitted in the belief that he was a licensed professional performing these procedures in the legitimate course of therapeutic treatment.

Did he commit any sex offense? Did we have a crime to prosecute? No, although I would be the first to agree that each of the women he examined was sexually abused. Every patient had given Richards her consent to be examined—not one claimed it had been accomplished against her will. Sexual contact by deceit and fraud? Certainly, because the *sole* reason each patient had allowed the intimate touching was because Richards had maintained that it was an essential part of the therapy or "medical" treatment.

By 1991, however, because he had breached the Education Law of New York, that is, he was practicing medicine without a license, there was a violation with which he could be charged. Not a sex crime, just a licensing fraud and perhaps a successful civil lawsuit against this "healer" whose patients had sought his aid for a wide variety of problems and vulnerabilities that he could only have exacerbated.

Some states—New York is *not* yet one of them—offer protection under the criminal law when licensed physicians engage in medical exams or treatment that are "unethical or unacceptable." Thus in New York, if a patient submits to an act of intercourse with her radiologist or brain surgeon because he tells her it is part of her treatment plan, the fact that she has consented to the act, although for a fraudulent purpose, means no crime has been committed. Yet even in the states that have protective laws, the courts have been ridiculously reluctant to punish the professional offenders. In a 1980 Michigan case, a physician was convicted of committing cunnilingus during a medical examination. The Michigan Supreme Court reversed the doctor's conviction—the patient's credibility was never challenged, but the Court held that the prosecution had failed to present medical testimony to prove that such a practice does *not* fall within medically accepted standards!

That decision—that the Court had needed the testimony of an expert to say that a proper medical exam doesn't include the need for the physician to place his mouth on the patient's vagina—was met with great incredulity by most of my colleagues in the legal profession. On a memo of recent decisions circulated in the office, a quip by then New York State Supreme Court Justice Albert Rosenblatt had been added:

> Suggest that if and when you're ever ill in Michigan, it is probably better to simply suffer through with it, or wait until you cross over the line into Ohio!

Occasionally, even without an applicable section of the penal law to invoke, we attempt to fashion an innovative prosecution. In 1981, students in the theater departments of New York University, Hofstra University, Fordham College, and other local schools noticed postings of ads offering acting jobs to co-eds for productions to be filmed on exotic locations in the Caribbean. Those interested called the number and asked for the producer, Steve King, who explained the project to them. King was auditioning for ingenue types to appear in a movie about a sorority whose members were accompanying a college basketball team to a tournament. During the trip, some of the girls "misbehaved," and were playfully spanked by the teacher who had been sent to chaperon the tour. The women were promised excellent pay—fifteen hundred dollars per week, plus the tropical travel expenses.

The auditions were held in a midtown studio, which seemed perfectly legitimate to the women since many music and film groups rent studios there hourly for just such purposes. Scores of eager students scheduled one-hour auditions with King over a period of several months. There was a small dressing room where each was instructed to change into the "costume" he provided—a red miniskirt and demure-looking white blouse with a Peter Pan collar.

Then they were to go into the studio, where the genial King sat on a stool and explained that the self-timed camera across the room would record the audition. Each woman leaned over his lap and allowed herself to be spanked by him on the derriere. Each had been told to scream as loudly as possible during the spanking. The performances would be judged on the appearance of the actress and how realistically she vocalized as well.

As far as we could ever determine, King never paid any of the women a penny, since not one of them was ever hired. The jobs, the production, did not exist. The scheme came to an end when a group of the students went to the NYU Placement Office to find out which of their lucky peers had been chosen for the Caribbean vacation. When the woman in charge of placement tried to check with King Productions, she came up with a dead end, and rumors began to spread that the "scream tests" were not connected to any legitimate film project. Our office was contacted.

Our investigation began with an attempt to locate and identify Steve King. Perhaps he was for real and these girls simply hadn't filled the bill, or perhaps (as the school officials feared) he was a sex offender who was on his way to more violent behavior. It took a while until we found another series of ads, but once we did, we assigned two detectives to track him from the audition studio to his next stop—hoping he would lead us to his home or some other means of discerning his identity.

Imagine my surprise when the detectives called in to me at four o'clock one afternoon and told me they had solved the mystery. Steve King, who was actually Steven Davidson, was an agent of the Internal Revenue Service, employed just down the block from the courthouse at the Church Street offices of the IRS! Almost every afternoon, the forty-four-year-old Davidson would sign himself out in the field and set up shop in his rented studio—all on taxpayers' time and money. For months he had been turning his sick fantasies into reality with clockwork regularity, and without suspicion on the part of the bureaucrats who worked beside him every day.

Again it was my friend and colleague Steve Saracco who worked on the case. There was no sex crime, because the women had consented to have their buttocks touched. There was no physical assault charge, because no injury had been caused to the women. Saracco finally came up with the idea to charge the crime of scheme to defraud—a felony that accused Davidson of engaging in a "systematic ongoing course of conduct with intent to defraud ten or more persons by false or fraudulent pretenses, representations or promises and so obtain *property* from one or more of them"—the property consisting of the videotaped performance. Davidson pleaded guilty to the crime was given five years' probation, and, of course, lost his job with the IRS.

Perhaps you will say that the men who created and carried out these scams didn't physically injure or maim these women, and that these are just extremes of the games that members of both sexes use to outwit and trap each other. And perhaps you will say that had the women involved "used their common sense," they would not have fallen victim to these perverts. Sadly, it would seem to be true that no woman will ever have a protector like her own good sense, even though it often fails us when we are most vulnerable and in need of its armor. The variety of con games that concern sexuality, which part a woman from her self-respect or dignity, are just as infinite, and wrongful, as those that concern money.

Once again, this is what makes our jobs so interesting and, at the same time, so impossibly frustrating. We deal with a thicket of human emotions that twist the healthy around the sick, the vital around the decadent, the creative around the deadly. These instances of sexual abuse, nonviolent crimes quite distinct from other categories of sexual assault, also reveal that the world of human sexuality is extraordinarily complex—and that applying law to that world involves understanding not only of right and wrong, but also of sicknesses and strengths, hope and loss, reason and confusion.

I do not expect that the solutions will come quickly, if ever. It is my belief that more legislation is needed to control some of this misconduct, especially when the victim is vulnerable to the offender precisely because he is serving professionally as her caretaker—as a health care provider, religious counselor, teacher, or in some similar position of trust. While these men do not exhibit the life-threatening physical violence of forcible rapists, they practice a form of abuse and violation that should subject them to criminal liability in a court of law.

CHAPTER SEVENTEEN

IDENTIFICATION OF ATTACKERS: RAPE AS A UNIQUE CRIME

THE EVOLUTION of sex crimes prosecution seems pretty linear up to this point: improving the ability of our legal system to recognize and appropriately punish the evil that rape is. Any study of the history of rape prosecutions would lead to the same conclusion that most of the general public, uneducated in this legal history, holds—that victims of these crimes have always been more harshly treated within the courtroom than victims of any other kind of crime.

From the time of the early English common law opinions urging the cautious review of rape complaints, a great deal of legal energy has been spent on the assumption that many women falsely report this serious crime. As the corroboration requirement was eliminated across this country in the 1960s and 1970s, many of the reformers argued that false reporting never occurred and was not a danger in the prosecution of rape cases. Neither of these arguments is correct.

False reports of rape *do* occur. Historically, these reports have made it difficult for legitimate victims to be taken seriously—a prejudice that was born centuries ago and persists to this day. Once someone has encountered an accuser who has lied, and realizes how great the jeopardy for the accused is, one must look at the subsequent complaints with skepticism. For all prosecutors, then, it is critical to acknowledge that false accusations of rape *are* made, and I believe in emphasizing also that they are made very rarely. The way to deal with false reports is to identify them at the earliest possible stage and to purge them from the system, for they harm no one as much as they harm the true survivors of sexual assault.

The obvious first question is how one can recognize a false complaint. This is where specialization in training, both in police and prosecutorial units, is exceptionally valuable. Because my colleagues and I deal with the crime of rape in such volume, and exclusively, the rare false claim usually strikes a discordant note early in its presentation. Whether that note results from factual inconsistencies in the story or important information supplied by other witnesses, there is a bright red warning light that goes off in the skilled investigator's mind that alerts her or him to the need to proceed with a more critical eye.

Everyone who presents herself or himself to us is presumed to be a "survivor," and therefore telling the truth. Everyone is treated with the appropriate dignity, respect, and compassion. The decision that a particular case is unfounded is *never* made by our office simply because we did not like a witness's story or had a hunch she might not be telling the truth. The only way we will label a complaint as false is by proving it so—whether that occurs because we present the results of our investigation to the complaining witness and she admits her perjurious attempt to us, or because we have exonerated the accused by other means during the course of the investigation.

Legitimate cases, which form the majority of our workload, are usually quite straightforward. As you know from earlier chapters, we need no evidence beyond the word of the complainant. In order to unfound a case, since that decision must be based upon proven facts—not just a prosecutor's hunch—we inevitably use more time and resources. And that is the reason for my hostility to false reporters: They divert the very limited resources of the police and prosecutors' investigative teams from the needs of all the real survivors we should be helping, and they are responsible for the disbelief with which so many real survivors are thereafter met.

Before I go on to describe in the next chapter some unfounded cases and explain why they were reported and how they were uncovered, I think it is important to distinguish them from other forms of problems with which they are often confused. I will here discuss these problems, which are primarily questions of correct suspect identification and a victim's "incomplete" version of exactly what happened prior to the rape.

When I speak of false reporting, or cases in which a "victim" has completely fabricated the occurrence of a crime, I am *not* speaking about cases of mistaken identity.

The problem of mistaken identity, which can be an issue in any kind of criminal case, is not at all like an unfounded complaint. The survivor has actually been sexually assaulted in this instance—the complaint is real—but the person who has been charged with the crime did not, in fact, commit it. The victim is a victim, but she is mistaken in her identification of her assailant—and it is an honest mistake.

The fallibility of eyewitness identification has been the subject of much study and practice in the criminal law. Every one of us has probably had the experience of seeing a person across a street or on the opposite side of a crowded room and thinking that person to be an acquaintance. As we move closer, we realize our mistake, that the person merely looks like someone we know. Defense attorneys use that simple kind of example over and over again before juries to argue that the witness who has identified his or her mugger or burglar is not doing so out of malice, but is just plain mistaken.

One of the reasons for the greater reliability of identifications in rape cases, as compared with other crimes involving only a single eyewitness, lies in the very nature of the crime. It is, obviously, a *contact* crime, and it is the most intimate kind of contact that human beings can experience. The survivor has been forced to undergo contact with her assailant in ways that no other crime victim has—usually involving every one of her five senses, and for a longer time than the occurrence of most other criminal acts—and the trained sex crimes investigators skillfully probe to retrieve from her memory the information a survivor has recorded, consciously or not, during her ordeal.

In every jurisdiction of this country, people are convicted daily of crimes like muggings based on the testimony of a single witness. And in most of those cases, the crime has taken place in a matter of several minutes—a victim is confronted by a knife- or gun-wielding robber who says, "Don't scream—I've got a weapon—give me your money"—and the transaction is completed. The attacker is seen briefly if at all (since some robberies occur from behind the victim) and his voice rarely says more than his threat and his demand. Those victims look through mug shots and at lineups, identify their attackers, and testify successfully at a trial.

Rapes and other sexual assaults are not accomplished, as robberies often are, in a matter of three or four minutes. A "short" sex offense is a ten- or fifteen-minute encounter, and a victim and her attacker are rarely together for less than twenty minutes. And more frequently, when an assailant has his prey in an isolated location where they are not likely to be disturbed—her apartment, a remote rooftop, or a wooded ravine (in New York's Central Park a jogger was attacked by a series of vicious marauders without interruption)—then the attack may go on for more than an hour.

So the time factor as well distinguishes this category of crime, and as awful as it is for the victim to experience, precisely that *extended exposure* so unique to sex offenses is what we use to enforce and validate the survivor's identification. Think how much more reliable the character of the crime of sexual assault *forces* its survivors to be.

SEXUAL VIOLENCE

What we attempt to do is to use that time *against* the greedy offender because he has given his victim more opportunity to record detail about him, and to do so through every one of her senses. She has seen him face-to-face, often before any violence occurs, for example, on a ride up in an elevator or passage in a hallway as he recognizes his opportunity and turns to act on it. Even in the cases in which a rapist covers a woman's face or blindfolds her, he has had at least some visual exposure—and in most instances it is prolonged. The victim knows not only facial features but can also give a more accurate description of his body and size. No, she may not be able to say a height and weight in inches and pounds, but she has had his body against hers, on top of or beside her, and can tell how much larger or smaller, how heavy or slight the frame, in a way that professional investigators can thereafter reconstruct his size. And she may have been able to see what victims of a bank robbery would not have a chance to notice—marks and scars and even distinctive clothing on parts of his body that would be visible only with his clothing lowered or removed, during criminal activity. Probing the victim for detail, we often learn of surgical scars on an offender's thighs or abdomen, birthmarks or growths, unusual underwear (sometimes still on him at the time of arrest), and tattoos. My easiest investigation occurred more than a decade ago when a survivor described the tattoo of a scorpion on the rapist's penis. When he was apprehended months later and identified (fully clothed) in a lineup, he pleaded guilty to the crime because the detective had photographed his unusual tattoo and his lawyer had no defense to counter that unique marking.

And every other sense can be used in identification as well. An assailant is rarely silent when he attacks. He not only threatens and demands as a robber does but talks and questions during the sexual assault. Usually he tells his victim what to do throughout the encounter and often he questions her about her experience and personal life, although he is a complete stranger. Again, by language, diction, accent, dialect, and speech defects he leaves a mark that distinguishes him from other suspects.

Less frequent but occasionally telling is an assailant's smell. I am not talking about the cologne a date rapist might have primped with, but some other body odor the close proximity may have imprinted upon the victim. Sometimes, as with homeless or street dweller attackers, the odor is no more definable than a strong, unwashed stench. But sometimes it is a direct clue to the whereabouts of the criminal. A man who committed burglaries and raped several women in their homes reeked of a fish odor, described by each of the complainants. When police investigated the famous Fulton Street market, they found the attacker—a paroled burglar—working a night shift unloading crates of smelly fish and placed him in a lineup. In another case, a woman had been accosted in the stairwell of her walk-up apartment near the Columbia University campus. She spent a long time trying to talk her assailant "down," to convince him that he didn't need to do this to women. She told him he was nice-looking and well dressed and surely would be able to find consenting partners, and as she struggled on making small talk, he told her the reason he smelled so good was that he used Coast soap. Unfortunately, she was unsuccessful and he raped her and eight other women before his arrest. When the police executed the search warrant for his apartment, which yielded the jewelry and wallets of several of his victims—they also photographed and vouchered five cakes of Coast soap in his bathroom cabinet.

There is also, obviously, touching in these crimes, as in no other. The defendant has touched—with his hands and private parts—much and sometimes all of the victim's face and body. Similarly, he has often forced her to put her hands on him. Again, though not in every case, there may be something that signals a peculiar recollection to the survivor—a physical deformity on the body, raised scar tissue, jewelry on the wrist or fingers. In one instance an artist described touching her assailant's hands and noting that the lines in his palms formed unusually deep ridges. The police and I were skeptical about the feature she described, but when he was apprehended, apart from the lineup identification the witness made, we were all able to observe and feel the pronounced indentations to which she had been so sensitive.

The rapist, unlike every other criminal, compels his victim to experience him through every one of her senses— sight, sound, smell, touch, and taste—and it is by probing her memory for the impressions he has indelibly left upon her that we can connect him to his crimes and provide that evidence to a jury. Single-witness identifications in sexual assault cases—without fingerprint evidence, without DNA testing—should be the most reliable, stable, and convincing proof with which a jury can be presented.

There is another type of problem that presents itself in many rape cases which must also be distinguished from false reporting. Although it has no formal name, when it occurs I usually refer to it as the "gray area" of a case that needs to be resolved before the survivor and prosecutor can proceed to a courtroom.

Frequently when witnesses and victims first encounter law enforcement figures, which often is for the first time in their lives, they misrepresent some aspect of what has occurred even though they have truly been the victims of a serious crime. Why would anyone do that when seeking help from the police? For more reasons than I will ever be able to suggest to you, although a few may seem obvious.

For example, as you know, many rapes occur, especially in acquaintance rape situations, after both parties have been "getting high" together, situations in which the woman had *no* intention of becoming sexually involved with her companion. Sometimes, in reporting the crime, the women will deny that she had been snorting cocaine that evening—fearful that the police officer may have to charge her for illegal drug use, or just as fearful that the officer will not take her complaint seriously for a similar reason. Women with histories of prostitution will often lie about their criminal background, also

205

doubtful that they have a chance in the system if they present their occupational credentials. Most of the untruths are viewed as even more benign by their tellers. We have cases in which married women go to the home of a male acquaintance for a perfectly legitimate purpose and become rape victims as a result—and in some instances, they will tell a different story about how they came to be in the rapist's home (like "he forced me there at gunpoint"), because they know their husbands will "blame" them for having "allowed" the crime to occur.

For the most part, we are dealing with criminal acts that should be prosecuted, and yet, we cannot go into court when a witness is not telling the truth, even about one aspect of the story that seems irrelevant to her. "What difference does it make that I was snorting cocaine with him?" a woman might angrily ask me when I confront her about the issue. "He still raped me!" About the latter she is absolutely correct, but about the former—whether or not she has to admit what was happening between her and her companion before the attack—any prosecutor would have to tell her that her candor *does* make a difference.

The first problem with her question is an easy one. As assistant district attorneys, we are officers of the court, and it is our obligation not to allow perjured testimony to be presented in the courtroom. Most witnesses fail to realize that when they testify at a trial, under oath, they are actually committing the crime of perjury if they testify falsely. If that fails to move them, there is a more practical feature that usually hits home. Many witnesses have no reason to know what occurs at a trial, since for many this experience is their first contact with the criminal justice system. We explain that when they testify before the jury, the defendant is present in the courtroom, with his lawyer. Not only does the victim tell the story directly, through questioning by the assistant district attorney, but then she is cross-examined or questioned by the defendant's lawyer. After the entire prosecution case, the defendant has the choice to take the stand in his own defense.

That's the part that often comes as a surprise to people not familiar with the system. And in the overwhelming number of acquaintance rape cases, the defendants have no criminal records and often do take the witness stand to testify. If the victim has lied about some aspect of the time leading up to the assault, and the defendant's version of events sounds more credible, the jury may believe that "something happened" to the woman, but they will often fail to convict the defendant of any crime because they have reservations about the credibility of the victim. Thus the danger is real that the rapist can be found not guilty of the crime—even though the victim has been candid about every moment of *that* part of the encounter—because the jury has rejected *other* parts of her testimony as untruthful.

There is only one way to resolve this problem, which is to attack it at its earliest stage. Sometimes it is a very simple thing to do. In those cases where we have a valid reason to believe that the survivor is minimizing her drug use, we are quick to make her understand that she will not be arrested or punished for her substance abuse or possession. Again, our questions are not based on mere hunches but might arise from an experienced detective having told us that the crime occurred on the rooftop of a building that is a "crack den" or known drug location, but otherwise abandoned. If the victim has claimed she went to that address at three in the morning to look for her girl friend's apartment, I would certainly offer her the opportunity to change her story, once I have tried to make her comfortable with the understanding that she is not in jeopardy of punishment, and that her rape charge *can* go forward if she is candid about all of the circumstances.

Keep in mind that we are not hiding this change in the story from the defense in any case. By the time of the trial, the defense will have received all of the investigative reports in the case, which will obviously contain the original version of the events. The witness will have to explain—as she should—why she originally misrepresented the facts. It is part of *our* job, as prosecutors experienced in the issues unique to this crime, to make the necessary arguments to the jury that will enable them to understand the prejudices confronting the victim as she first reported the attack and to distinguish those circumstances from the violent criminal act that occurred.

Two of our trials help to illustrate the dilemma of the victims, as well as the probability that if the problems are confronted directly they can still result in successful prosecutions. For too long, when confronted with these "gray areas" in victims' stories, prosecutors simply exercised discretion *not* to take the cases to trial, or took their chances in the courtroom, only to see the women torn apart on issues seemingly irrelevant to the rape but essential to the jurors' ability to credit their larger stories.

This story of a sixteen-year-old high school student, Janice, may make clearer the range of reasons why victims find the need to change some of the facts when they initially report the crime. Janice took the train into Manhattan from her suburban home early on a Saturday morning to attend a "smoke-in" rally in Washington Square Park, an effort aimed at the legalization of marijuana by some NYU students. It was a beautiful spring morning and the large gathering of teenagers and college students mixed easily with the local street types. Janice's parents had been vehemently against her trip to the city, and their worst nightmare seemed to have come true when the phone rang at five o'clock and a New York City detective came on to say that "Janice is okay, she's not injured, but she has been raped and we are here with her at Roosevelt Hospital. How soon can you be here?"

Her horrified parents raced to the city to find their child, still tearful and trembling, in a cubicle of the hospital's emergency room. She had already told the police her story, directed them to the scene of the crime, and a suspect was in custody. Janice had described how she had tried to leave Washington Square by two o'clock, when a man had held a knife to her side, threatened to kill her if she made a sound or signaled to anyone, and abducted her from that area. He forced her to get on the subway and they rode to the Upper West Side, where he took her into Riverside Park—almost one hundred city blocks north of where he had encountered her—into a small cave formed by enormous rocks, and sexually assaulted her at knife point. Janice was seen by a police officer on patrol as she struggled to find her way back to the street, dirty and dazed from the attack.

The defendant had been arrested immediately thereafter, still in his cave, and had told the police a different story—which is not unusual for suspects charged with any type of crime. He was homeless, and his shabby, toothless appearance was in sharp contrast to the preppily dressed teenager who appeared in the District Attorney's Office two days later for her testimony before the grand jury. Yet the defendant continued to insist that Janice was his friend (even calling her by name), and that she had accompanied him to his "home" quite willingly.

One of the experienced lawyers in the Sex Crimes Unit, Nancy Paterson, was assigned the case. Before she headed for the grand jury, she came to my office to discuss it with me. There was no question that Janice had been the victim of a life-threatening rape—her description of the events in the cave was harrowing. But Nancy had good reason to question exactly *how* the young woman had gotten uptown, and whether she would have any motive to misrepresent any part of her story.

What were the clues to Janice's unreliability about the earlier events of the day? Although abductions can happen anywhere, in theory, it was unlikely that a knife-point kidnapping had occurred in broad daylight in front of hundreds of people in Washington Square Park. Especially since, as Nancy and I knew, the park had been saturated with uniformed police officers for the purpose of controlling the rally. Add to that the fact that Janice and her attacker then had spent at least half an hour on well-populated and fairly well policed subway trains to get to the actual location of the crime. Had she not been able to signal her distress to anyone throughout that ride? We are keenly aware that most offenders will lie for their own self-preservation—we always examine their statements—although occasionally there is a kernel of truth in their stories that cannot be ignored. So we went over the suspect's statement. In it he kept repeating that he had been "very good" to Janice before they went uptown—she had been hungry and he had taken her to a bodega to buy her a soda and sandwich. Was he lying, or had she chosen to omit this from her narrative? We needed to know, for if we could locate the particular store, we might find witnesses who could either support, or contradict, that part of Janice's report.

It made sense for me to be the one to question Janice. Nancy was going to be the prosecutor from this initial stage throughout the trial of the case, and they had already, in just a few hours together, established a rapport. We thought it was essential that Nancy maintain that relationship and that I be the "bad guy" who would probe more deeply into the events leading up to the assault.

Nancy introduced me to Janice and then left us alone together. The teenager was quite brave and understood the importance of the testimony she was about to give that afternoon. I prefaced my remarks with an expression of my appreciation for what she had been subjected to and her intelligence in getting away from her assailant and reporting to the police. I made it very clear that we *believed* that she had been raped and that Nancy was going to do everything possible to convict her attacker, as well as make Janice as comfortable as possible in getting through everything. Then I went on to explain that the only way there could be a problem was if she had not told the truth or had exaggerated some point, for whatever reason, even if that point seemed inconsequential to her. If she gave the jury any reason to distrust any part of her story, then we would have no way to protect her. Only two people knew what actually had happened during all those hours—Janice and her rapist—and no matter how violent and unprovoked his crime had been, if his lawyer could make half of her story seem incredible, then the jury could choose to reject it all.

It didn't take long for tears to well up in Janice's eyes, and she didn't hesitate too long before telling me what the problem had been. Most of the time, when survivors create this "gray area" of untruth, there is a motive that has driven them to lie—one that seems quite reasonable and necessary to them, just as they think it is unrelated to the case. Once we pierce that motive, we can understand the fabrication and attempt to resolve it before it results in a greater miscarriage of justice.

"I can't testify to what really happened," Janice pleaded to me. "My parents will absolutely kill me if they find out—they'll never let me leave the house again." I tried to assure her that her parents were glad she was alive and were not being judgmental, and that Nancy and I would work with them to make certain there would be no repercussions. Once I explained to Janice the risk she took by withholding the truth, and that we could not go forward with the case unless she gave us everything, she reluctantly agreed to tell Nancy and me the story.

It had started the way she described, and by late morning she had met the defendant, who had called himself John, as she mingled with many of the people in the friendly crowd. After a few hours of hanging out on the grass with the same group of on-lookers, John explained to Janice that he had some marijuana he kept stashed in Riverside Park, and he wanted to go uptown to get it to bring back to sell. But it was loose in a bag, he explained, and if she accompanied him, he would give her fifty dollars if she helped him roll joints to sell. John was friendly and calm, the day was magnificent, Janice felt safe—and excited at the prospect of making more than a month's allowance in an hour, simply by helping her new friend.

So it was quite true that she had not been abducted from the crowded mass of people and police, and that John had never shown her a knife or threatened her in any way. They walked out of the park together, with John's promise that he would get her back to Grand Central Station in time for her afternoon train home. And yes, she had asked him to stop for something to eat, so they did go to a small shop for a sandwich. Even though John was homeless, he had some cash from his petty sales of grass, with which he treated her to lunch. He was a nice guy . . . then.

They rode uptown on the subway, and Janice never thought twice about going into Riverside Park. The walkways and grassy patches were filled with walkers and runners and people enjoying picnics. John walked to a more isolated area which had several large rock formations and explained that he kept his stash inside under the rocks. Janice wasn't even apprehensive as she entered the cavelike boulders—she had been in John's company for close to three hours; she was sympathetic to his plight as a homeless person; he had been casual and impersonal with her; and he had never so much as touched her or made any references to anything sexual. But as soon as she passed through the mouth of the cave, John grabbed her around the neck and covered her mouth with his hand, and for the first time she saw the glinting flash of a knife as he raised it to stick into Janice's neck.

Thereafter, the story of the sexual assault, which continued for more than one hour, was exactly the tale of terror that Janice had told the first police officer. Now, we explained to her, when she testified, she would also have to explain that she had lied about how she came to be with John—fearing her parents' reaction—and then tell the true story. She did just fine, and as in almost every case in which the jury is able to understand and accept the motive for the fabrication, they indicted the rapist.

Janice asked Nancy and me to break the news to her parents. They were both intelligent and sensitive enough to recognize that their child had been through a terrible ordeal and did not need any more "I told you so's" or reprimands. They knew she was lucky enough to be alive.

When we examined John's criminal history, we noted that scattered among his many drug-related arrests, he had twice been charged with rape and twice beaten the charges— each time the victims had lied about their drug involvement with John, and juries had rejected their stories. Janice testified at this trial, and John was convicted of rape in the first degree, for which he received the maximum sentence.

Janice's initial exaggeration may appear to be just a schoolgirl's error and therefore an uncommon problem. But this adult version will help illustrate what tangled webs even the most severely victimized survivors can weave to complicate matters.

This case, which was unfortunately sensationalized in all the local tabloids, had a similar background: the occurrence of a devastating rape, but under circumstances that preceded the crime, embarrassed the victim, and caused her to become enmeshed in a series of obvious lies.

Karen was a thirty-five-year-old businesswoman who commuted daily to Manhattan from her Westchester home by train. On a regular basis, she found herself sitting beside an accountant named Harry, and they began to exchange stories about their lives, their spouses, their jobs and homes. After six months of "train socializing," Harry invited Karen to meet him in the city for a drink before heading home and she accepted. He revealed how attracted he was to her, and they both opened up about their feelings for each other, even though they both wanted to stay in their own marriages.

Before parting, Karen and Harry made a date to meet at lunchtime the next week, to go to a hotel room for a few hours and take the romance to its next stage. They met near Park Avenue and Fortieth Street and walked to a small hotel on the East Side, where at the sign-in desk Harry registered with an alias and paid for three hours in the room.

The couple was hand in hand as they walked down the third-floor corridor toward their room and didn't even notice the well-dressed man carrying a briefcase approaching them from the other end of the stairwell. Just as they reached the door of the room—Harry, with the key in his hand, about to unlock the door—they were passed from behind by the other man, who held a gun to Karen's head and told Harry to open the door or he would kill them. Their secret tryst became a living hell as the gunman took them inside the room, forced them onto the bed, and opened his briefcase to reveal handcuffs and a camera. With Harry handcuffed to the bedpost, the rapist began a series of sexually assaultive acts on Karen. When he had completed them, he secured Karen as well and took photographs of both his captives. He also took identification cards from their wallets so that he could blackmail them thereafter.

It is impossible to even imagine the violation, fear, humiliation, and related range of emotions that Karen—like every survivor—must have felt in those minutes after her tormentor closed the door behind him.

Now, add to that one element that made the pain even more excruciating. Harry, after comforting Karen briefly, realized that if *he* accompanied her to the police station and told the true story of the crime, then both of their spouses would learn of their attempted infidelity. With some incredibly weak line like "It will be easier for you if you do this alone," Harry convinced Karen to report the crime by herself, and to say that her attacker forced her off the street and into the hotel at gunpoint . . . changing the facts just a bit.

Karen had little choice in the matter as it became obvious that Harry was not going to stand up beside her. They dressed, Karen became more composed, they left the hotel, and Harry put her in a cab headed for the local precinct.

The police were terrific—they questioned Karen gently but thoroughly and took her to a nearby hospital where she was examined, tested, treated, and offered counseling. She called her husband, whose response was also wonderfully caring and supportive, and who drove in from the suburbs to take Karen home.

The detectives assigned to the case went back to the hotel, and although it was now early evening and the staff had turned over, the room—"the crime scene"—had been secured and was scrutinized for any kind of evidence that might aid in the investigation.

A day or two later, Detective McCarthy returned to interview the desk clerk in case he could augment the description of the gunman, whom the detectives assumed must have registered for the room shortly before taking his victim there, since she had described being accosted on the street and taken directly to the room. McCarthy, who doesn't shock easily, was rather surprised to hear the desk clerk tell him, "That isn't the way it happened. I don't know who raped her, but she stood here at the desk, hand in hand with the guy who paid for the room, and it didn't look like nobody was forcing her to do nothing at that point!" The description he gave of her companion could not have been more different from the way Karen had described the rapist if they had been from different planets.

The detective began to figure out that Karen was hiding something, and so he attempted to talk to her again—alone—to see if he could gain her confidence. She didn't budge and kept insisting that the clerk must simply have confused her with another guest.

The investigation stalled for a few weeks. Then Karen got a phone call from her mother-in-law, with whom she and her husband used to live, telling her that some mail had come for her to that address. Without thinking, Karen asked her to open and read it. It was the first blackmail letter from her attacker, since Karen's stolen identification card still had her former address on it!

Karen realized that the moment of truth had come, and the full story had to be told. The detective and I had a meeting in which we decided to arrange a sting-type operation, with Karen's involvement. She was to respond to the extortion scheme, which she did, and when the defendant arrived at Grand Central Station with his briefcase of photographs to pick up his ten thousand dollars, he was met by police officers—not by a blackmailed wife. The defendant was arrested, and at the trial—prosecuted by Steve Saracco—amid all the screaming headlines about "Terror at the Hot Sheet Hotel," the exceptionally courageous woman had to testify to all of the events, including her fabricated efforts to keep her indiscretion from her husband. The defendant was, of course, convicted and sentenced to twenty years in state prison.

I will never be able to list for you all the reasons for which survivors complicate their efforts to bring their assailants to justice by telling the police or prosecutor a "little white lie"—a fabrication or exaggeration they think is unrelated to the crime or not fatal to their cause. From any point of view as a prosecutor, such lies cannot be tolerated. The criminal justice system is *not* a game and the stakes for the accused are very high. If a crime has, in fact, been committed, then everything leading up to and around its occurrence must be told as the truth.

The two examples I gave are not rare happenings. We see this "gray area" whenever a survivor wants to minimize some part of her conduct or prevent a loved one from hearing facts that will cause him or her to be less supportive. It is a mistake made, in my opinion, by prosecutors in many jurisdictions to let a case go forward to trial when it is pregnant with internal inconsistencies and falsehoods. When those are exposed on the witness stand—as they inevitably will be—the victim is crucified before the jurors, who often are left so confused by the juxtaposition of truth and lies that they are left no choice but to find the defendant not guilty.

These cases *can* be tried and they can be successfully tried. It is essential that prosecutors identify any inconsistencies at the earliest possible stage, confront the witness about them and assure her that her assailant can be convicted, but that he will be convicted *only* if she is honest about every detail of her story.

CHAPTER EIGHTEEN

FALSE REPORTING—A TERRIBLE FOE
OF THE RAPE VICTIM

THE RAREST CIRCUMSTANCE in the field of sexual assault crimes—but by far the most pernicious—is that of false reporting. By this, I am speaking of those instances in which *no* crime, *no* sexual assault occurred, and yet for some reason an individual has reported to the police that she was raped and started the process that results in the arrest and incarceration of another human being.

It is hard to imagine what forces would drive someone to contemplate making such a claim, no less to carry out the entire deception. Aside from any ethical compunction, the stigma of being a victim is still a deterrent for many legitimate victims, as is the possibly rigorous path of a survivor through law enforcement agencies and medical protocols.

I had been in charge of the unit for several months before I encountered my first incident of false reporting, at a time when I was still imbued with the satisfaction of being a part of such a significant improvement in the criminal justice system, and enjoying the greater access we were offering survivors to the process.

A woman appeared at the Manhattan Sex Crimes Squad detective office to make a complaint. Louisa was a twenty-

217

eight-year-old Brooklyn resident who lived with her parents and had worked until recently as an executive secretary to Gary Branch, a senior partner at a prestigious Manhattan law firm. She was soft-spoken and delicate, and told the detective that she had been assigned to work with Branch for more than three years. He had always been respectful to her, and although he often made "sexist remarks" about her attractive appearance and dress, she found that to be a fairly common practice at the Park Avenue firm.

Louisa was often called upon to work long hours when deals were being made or briefs were being prepared for submission, so she never thought twice about Branch's request that she stay late on that particular October evening when he planned to have dinner with a client before returning to the office to edit the brief Louisa was typing that afternoon.

Louisa was at her desk at ten that night when Branch came back to check on the work. On his way past her cubicle into his plush office, he leaned over her shoulder to see how far along she had progressed, and Louisa thought the odor of alcohol was strong. Branch went inside and the phone console lit up as he made several calls. Then, Louisa told the sympathetic detective, Branch summoned her to his office, began to "come on" to her verbally, grabbed her in an embrace, and began kissing her. When she pushed away and smacked him across the face, he became enraged and pushed her backward so that she fell onto the large leather couch in the corner of the room. And there, she explained quietly, he raped her.

When she was finally able to clean herself up an hour or two later, Louisa took a cab home and cried herself to sleep. She kept reviewing the events in her mind, knowing that she had never done anything to invite Branch's advances and that she had always maintained the relationship on a professional level.

The shocked secretary did not report the crime immediately. In fact—as is common in many acquaintance rape cases—she told no one. She continued to come to work, for fear that if she made any trouble for Branch at the law firm, *she* would be the one to lose her job. It was impossible to talk to her parents about it because they were old-fashioned immigrants who thought Louisa was very fortunate to have such an important boss to work for. Add to that that Branch had a wife and children, and a professional reputation—those things had caused Louisa to give a great deal of thought to the position in which she finally found herself: reporting this crime to the NYPD and urging the detectives to arrest Gary Branch.

Louisa was a good witness—she seemed forthright and calm, all of her actions and reactions were consistent with those of a rape survivor, and the detective assured her he would go ahead with the arrest. Since Branch was not a fugitive nor did he have a criminal record, the detective called the lawyer at his office and asked him to surrender to the precinct to face the charges.

Branch was incredulous, but that, too, is the anticipated reaction of the professional defendant accused of this kind of crime. He was extremely cooperative and took a taxi to the Sex Crimes Squad office on West Eighty-second Street immediately.

He was advised of his rights and told he could, of course, have a lawyer present before he made any statements. He was quite anxious to tell his story, which he volunteered to do in great detail.

Branch had done well in his legal career. The forty-eight-year-old partner lived in Kings Point, Long Island, with his wife and two children, and the appropriate "toys," as he called them, his two Mercedes and a forty-two-foot fishing boat. Louisa had been assigned to him from the office secretarial pool, and within a month of their meeting, they had started an affair. On many of the occasions he had told his wife he was working late, he and Louisa were in a hotel room on Fifty-fifth Street, one block from the office. He wasn't proud of the betrayal, but the marriage had been a rocky one in recent years, and he and Louisa had found great pleasure, physically, in each other's company. In fact, in the last several months, his secretarial lover had even accompanied him on overnight business trips to a number of cities.

It was only a few days earlier that Branch had decided to end the relationship. Louisa had started to make demands that he leave his home and get an apartment with her, divorce his wife, and start a new life together. He had no intention of doing that, so he had admitted the whole story to his wife and entered marital counseling with her, and at the same time suggested to Louisa that she try to find a new place to work so they could each "go on with their lives." Louisa had threatened to kill Branch, to kill herself, to kill his wife— she was irrational and inconsolable—and Branch assumed that this was the reason for her desperate cry of "rape!"

The detective went into another room and called me. What should we do? A seemingly credible victim was alleging a terrible crime, and her accused, a man with impeccable business credentials, if somewhat vacant morally, was using the oldest line in the book: that his "scorned woman" was fabricating this mess to get back at him for a soured romance.

Was it possible that Louisa and Gary did have an affair, but he raped her after they had split up? Sure, but she had denied any sexual history or personal involvement with him. Further, Branch insisted to the detective that he could prove—through independent witnesses—that his story was true.

The detective and I shared quite a dilemma. We wanted to help Louisa, whom he had initially believed. And yet, to charge a man with the crime of rape, if *no* criminal act had ever occurred, is a course not to be pursued capriciously. I decided to let Branch return to his office and to follow up by meeting with Louisa at my quarters.

As the interview proceeded, I had to agree that she was very convincing in the telling of her tragedy. When I asked her whether she had carried on an affair with Branch, she looked me straight in the eye and denied it. When I asked

whether she thought he could produce witnesses to contradict her, she hesitated before insisting that he could not.
I read to her a section of the penal law called "Filing a
False Report" and explained that she would be committing
a crime if she was making up this story. Not a problem, she
assured me.

Branch appeared the next morning. He carried with
him the receipts from all of their air travel together and
various hotel bills from around the country. She was right, he
said, about the fact that there would be no witnesses in New
York. He had not wanted to diminish his reputation in the
eyes of his prominent partners who believed him to be a
happily married man, so all of their dinners in the city were
planned at secluded places where Branch was not known.
But there were certainly airline tickets in Louisa's name, and
there were several occasions on their out-of-town trips when
Branch had conducted business meetings at breakfast, in
their hotel room, at which Louisa had been present . . . often
in her negligee.

After a day of phone calls to many of Branch's business
associates, his story held up well. Several of the men with
whom I spoke had assumed the woman in the hotel room was
Mrs. Branch, but the description they gave fit Louisa in perfect detail.

Once more, we had her return to the office, and this
time we presented the results of our digging. For the first
time since either the detective or I had seen her, Louisa
lowered her head and began to cry. "You shouldn't be talking to people in Florida about this, they're not in your jurisdiction," she whined to me. The little bit of law that she had
picked up at the firm was sadly misunderstood by her, and
couldn't protect her from our attempt to see that no one was
unjustly charged. It was as though she had thought we had
no right to investigate the charge, or that we would be too
stupid to look beyond our noses.

The story was the most simple, most obvious case of
"revenge reporting" I have encountered. Louisa finally ad-

mitted to us, in the presence of her father, who had brought her back to us on this visit, that she had commenced the affair with Gary and had fallen in love with him. From time to time, when they talked about the future, he promised that there would come a time when he would leave his wife and marry Louisa. She, too, wanted children with Gary, a mansion in the suburbs, a fancy car, and a yacht of her own. And when she learned that the romance was over and her dreams were dashed, she wanted to hurt Gary in the worst possible way.

Louisa acknowledged that she hadn't thought she would get all the way through a trial before the truth was revealed. But the one thing that she completely had not anticipated was that Gary had *already* admitted his involvement with Louisa to his wife when he attempted to put their marriage back together. Louisa was sure that once arrested for rape, Gary would be cast out by his partners and lose his job; and even worse, that when the truth was revealed, his wife would walk away from him. If Louisa couldn't have happiness with Gary, then he should have nothing without her—nothing except misery and failure and heartache.

I am aware that if someone wrote this as a script for a soap opera, it might well be rejected as too trite or incredible. It is a true story, and a rare one in that the false accuser actually admitted the fabrication and the motivation for it.

The circumstances of false reporting are not always so obvious, and are frequently bizarre.

On May 26, 1989, a twenty-seven-year-old woman named Shelley called 911 from a pay phone on Central Park South and reported a rape at 2:00 A.M. Police responded immediately and learned from the woman that she had just arrived in Manhattan by bus and had walked from the Port Authority Bus Terminal to Columbus Circle (at the southwest corner of Central Park), where she had a pre-arranged date to meet a friend—her only connection in town from her home in Greensboro, North Carolina. As she waited in the dark, she was approached by a man who grabbed her arm, threatened her with a gun, and took her inside a wooded area of the park, where he raped and sodomized her. He left her facedown beneath a tree and directed that she wait there for five minutes. She did that before fleeing the park to call the police.

One of the most significant things about this report was its timing. Shelley's outcry was made exactly one month after the rape and attempted murder of the investment banker who became known to the world as the Central Park Jogger. New Yorkers were outraged about that crime, of course, and it heightened concerns about the normally safe park which is so well used by residents and tourists alike.

So police responded promptly, and when Shelley pointed out a hot dog vendor working his territory down the street, they arrested him as the rapist—even though he denied ever having raped anyone and even though he did not have a gun in his possession. The police knew that this new Central Park rape would get a lot of play in the press, and that it would heighten public tensions about the safety of the landmark location, because of its close timing to the previous month's terror in the park.

Shelley was taken by the police to Roosevelt Hospital, where she was examined by doctors and offered counseling by the Rape Crisis Intervention Unit. The concerned officers waited throughout the night with their recovering victim, and since she had no place to stay in Manhattan, they arranged to take her to a women's shelter and even bought her some clean clothing when the shops opened the next morning.

A day later, the same case officers picked her up to bring her to the office of one of the senior assistant district attorneys in our unit, Melissa Mourges, who was going to prepare the case for its grand jury presentation.

By this time, tabloid headlines indeed blared the story of "Gunpoint Rape in Central Park" as corresponding editorials questioned the seeming wave of crime escalating in that popular site, just as summer approached.

As Shelley was led into Melissa's office, another detective was leaving there, having prepared an unrelated case for trial that same morning. He saw Shelley, whom he thought he recognized, and told Melissa that he believed he had handled a case in which she had been the victim several years earlier. Melissa brought the woman in and began the process of making her comfortable and attempting to explain what would follow, before starting to ask about the details of the crime.

Melissa then went on to ask for pedigree information—Shelley's name, her permanent address, occupation, date of birth—which we routinely gather in every instance. Then, because one of our smartest detectives—Bruno Francisi—had alerted Melissa to the fact that Shelley may have been attacked previously, Melissa asked her if she had ever been to our offices before. Shelley said that she had not, and that she had been in New York City only once in her life, for a brief, uneventful stay. In response to other questions, she told Melissa that she had never been the victim of a crime before, and thus, obviously, never sexually assaulted until this attack.

Melissa left the room to tell Bruno that he must have been mistaken. He was not only insistent that he had seen the woman years ago—but he was also sure that her name was Shelley, and that the rape she had reported to him took place in Central Park!

While Melissa got to work on the new case, she suggested that Bruno go to my office to see if we could jog each other's memories about Shelley. The unit has a filing system with which we can track cases back to my first year in charge, 1976, and the records are cross-indexed by the last names of both survivors and offenders. When Bruno reminded me of the circumstances of the first case involving Shelley, which he said I had worked on with him, it did sound familiar to me. But since the surname she was using this time was not, according to Bruno, the name she had used before, our files were useless to solve the dilemma.

During Melissa's interview, she learned that Shelley

claimed to be separated from her husband, which was the reason for her trip to New York, to start a new life. That gave Melissa the reason to inquire about Shelley's birth name, which she immediately called over to Bruno, but still our records showed nothing. Bruno was adamant, however, and so he started my two paralegals on a *hand* search (our files had not yet been computerized) through thousands of our old case reports, starting in 1987 and working backward, to look for a case in which a witness named Shelley had reported a gunpoint rape in Central Park.

Before they got very far, Melissa had another breakthrough. She and Bruno decided to check with the FBI, using both of the names Shelley had given, to see whether they had any information about her. They certainly did.

Shelley had been arrested more than fifteen times, in ten different states, using a variety of aliases. She had two arrests for prostitution and two for armed robbery—neither of which would automatically cast any doubt on her current claim of victimization. However, the startling fact was that she had been arrested more than ten times for the crimes of falsely reporting an incident and false imprisonment—and in each instance the crime she had falsely reported was rape.

We had never had a case quite like this one. As in every falsely reported crime, the time, concern, interest, and professional attention of an experienced prosecutor, many police officers, medical personnel, and caring counselors was engaged in efforts on the survivor's behalf. She was "the victim" unless there was compelling evidence to the contrary. The distinction here, though, was a documented history that included this woman's criminal convictions for fabricating cases of sexual assault.

How to proceed? We had to explore the possibility that in *this* case, the crime actually occurred. We also had to confront Shelley with what we were learning about her history and ask her to explain it.

At the heart of this, as well, is the disturbing fact that for the five days between the suspect's arrest and his first court appearance, a man had lost his liberty and was incarcerated because of Shelley's accusation.

Melissa brought the woman to my office for the next round of questioning. Like Bruno, I recognized her too. Armed with the many aliases provided in the FBI check, my paralegals had found Shelley's first New York case, which had been reported in October 1984. "We meet again," I greeted her as Melissa walked her in. But Shelley continued to deny she had ever been in my office and assured me that both Bruno and I were mistaken.

I picked up a piece of paper from my desk and read to Shelley from what I told her was a police report: "The complainant stated that she was to meet a friend near the park at Columbus Circle. A man approached her, placed a gun to her back, threatened her not to scream or make a scene, and took her into the bushes in Central Park, where he raped her."

Shelley said, "Yeah, that's exactly what happened."

I leaned over to let her look at the paper, because I had been reading from the 1984 case that she had reported to Bruno—and yet that described the very same facts, in exactly the same location, as in the new case. None of us believed that lightning struck twice in quite that way—it was obviously time to confront Shelley with what we knew about her.

As we started to lay out the facts, Shelley admitted that she had lied about much of the information she had given to Melissa. She finally acknowledged that she was the woman who had made the report in 1984, a case Bruno and I had finally declared unfounded after Shelley had three different men, on separate occasions, identified and arrested for that crime.

In the meantime, Melissa continued to investigate the arrests and convictions from all over the country. Shelley's first false report (of which we are aware) was made in San Diego, California, in 1982. When she finally admitted that she had fabricated the attack, she pleaded guilty to the charge of false imprisonment. Instead of a jail sentence, the judge recognized her mental instability and placed her on probation, mandating some kind of psychiatric treatment. It was, I think, the appropriate response. But instead of availing herself of the much-needed help, Shelley simply left the state and never got the medical care that might have identified the underlying problem.

It is interesting to see the note made by Shelley's probation officer at the time of that first conflict: "This lady is sick—this type of case, false reporting, makes *all* rape cases more difficult!"

The FBI history revealed that Shelley was arrested for similar charges at least once a year thereafter as she traveled around the country—Texas, New Jersey, North Carolina, and Oklahoma. In January 1988, she was convicted again in the town of Middletown, Delaware. In that episode, she had been employed for several weeks as a housekeeper for a family with several small children. When she was fired, because of drug use in the house, she made up the rape charge to "get back at" her employer, who was incarcerated until Shelley admitted that she had lied in revenge for her dismissal.

By October 1988, she had moved on to Florida and in Sarasota she had reported that a man followed her home after a dance and had forced his way into the house at knife point, raping her there. Shelley's roommate told police that she had been sleeping fifteen feet away from the victim's bed—with her German shepherd guard dog at the door—and had heard no noise or commotion.

When the police in Florida asked Shelley to take a polygraph test—something we do *not* do in New York—she refused to and finally admitted that she was lying. (I neither approve of the use of a polygraph nor do I think it has much value, but as this example illustrates, it is often the suggestion of its use that encourages a liar to tell the truth.) Shelley then confessed her lie to the Florida investigators and said that she had made the report "just to get attention."

That last admission was the most useful point of information for us to attempt to understand why Shelley might have made up the current allegations. I do not know of anyone who would agree with the judicial admonitions of seventeenth-century British writers who stated, as I mentioned in the Introduction, that rape is a charge that is *easy* for a woman to make. For most of us who have heard the sad stories told by women who have been stigmatized by reporting having been raped, it is impossible to imagine what circumstances would compel anyone—without necessity—to take on the system and make up such a crime.

When Shelley finally confessed, she admitted that she had found, in the past few years, that most communities had developed very supportive services and systems for survivors of sexual assaults. In New York, for example, she was able to arrive in the city with thirty dollars, and because she had convinced everyone in the system that she was a victim of a violent crime, she was provided with housing and board, and even access to welfare eligibility on an emergency basis—thus she was given money too—and she was getting a lot of empathetic attention from advocates she met at the counseling programs. She even abused those services by enrolling in three of the programs at the same time, each without the knowledge of the others.

Clearly, this case involves a woman who is pathologically disturbed and in need of intensive psychiatric intervention. And while it is extreme and an extraordinarily rare occurrence, it illustrates that false reporting does occur, and does have devastating effects on the lives it touches. What was Shelley's diagnosis upon examination by the court-appointed psychiatrist? "Personality Disorder with Borderline Antisocial Traits." Quite an understatement, it would seem to me.

Some of the false reports are motivated by less complicated reasons. Among the adolescent population, we occasionally encounter teens who have reported rapes several months after their occurrence, with the parents demanding the arrest of the survivors' boyfriends. Obviously, the overwhelming number of rape complaints are real—most law enforcement officials equate the amount of false reporting of sex offenses with that of every other category of crime, at approximately 5 percent of the total number of reports. So every now and then, once my colleagues or I conduct our interviews of the young women, out of the presence of their parents, we get an admission from a frightened "victim" who will urge us *not* to go forward with the prosecution. Why? Well, she can't tell her mother, but the sexual intercourse was entirely consensual, and she became pregnant, and when her mother learned of the pregnancy, the girl lied and said she was "forced" to have sex so that *she* wouldn't be punished by her parents for her promiscuity. Most of the teens who report in this manner never think their stories will result in criminal cases; they are just seeking to protect themselves from parental wrath. The truth usually outs the moment they hit the police station or prosecutor's office.

And finally are the cases of false reports prompted by greed, of all the unlikely factors. From time to time, we confront cases in which the accused are very prominent men—celebrities, politicians, businessmen—whose lives and careers could be ruined by just the hint of scandal, no less an arrest for an allegation of rape. We have actually had cases—thankfully very few—in which women have attempted to extort such men by threatening to charge them with sexual assault unless they pay exorbitant amounts of money: blackmail. In some of these rare instances, we have been able to tape telephone conversations between the two parties, proving the women's attempt to "set up" their prey. (I am by no means suggesting that such public figures cannot or do not ever commit sexual assaults, rather, though, that they are very easy targets for those women who are using the false report as a means of illegally extorting money from them.)

For at least three reasons, then, I think it is critical to acknowledge, rather than deny, the existence of false reports of sexual assault, and to develop effective ways to eliminate them from the criminal justice system before arrests are made and before reporters infect the attitudes of the public who learn their stories.

First, these fabrications (which are themselves criminal acts) waste the time and resources of an already overtaxed justice system. Most municipalities do not have the manpower to respond to and fully investigate many real crimes, and therefore for each false alarm that is sounded, some legitimate victim goes unaided.

Second, for each false report that results in an arrest, a man is imprisoned—whether for hours, days, or months—when he has committed no offense.

And most important, to me, is that these falsehoods degrade and trivialize the experience of every legitimate rape survivor who will ever tell her story to a police officer or jury. They encourage the ignorance and callousness of people who still fail to see the extent and significance of the problem of rape. Each false accusation makes too many skeptics think that every accusation is a false one—which is a danger that cannot be overstated. False reporters are among the worst foes of real rape victims, and the deadliest enemies of legal protection for women everywhere.

CHAPTER NINETEEN

SERIAL RAPE—THE MIDTOWN RAPIST IS CAUGHT

PATTERN FIVE 1985—Manhattan Sex Crimes Squad.

That's how the rapist who attacked Lois Lusardo on May 24, Sylvia Becker and Tanya Johnson on July 3, and Marina Lamb on July 9 was known to the police department. He was the fifth serial stalker of the year to develop an identifiable routine. It was the tabloid press who gave him the name "Midtown Rapist."

One of the more difficult decisions in policing is the point at which a number of distinct criminal acts are labeled as the work of a single individual. It often seems simple and obvious in detective fiction or thriller movies, in which the criminal leaves some signature piece of evidence at each crime scene or calls his favorite radio talk show host with a clue to his acts. But in a large metropolitan area, divided into more than fifty police precincts and dozens of specialty investigative squads, experienced cops sort through police reports and forensic evidence for the much more subtle factors that suggest that one actor is responsible for a series of assaults.

The Lusardo case seemed to be an isolated attack, at least at the time of its occurrence at the end of May. The uniformed cops who responded to the 911 call had referred the investigation to the Sex Crimes Squad. Since the squad detectives had reports of every sexual assault in New York County, they knew of no other recent strikes in commercial buildings by an assailant matching the description Lusardo had given them.

The detective assigned to her case proceeded in the usual manner. The initial questioning at the hospital was detailed but gentle, since the emergency room records logged the victim in as "mildly hysterical with nervousness and hyperventilation." Once a description of the rapist was elicited, the investigators left Lois to be comforted by her family and examined by the physicians.

Specialists from the Crime Scene Unit had been dispatched to the bathroom in which the attack had occurred to cover every inch of it for possible evidence that would eventually link a suspect to that remote location. The two-man team photographed the area and then "processed" the bathroom to determine the presence of fingerprint evidence. They found partial prints on the outside of the toilet door and on the towel rack over the sink. Were they hers? Her assailant's? Or any of the people's who had been in that room? That question could not be answered without hours of painstaking comparisons between the whorls, swirls, and ridges that make up the unique characteristics of millions of fingerprints.

Several days later, at the very end of May, Lusardo made her first trip to the West Eighty-second Street office of the Sex Crimes Squad. There she was interviewed in much greater detail by the assigned detective, who was looking for any hint or suggestion of something distinctive about the attacker that would lead to his identification. The lengthy debriefing was followed by Lois's viewing of scores of photographs, mug shots of men arrested throughout the city for sexual assaults, separated in rows of file drawers by physical characteristics like race and height, providing the general frame in which the search for a single face could begin.

She didn't find her assailant on that initial visit to the squad, and although she was unable to get the sight of him out of her mind's eye, Lois thought it unlikely that the police would ever be able to connect anyone to her case.

The detectives were only a bit more optimistic than Lois. It might be a long shot, but they doubted that a novice would attempt an armed rape in the middle of the day in a busy commercial building. He was unhurried, confident, and most likely experienced at his business. Sadly, they expected they would encounter him again before too long.

Throughout the month of June, although reports of sexual assaults made by women, men, and children came in to the squad at the rate of five to ten a day, there were none that seemed to bear any connection to the Lusardo case. On the third day of July, though, in a small office building on East Fortieth Street, just off the corner of Fifth Avenue, a woman was taken off an elevator by a man with a knife and forced into a stairwell, where he demanded oral sex after robbing her of her money and jewelry.

Lieutenant Richard Marcus read over the reports as they came in from the precincts around the borough. This new case called up the still-unsolved Lusardo crime. Although the incidents were separated by almost six weeks' time, the physical characteristics and clothing descriptions of the assailant were similar, and both attacks had taken place in office buildings in midafternoon in midtown Manhattan. If it was, indeed, the same man, had he been idle in between? (This is unlikely for a serial rapist.) Had he been out of town, or just unsuccessful? Had there been other victims who had not reported the crimes, or was this just an unrelated coincidence?

Marcus had the good sense to pursue the seemingly slim connection. A great homicide detective before his promotion to lieutenant—and one of my best friends in the police department—he called his counterpart at the Manhattan Robbery Squad, another specialized unit on East Tenth Street, with the mandate to investigate armed robberies, to ask whether they had any patterns actively ongoing in the mid-town area. The response was affirmative. There was, in fact, a man with a knife who was doing stickups in commercial buildings in the Thirties and Forties on both sides of Fifth Avenue. The robbery detective who spoke with Marcus downplayed the likelihood that this was the rapist: The robbery victims were men and women, there were no sexual overtones to the attacks, and the robber was so polite to his victims that the cops were calling him the "gentleman bandit!"

That last reason would have seemed to separate the suspects, but Marcus was not one to let the matter drop so quickly. He asked for copies of all of the investigative reports on the cases, and when that package arrived on his desk on July 6, he assigned his detectives to reinterview those women who had been robbery victims in midtown.

On July 8, Detective George Zitis had three of these interviews scheduled. The first two women with whom he talked described their episodes, both of which occurred as they were forced off office elevators. And both attacks seemed to have ended or been interrupted by the noise of someone else approaching, which sent the assailant running off. It was the third victim who confirmed Marcus's hunch. Like the others, she worked only several blocks from Lois Lusardo's building, and like all of them she was accosted at knife point as she got on her elevator during an afternoon break. But this woman insisted to Zitis that the man with the knife would have raped her had she not been "so obviously pregnant."

"It's not just that I got vibes about it. But he was really creepy, wanting to know when I got pregnant and when the last time I had sex was. I begged him not to touch me, not to hurt my baby, and he thought about it for a few seconds and then said he'd let me go. He had already taken all my jewelry, and finally the last thing he said to me was 'Good luck with the baby.' "

Marcus and his team were convinced. The soft-spoken,

articulate man with the knife, who brazenly stole from victims in well-populated offices and, when he had the opportunity, sexually asaulted them; who apologized to Lois Lusardo and wished another woman good luck, was indeed a serial assailant, a sexual predator. On an enlarged street map of the borough which he hung on the wall, Marcus pinned a red flag on every building site where a crime had occurred. He called police headquarters to arrange a meeting with the chief of detectives for the next morning to request permission to declare the case a pattern and release the news and composite sketch through the department's Public Information Office.

The decision to go public with the news is also a difficult one. There must be enough certainty to proceed, for the broadcast of a rapist loose in any community deservedly raises fears and has the potential to cause panic and create alarm, as it was to do in this instance.

On the morning of July 9, the day Marina Lamb was attacked, Lieutenant Marcus called to let me know that he had formed a task force or team to investigate the series of midtown rapes and robberies known as PATTERN FIVE/ 1985.

Of no help to Marina Lamb, news of the serial attacks was released to the local media. Details of the assailant's modus operandi accompanied the composite sketch that was broadcast, and copies of the drawing began to appear in lobbies and on bulletin boards in office buildings throughout the central business district of Manhattan. Women employees—those who had the luxury of working in places with staffs large enough to accommodate such changes—were going on their breaks in groups of two or three. Still others (more than five hundred people) called the police hot line to report the sighting of messengers or delivery men who bore even the slightest resemblance to the published description.

At the District Attorney's Office, my colleagues and I began to search, both by computer records and individual memory, for similar cases we had prosecuted. Each of us was aware of the recidivist nature of the serial criminal, and all of us were certain that if this guy was the pro Marcus believed him to be it was likely one of us had run into him in the past.

As each of us called in names of suspects, the Sex Crimes detectives pulled old mug shots out of case folders and added them to the photo arrays that were being displayed to the growing list of witnesses. The Latent Print unit requested the fingerprint cards of the same men and compared the inky blotches to the fragments of fingers and fingertips found at each of the crime scenes.

By the middle of July more than one thousand two hundred people had been interviewed—victims, witnesses, potential suspects, and ordinary office workers. At least ten thousand pamphlets had been distributed to women in the midtown area with advice on security precautions.

Sex crimes detectives working around the clock were stymied by the boldness of this stalker's success and alarmed by what seemed to be his increasing frenzy, with two attacks on the same afternoon. When the mystery was finally solved, it was not because of sophisticated forensic technology or hours of exhausting surveillance. The key was indeed human memory, that rapists *do* repeat their acts with greater frequency and in identical fashion when they have been successful in a particular pattern.

The hero of the story is a man I have never met: Dick Weber. He had been a detective in NYPD's Safe and Loft Squad but had retired from the department in 1967 after serving for twenty years. Like so many retired cops, Weber went into corporate security and was currently the chief of security at CBS. He had been out of the city for his summer vacation and returned on July 24 to read the headlines about the serial rapist terrorizing midtown office buildings.

The giant black tower that is the world headquarters of CBS looms at the corner of Fifty-second Street and Sixth Avenue, and the safety of the workers in that building was the responsibility of Dick Weber. It was with special interest, then, that he read about these daylight attacks that happened not only in small, unguarded commercial buildings but also in corporate landmarks like his own—the Chrysler and Pan Am buildings, which boasted security systems to protect the thousands who passed through the entrances each day.

And the eerie feeling of déjà vu that Weber later described was actually the instinctive memory of a good cop. He remembered his own nightmare of eleven years earlier, when a young man embarked on a string of knife-point rapes and robberies from late January through the middle of March in 1974—and one of those sexual assaults had occurred in a bathroom of the CBS building. Weber searched his files until he found the photograph of the man who had been convicted of that vicious series of crimes: Russell West.

Weber himself thought his tip to the police would be a long shot, but the coincidences were too great to ignore. "When he went away eleven years earlier, I figured that would be it. I never figured he would be back."

Someday I assume there will be a computer system in each state that will serve as a data bank for information about serial assailants. It will contain physical descriptions, details about the nature of the sexual acts performed, DNA or genetic fingerprint coding, and latent fingerprint data. It should certainly inform local police and prosecutors when a pattern criminal is released to parole and returned to a community, as Russell West was in May 1984.

Before Dick Weber's fortuitous call to the Sex Crimes Squad, there was no way to link West to the current crime spree, short of the laborious hand search that was being made through all of the old case records and histories. There were no members of the police team who had made the 1974 arrest still working in the squad office, and the District Attorney's unit hadn't been established until several months after that prosecution. There is no way to tell how many more women would have been victimized had Weber not acted on his hunch and called Marcus's office.

The Pattern Five team acted immediately when they received the West information. Had his picture actually been

among the hundreds viewed by the women and *not* identified? That would have been a bad indication, even though
one would presume that his appearance could have changed
over eleven years. But in fact, as George Zitis was about to
learn, West's photograph hadn't been in the office files for
almost a decade. At the time of his arrest, the Police Department mug shots had been taken in black and white. When
they switched to color photography in 1976, the photo files
were emptied of the old photos and replenished with the
seemingly endless supply of rapists in more accurate color
print. None of the victims had identified Russell West because none had been shown his picture. Zitis and his partners
raced to police headquarters, to the Photo Unit, to have copies of the 1974 arrest pictures made to be placed in black-
and-white arrays for identification purposes.

At the same time, Paul Lizio, George Zitis's partner,
called down to the Latent Print unit. He reached Jose
Vasquez, the senior technician who had been working with
the team and comparing hundreds of prints on record
against the bits and pieces from assorted crime scenes. Lizio
gave Vasquez the NYSIS—State Identification System—
number that had been assigned to Russell West when he was
arrested years ago. Vasquez forwarded the request for the
convicted rapist's prints so that he could begin his examination—which might provide the one irrefutable link between
the violent criminal and the cold bathrooms he seemed to
favor for his acts.*

Lizio then checked with the Department of Correction.
What had West's sentence been and when had he been released? Tips had come in before on dozens of other cases
only for the police to discover that the suspect was still safely
behind bars for his original offense. While Corrections
checked on his release status, we called West's court file up

---

* In 1992, the NYPD finally acquired a laser fingerprint machine that has made
these kinds of searches easier in so many cases. But the overwhelming volume of the
day-to-day identification is done by the careful technicians who transform the partial kernels of information into invaluable evidence for the prosecutorial team.

from the archives section of the District Attorney's Office records. The prosecutor who had handled the case had long since resigned to go into private practice. When the folder was located on the morning of July 25, it told a short and somewhat predictable story.

West's criminal involvement had begun when he was a teenager in the Bronx in the late 1960s. In 1972, he was convicted, for the first time, of the crime of attempted grand larceny. He was not sentenced to any jail time for that offense. A year later he was charged with harassment but was conditionally discharged on a plea to that violation. Also in 1973, he was convicted of coercion, for his effort to extort $350 from a woman—he had threatened to kill her children.

After his arrest for his midwinter rampage of sexual assaults, West pleaded guilty in November 1974. By that plea he stood convicted of three counts of rape, two of sodomy, and six robberies related to the sex crimes. In each case he had grabbed his victims in office elevators and hallways, taken them to nearby bathrooms, forced them to strip at knife point, and attacked them. Although the file did not offer any reason for the plea bargain, the crimes occurred before the corroboration requirement had been completely eliminated in 1974, and it may have been a necessary evil at the time. In any event, West was sentenced to several concurrent terms of five to fifteen years.

Lizio got his callback from the Corrections people. Although the state parole board had denied the prisoner's first four requests for release to an early parole, he was freed in May 1984 under New York's "good time" law, according to which, an inmate who has stayed out of trouble in prison is eligible for release after serving two thirds of his sentence.

The next call Lizio made was to West's parole officer in an effort to find out where he was living and what he was doing. His parole officer said he had seen his charge regularly. The quiet ex-con had been employed at a Selby shoe store as a stock boy until the previous week, when he had been fired after flunking a lie detector test after women's shoes had been missing from the store. What branch of the chain had he been working in? The one in midtown Manhattan.

The officer promised to look up West's address. He knew the thirty-four-year-old parolee had first taken an apartment in Brooklyn. But he doubted that West had resumed his habit of assaulting women—he had just married the "loveliest" young lady and moved into her apartment in the Bronx. Lizio knew, however, what so many people find surprising: that the great percentage of violent sex offenders live what appear, to the outside world, to be "normal" domestic lives.

Late in the afternoon of July 25, Jose Vasquez called Lizio and Zitis at the Sex Crimes Squad office. "It's a hit," he roared into the phone! After weeks of painstaking comparisons with more than *fifteen hundred* suspects, Vasquez found double the requisite number of characteristics to declare that the fingerprints of Russell West matched the partial prints left at the crime scenes of two of the rapes. And to the members of the Pattern Five team, if West committed two of the crimes, his signature acts and comments would undoubtedly link him to all.

It was almost evening. No new cases had been reported since the attack on Marina Lamb on July 9, the day West was fired, and if the team had made it through this day without news of another crime, they had to find West and put him out of business before the next workday. They got back to his parole officer, who confirmed the new marital abode: 811 Walton Avenue, an apartment in nearby Bronx County.

Lizio called me with the good news. With adrenaline renewing everyone, the team worked through the night— combining the forces of the Sex Crimes and Robbery squads—to plan the arrest strategy. I got started on a search warrant, hoping to be able to gain entry for the officers into West's home to look for the distinctive clothing he had worn on some of the assaults and perhaps even the "trophies" some criminals keep from among their victims' belongings.

Shortly before five o'clock on the morning of July 26,

1985, several unmarked police cars pulled into the eight hundred block of Walton Avenue. While most of the members of the Pattern Five team remained on the street, three detectives from the Manhattan Robbery Squad branch of the operation entered the apartment house and concealed themselves from view beneath the stairwell of the old-fashioned walk-up building. West was living in apartment number A-14, and they didn't want him to see them as he walked out the door and headed for the street.

The three men were rewarded for their patience at 7:15, when they heard footsteps on the staircase and saw West descend and turn in their direction. Detective Gregory Modica, who had studied the old photos of West the evening before, recognized him and alerted his partners as they followed him toward the main entrance. When Modica called out, "Russell West!" the parolee turned around and stopped, and was immediately surrounded by his three captors, who placed him under arrest, handcuffed him, and sat him in their patrol car for the ride to the Manhattan station house.

As I went before a criminal court judge that morning to have the search warrant signed, two of the team detectives from the Sex Crimes Squad remained in their cars in front of 811 Walton Avenue. At eleven o'clock, they got the radio call directing them to knock on the door of the West apartment and ask for permission to talk with West's wife.

Lauren West, a very bright and attractive thirty-year-old woman, opened the door to Detectives Thomas Belfiore and Ida Kilabru. It was in the steaming hot hallway that the pair told them who they were and gave her the incredible news that the man she had met eight months earlier and recently married was under arrest for the rape and robbery of a series of women. So stunned was she by their statement that her first reaction was to laugh in utter disbelief. She was assured that they were not joking, and the three went inside the apartment to tell Mrs. West the details of the investigation.

She was even more shocked to learn that the mild-mannered man she had taken into her home had just served ten years in state prison for a rape conviction. Yes, she knew he had done time, but he had never told her any more about his past than that he had stolen some things for which he had been caught and convicted.

Her shock turning to anger, Lauren West understood that the detectives were waiting for the search warrant to be signed and delivered to them, but she agreed to help them look for some of the clothing the victims had described in each of the police reports. They found the distinctive sunglasses, a baseball hat and a sailor's cap, black pants with white pinstripes, and a short khaki jacket. One cannot imagine the pain and betrayal this decent young woman felt as she heard the detectives list the items inextricably linked to the sexual assaults of complete strangers and know that each possession belonged to the man with whom she shared her home and life.

In the meantime, the 20th Precinct on Manhattan's Upper West Side became the center of the next vital stage of the investigation, as Lizio and Zitis were responsible for arranging a series of lineups in which the many women who had been victimized by Russell West would attempt to identify their attacker. The rules for lineups had been refined in hundreds of court cases over several decades, and these experienced professionals had to oversee how each witness was notified about her trip to the station house and how the separate viewings would take place.

As the women would later testify at the pretrial hearing that validated the propriety of the police work, each one received a phone call from the detective assigned to her case. The issue for a judge to ultimately decide is whether the officers did anything improper to "suggest" to the victim that her assailant was in custody, or to taint the array from which he could be selected. Each caller requested that his witness come to the precinct at a designated time for the purpose of viewing a lineup.

Anyone who has ever gotten such a call appreciates the frustration of the witness. When a detective asks her to come in for a lineup, obvious questions tumble to the surface. Have you caught the man who raped me? Did you find my attacker? Was he wearing the baseball cap? Did he admit it? And so on. But in order for the proceeding to be proper, the cops must be exceedingly cautious and uninformative, at a time when the witness is in need of much emotional support—the first moment she may have the occasion to see the rapist again.

Lizio and Zitis were allowed to tell the witnesses only what the procedures would be at the Sex Crimes Squad office, nothing substantive about the investigation. Each witness would be met by a detective and escorted to a waiting area. That was to ensure that none of the women knew that other women were there—each identification had to stand by itself, and no one would have the opportunity to know that a different victim had seen or had not seen her attacker in the room. The men to be viewed were in a special room closed off from the one in which, separately, the victims would stand beside Paul Lizio, each secure in the fact that although *she* could see the six suspects through a small window, none of the men could see through it to identify her. The lineups were conducted through a "two-way mirror," so that all that the rapist could see was his own reflection in the pane of glass. The women were told that they could have no more information about the ensuing events after the viewing, to protect the integrity of the investigation, and thus to ultimately benefit them.

One by one at slightly staggered intervals, the rape and robbery victims appeared at Eighty-second Street throughout the early summer afternoon. They came from their homes and offices, some with relatives or friends for moral support, others alone, and all with apprehension about whether they would be able to recognize their assailant if he were actually in the room. Each woman was led to a different office in the multistory station house while cops scrambled to find men who bore some physical resemblance to Russell West to stand with him as "suspects" for the purpose of the multiple lineups.

When all of the participants were in their places, the actual viewings began, with the rape victims the first to be brought into the small darkened room by Lizio. Lois Lusardo came in first and approached the window to look at six men, all the same approximate age and size and shape as the knife wielder she had described to the police two months earlier. Each of the six men was bearing a card with a large number affixed to his chest—numbers one through six, marking his position in the array. Lizio spoke to her quietly, directing her to look into the adjacent room and tell him whether anyone inside was familiar to her, asking, "Do you recognize anyone in that room?"

Lusardo looked through the window at the group of six men and instantly said, "It's number three—it's the man who raped me." Russell West had chosen to be in the middle, as number three among the six seated "suspects."

The identification that Lois Lusardo had dreaded took only seconds. She had immediately known the face that she had not been able to get out of her mind the instant she saw him. Incredulous that he had been found, and quite relieved, she was escorted from the lineup room to the precinct garage to be driven home without any of the other women knowing the results of her viewing.

Marina Lamb had walked to the station house with a girl friend after her notification and waited only fifteen minutes before Lizio accompanied her into the viewing room. She looked at the six men and also recognized Russell West, still wearing the number three. Then she asked Lizio if she could see the men with hats and sunglasses on—her assailant had worn a sailor's cap on July 9—and the window was closed as all six were given the hats and glasses that had been purchased for the stand-ins to wear that day.

Lamb looked again, and as she said, "knowing the consequences and being a careful person," the hat and glasses confirmed her original instincts: The rapist was number three. "I studied him carefully and I looked and everything matched—the physical stature, the muscular body, the

height, complexion, eyes, and face." When asked what was
the most significant difference between his appearance two
weeks earlier and the day of the lineup, Marina Lamb told
Lizio, but would not be allowed to tell a jury because it would
be deemed too prejudicial: He looked so benign and un-
threatening in the police station, but he had the mien of a
"predator" when he encountered her on the day of the rape.

Marina Lamb made her identification and just as swiftly
left the precinct to return to her office.

She was followed by Sylvia Becker, who named number
three immediately. Then she asked to see the men in hats—
baseball hats, like her assailant had worn. She stepped away
as the window was closed and the six hats were distributed.
Back for a confirmatory look, she was positive that Russell
West was the attacker. Lizio asked if she wanted to see him
closer up or standing and she said, "Not necessary—that's the
man."

The woman who had been raped just minutes after
Becker's assault, Tanya Johnson, was led in next. As Lizio
walked her up to the glass window he was surprised by what
happened next. She raised her face to the window, then
turned and bolted past the startled detective and actually ran
to the door of the squad room to try to leave. Lizio chased
after her, calmed her down, and led her to a quiet alcove,
where he gave her a glass of water. She was frightened, she
said, as well as nervous, and Lizio was afraid she was going to
pass out in the office. He comforted her for fifteen minutes,
reassured her that the men could not see or know who she
was, and explained that this had to be done if the case was to
go forward. She composed herself and bravely walked back
into the room with Paul Lizio and told him that number
three, Russell West, was the man who had raped her.

The lineup arrays continued for the robbery victims,
several of whom also picked out West, but the great sense of
satisfaction felt by the Sex Crimes Squad detectives that day
was because of the four solid identifications by the women
who had been sexually assaulted.

At the end of the very long day of July 26, after all the lineups had been conducted and all the arrest-related police paperwork had been prepared, the detectives took Russell West downtown to the detention cells in the basement of 100 Centre Street. While I drafted the complaint—the list of charges against him—to be presented to the judge that night, West was fingerprinted and photographed like all the other prisoners detained with him on other felony charges.

When he was brought out to appear before the judge, he did not have an attorney. The Legal Aid Society was designated to represent him, and a young lawyer stood up on West's behalf to request that he be released on the modest amount of bail that the lawyer believed West's family would be able to raise for his client. The judge agreed with our position: that the charges were far too serious, the strength of the People's case too overwhelming, the defendant's criminal history too egregious, and the likelihood of his returning to face trial too remote to fix bail in any dollar amount. Russell West was remanded to the Department of Correction. He was to be incarcerated until trial on Riker's Island and not eligible for bail.

In order to spare the four women the need to testify at a preliminary hearing—in West's presence, subject to cross-examination by his attorney—we worked speedily to present the case directly to a grand jury. On the mornings of July 29 and July 30, I met with each of the women for the first time. I introduced myself and the other members of my staff who would work on the case with them—John Dalton and two paralegals—and explained the nature of the proceedings. I spoke with each of them alone and prepared them for the grand jury presentation that occurred on those same two days.

This quartet of women, randomly chosen by West as are most serial rape victims, seemed to have no other common thread. There was a forty-year range in age, they were all of different ethnic and racial backgrounds, different levels of educational training, and different socioeconomic classes.

When interviewed separately they had very similar concerns: How difficult would this process be for them? And did we have enough evidence to convict Russell West?

In this case, typical of most stranger assaults, there were many assurances I could give at the outset. To begin with, we intended to make the courtroom experience as comfortable as it could possibly be. I knew, because of the rape shield laws that had been passed almost a decade earlier, that these victims could *not* be cross-examined about their prior sexual history, which had no relevance in this case. So from the first day that we worked together I was able to tell them that their personal lives were safe from inquiry—the only period of time that was open for examination was the time of the occurrence of the crime. There would be, at most, three court appearances: the very short grand jury presentation, a pretrial hearing limited to the issue of the lineup identification, and the trial itself. And unlike in every trial depicted in made-for-TV movies about rape, I did not expect any of the witnesses to be on the stand for more than an hour.

What of the outcome? Of course, I could make no promises, since it was ultimately a jury of twelve that would decide whether the State had proved the guilt of the defendant. But this was an exceptionally strong case—as are, in fact, the overwhelming number of stanger rapes if they are properly investigated—because it included some forensic evidence that linked the suspect to the crime scene and enhanced his identification.

I needed to gain the trust of each of these women, to have them relate to me all of the details of the assaults, and to believe that our team of witnesses, experienced and compassionate detectives, and prosecutors were working together for the same goal: to see that justice was done.

On July 29, Lois Lusardo and Marina Lamb both testified before the grand jury. Lusardo, the twenty-year-old who was West's first victim in this string of attacks, was the first to be questioned. She sat before the twenty-three-juror panel while I asked a series of questions about the events of May

24. She knew she would not be questioned by anyone else—no judge, no defense attorney—and she knew that she did not have to tell her story in front of her attacker, which also gave her more comfort. Like the women who succeeded her, she was pleased and relieved that the entire appearance took less than ten minutes' time, and was far less arduous than she had anticipated.

Sylvia Becker and Tanya Johnson, followed by Detective George Zitis, completed the grand jury presentation on July 30. After I charged the jurors on the applicable counts of the penal law and read the definitions of the crimes submitted for their consideration, I left the room while the panel voted. In a short while, the warden informed me that a true bill had been voted: The grand jury had indicted Russell West for the sexual assaults and robberies of the four women who had testified briefly before them.

The period of time between Russell West's indictment and the commencement of the trial proceedings on July 1, 1986, was perhaps the greatest frustration for the victims of his assaults. Although the arrest of one's assailant provides some satisfaction and relief, it is the ultimate verdict in the case that allows the *closure* of the attack, at least in regard to the criminal justice system. No matter how many reassurances a prosecutor may give about the course of the trial, it is understandable that almost every victim anticipates the actual courtroom confrontation with much apprehension. And it is not until that experience has been completed that the witness can move on with that piece of the recovery process.

West's case moved through the system more slowly than I would have liked. After his Supreme Court arraignment in August 1985, because of the extraordinarily serious nature of his crimes, one of the most competent and experienced Legal Aid attorneys was assigned to represent West, who did not have the financial resources to retain private counsel. Geoffrey Abrams, a contemporary of mine, was a member of Legal Aid's STAB—Senior Trial Attorney Bureau—staff. Geoff is smart and diligent and has had a lot of practice in the courtroom. But there is no question that I had the "better" case—with four intelligent, independent eyewitnesses, a defendant whose criminal history would make it unlikely for him to be a successful witness in his own defense, and fingerprint evidence that would be difficult to discredit.

It is almost impossible, as you might imagine, to lose a case with fingerprint evidence, unless the defense convinces the jury that the police "framed" the defendant and planted the prints, or the lifting was improperly performed, or the match was inaccurate. Since there were prints in the cases of two of the four women who would testify against West, those two were overwhelmingly strong evidence. But it is simply impossible to guarantee any witness what a jury will do, no matter how strong the prosecution case.

The description of the course of the trial, then, is not a story about the skills of the lawyers. Quite simply, this case is illustrative of the course of many thousands of rape allegations through the system. The participation of a victim in the trial of a *stranger* rapist need not be the ordeal that it had been for so many hundreds of years. While I would never minimize the experience of facing one's assailant in a public courtroom to describe the crime he committed, the legislation of the last two decades has protected the survivor from being re-victimized in the process.

With such a compelling case, though, why must there be a trial at all? Of course, the Constitution affords each of us the right to a trial by jury. As any experienced lawyers would, Geoff Abrams and I discussed the possibility of a plea in this case. Had Russell West been willing to plead guilty to each one of these attacks and had the sentence range been appropriately severe, the four women would have been spared their trial appearances. Unfortunately, though, all a defense attorney can do is explain the options to his client and advise him which route to take. It was not a secret that Abrams recommended a plea to West, but it is my belief that a combination of factors made such a disposition impossible.

First is simply that the plea I offered was no bargain—I

had cooperative witnesses and there was no reason to let West off with a light sentence, as I might consider doing in a much weaker case. Second, I have always found that defendants are more likely to "test" the witnesses in rape cases than in other kinds of cases. Because violent sexual crimes' sad history is that many women were reluctant to report these crimes and follow through with the prosecutions, defendants continue to anticipate that their prey will not have the courage to appear. Failing in that hope, many sadistic rapists, I think, view the trial as a further opportunity to humiliate the victim by forcing her to sit before him and talk about the details of the crime. And finally, for many criminal defendants—especially those, like West, who have spent an inordinate amount of their adult lives in the communal prison society—the trial is their moment in the sun. It is the only event that revolves completely around them, where their presence is required throughout, and as twisted as the psychology is, their only opportunity to be the center of everyone's attention.

The preparation of a criminal case is an all-consuming experience. Whether prosecuting or defending, an attorney must be as conversant with the facts of the case as every person involved in every single aspect of the crime and the subsequent investigation, whether or not all of the details are admissible at the trial. We train our assistant district attorneys to think as though the best adversary and most thorough investigator are their opponents, and to understand the critical importance of trial preparation.

The Crime Scene Unit had photographed each location, and with the help of the Sex Crimes Squad detectives I spent time as well thoroughly familiarizing myself with every stairwell, elevator bank, office hallway, bathroom, and building where each assault had occurred. They had to be imprinted upon my memory so that I could make them visible to each juror through the testimonial re-creation, not just with one-dimensional drawings or photographs.

Most important was probing each of the women for the

excruciating details of what had to be elicited at the trial. Not one minute fact can be omitted, and the questioner has to know the information as well as the witness, for the witness might skip or forget a point out of nervousness or discomfort, and the prosecutor has to be ready to see that every gap is filled so that the jury has every salient bit of evidence with which to work.

Both lawyers also have to contend with all of the procedural requirements, the careful framework into which the evidence must fit. There must be proven relevance to each piece of data presented to the jury and a proper foundation laid for the introduction of every physical item. No part of the jigsaw puzzle can be introduced without the right part preceding it. I think many litigators would agree that the most difficult part of a prosecutor's preparation is structuring a direct case that is logical and coherent as well as compelling and persuasive. That was the goal we worked for in the months before the trial began.

Then after eleven months of pretrial adjournments, during which time Abrams and I completed "discovery" and the rest of our preparations for the case, as well as tried an assortment of our other already indicted cases, both sides were able to answer "ready for trial."

CHAPTER TWENTY

A SERIAL RAPIST GOES TO TRIAL

THE TRIAL of Russell West took place in Part 42 of the Supreme Court of New York County, Criminal Term, in a courtroom on the fifth floor of a courthouse at 111 Centre Street, across the street from the building in which I work. Constructed originally to house civil trials, most of its floors have since been devoured by the enormous overflow of cases from the crowded criminal court docket in our older building.

The presiding judge was the Honorable Joan Carey, a fortunate draw for both sides. Judge Carey, a former prosecutor, was appointed to the bench in 1979 and has subsequently been elevated to the position of Chief Administrative Judge of the Criminal Term of Supreme Court in 1992. Early on she established a reputation for fairness, and Abrams and I knew she was intelligent, strong, and attentive to detail. We both recognized that we would get a good hearing before her, and that West's trial would be a just one.

Our first order of business was the resolution of the issues concerning the propriety of the police investigation. Had the identification proceedings been conducted fairly? Were the items of clothing taken from West's apartment the result of a legal search? One of the most important points was the one decided first. The defense wisely moved to sever the four cases, or counts, of the indictment. Abrams argued that the prejudice to his client would be heightened by the cumulative effect of the testimony of four women with separate cases. But the Court had ruled that the case could indeed be heard by one jury, which was a distinct advantage for the prosecution. It also gave the women extra confidence, for although none of them knew the others, each was psychologically buoyed by the fact that she was not in this alone.

To resolve the other outstanding issues, Judge Carey conducted a pretrial hearing. Detective Paul Lizio was the first witness to appear on behalf of the People, a role he had assumed frequently in his nearly twenty years with the NYPD. He described how the lineups had been conducted and we offered into evidence the photographs Lizio had arranged to be taken of the six men viewed by all the witnesses. The jury would eventually be able to see for themselves, if the Court so ruled, that the procedure had been a proper one and that West's victims had been able to identify him without hesitation even when he was alongside other men who matched his general description.

After Lizio's testimony, it was necessary for me to present the four women. Again, I was able to reassure them that the Court would limit the inquiry to a single topic: the identification procedures. They would not be asked any questions about the crime itself, and each one would be on and off the stand in less than half an hour. This would, however, mark the first time that the witnesses would have to confront Russell West face-to-face, in a courtroom, and the first time his lawyer would be able to question them.

Sylvia Becker was the first to take the stand. To give you an idea of how I was able to keep my word to her, that she would not be exposed to the humiliating kind of examination she had come to expect in a rape case, the sole question she was asked about her encounter with Russell West was by me: "Were you the victim of a crime that occurred on July 17 of 1985?" Abrams did not even mention the sexual assault when he cross-examined Becker—there was no need to because the issue of the hearing had another focus, to which Judge Carey held us strictly.

My direct examination was short and simple. Abrams then took her through the afternoon hours of July 26, trying to get her to say that the police did or said something that forced her to pick West out of the lineup, but Ms. Becker stuck to her guns and was emphatic that she had needed no help in recognizing the man who had molested her several weeks prior to the lineup. Her first foray into the courtroom, lasting barely half an hour, was much more comfortable than she had anticipated and helped steady her, she told me, for the more complete testimony she would have to give before the jury.

She was followed by Lois Lusardo, and the visual contrast was extraordinary, simply because of the forty-year difference in age between the women. Both Lusardo and Johnson were just as surprised by the neutral and speedy questioning. Marina Lamb was last among the four, and it seemed to both of us that she was pushed quite a bit harder by Abrams. Part of it was legitimate, for Lamb had selected a "look-alike" from police photo files during the investigation. She had pulled a picture from among the hundreds she had viewed and told police that although that man was *not* the rapist, he did bear a physical resemblance to her attacker. Abrams tried to build that into more ambivalence than the other women had exhibited, just as he tried to with the fact that she hadn't expressed her certainty of the lineup ID until after the men had put on sunglasses and hats. Finally, he relied on her professional status, that she was a lawyer (although not in criminal practice), to argue that she must have assumed the police had a man under arrest if they had invited her to come to a lineup. And although Ms. Lamb's time on the stand was quite a bit rougher than that of her co-complainants, she handled it with great poise and intelligent responses.

The hearing went on to include police testimony about

West's arrest and the subsequent search of his home. To counter the police version of events, Abrams called Lauren West to the witness stand. The defendant's wife countered the detectives' story that she had cooperated with them by saying she had only done so because they had approached her at gunpoint (though all had denied ever drawing guns), and that she had never seen a search warrant when they were in her home. When cross-examined, she did admit inviting the officers into the apartment because once they had told her Russell was under arrest, she had not wanted any of the neighbors to learn of his trouble. She also acknowledged showing the police the twelve different hats and caps that West kept in his closet.

The most poignant moment of her testimony came at the end, when Judge Carey asked the deceived young wife, "Were you angry when they told you your husband had been arrested for a series of rapes and robberies?"

Lauren West: "I can't say angry. I was shocked. But I wouldn't say angry."

The Court: "Any time during that day were you angry over that?"

Lauren West: "Yes, it was later on that day after it really hit me, what they were saying to me. . . . I felt I was angry at the world."

At the conclusion of the hearing, Abrams moved to suppress the evidence, that is, to prevent the jury from seeing the items of clothing taken from West's apartment and to preclude the People from telling the jury about the four strong identifications that were made so soon after the crimes. He cited higher court cases in support of his arguments, urging that the police search was invalid because Lauren West had not allowed the officers into her home voluntarily, but merely in submission to police authority and fear that her home would be ransacked if she did not comply. Our arguments to the Court on these issues took longer than the questioning of the four survivors.

On the morning of July 10, Judge Carey put her rulings

on the record. She denied the defendant's motion to suppress in all respects, based on her finding of facts. The police testimony about the search was entirely credible, and the Court also noted that Lauren West was a "mature and intelligent person," whose consent was freely and voluntarily given to the police. With regard to the lineup and photographic arrays, the procedures used had been appropriate and proper and it was clear that the detectives had taken "painstaking efforts" to keep the victims separate from each other and unable to communicate about their respective identifications. The fill-ins for the lineup, as the pictures and records confirmed, had all been within the age range of the mid-twenties to the mid-thirties (West had been thirty-one at the time), and of similar weight, height, and general appearance. West had been treated fairly by the police.

By midmorning on July 10 we were ready to begin the selection of the jury. The courtroom was filled on both sides with a panel of prospective jurors, from among whom Geoff Abrams and I would agree upon twelve men and women to hear the case and two alternates, who would participate in every phase of the trial in the event any of the jurors were disqualified or became ill. In turn we questioned jurors about themselves and their families, their occupations, prior jury service, and related topics. It was important to know whether they had read or heard media accounts of the case since they would ultimately have to reach their verdict based solely on the evidence elicited in the courtroom, not because of an opinion already formed from tabloid coverage of the events.

Each side in a rape case, in New York, is allowed fifteen "peremptory" challenges to the jury pool. A "peremptory" challenge is one a lawyer can make without having to state a reason for doing so. They are usually based on an adversary's instincts, which don't have to be articulated to the Court or one's opponent. Challenges for cause, on the other hand, are unlimited and are made when the answers elicited by an attorney from a juror demonstrate that juror's inability to render a fair verdict. Some jurors on their own recognize their unfitness for a case, as the woman who announced to us all, upon hearing the charges in the case, "I have an emotional problem as far as men are concerned—I can't stand my husband, so I doubt I'll like this guy very much." Excused.

Whatever the category of crime or the nature of the particular charges, lawyers for each side look for whatever qualities in a juror they think will serve their ends. In many sexual assault trials, especially those acquaintance rape cases in which the defense makes an issue of the victim's lifestyle or behavior, prosecutors must probe jurors to try to determine whether they harbor such attitudinal biases that they will, indeed, blame the victim for whatever events she claimed occurred. Sadly, it is often *female* jurors who are most critical of the conduct of other women, just as it is female jurors who are more likely to make judgments based on the physical appearance of the accused.

In a case like that of Russell West, that complication did not exist. As with most stranger rapes, the crime is viewed by almost everyone as the worst nightmare one could imagine happening to oneself or a loved one: a forced sexual attack by a stranger, life-threatening because of the presence of the knife, in a setting we all would think of as secure. Jurors can imagine this happening to themselves, through no fault of their own (a complicating factor in many acquaintance rape situations, though not here), and thus they are generally empathetic with the witnesses. Abrams's attack would *not* be on the character or credibility of these women, but simply on their ability to recognize, describe, and identify. As the prosecutor in this case, I needed intelligent people with good common sense.

After examining almost two hundred prospective jurors, we swore in a panel of seven men and five women (plus the two alternates), ranging in age, as my witnesses did, from their twenties through their sixties. Five jurors were black, like West and one of his victims, five were white, and two were Hispanic. Their occupations ranged from dance in-

structor to homemaker to actress, postal clerk, and school-
teacher. After Judge Carey swore them in, she carefully
instructed them on the rules they would have to follow for
the course of the trial.

Then, out of the presence of the jury, Abrams raised the
last of his procedural issues with the Court. Appropriately,
he sought a pretrial ruling to decide how much of West's
criminal history the prosecution would be allowed to elicit if
the defendant chose to testify on his own behalf (presumably
to deny his participation in any of the crimes).

Judge Carey listened to our arguments and agreed with
Abrams that I would not be able to go into West's three
earliest arrests. They were too remote in time and did not go
to his veracity in this matter. But the prior conviction that
most troubled Abrams, of course, was West's plea to multiple
rape charges a decade earlier. Ironically, it is very rare for a
Court to allow a prosecutor to cross-examine a defendant
about a sexual assault conviction. The point is simply that
when the prior offense goes directly to the veracity or credibility of the witness (in crimes such as forgery, perjury, or
larceny), then it is proper to cross-examine on it. But when
the crime would merely reveal a person's violent or impulsive
nature, the courts have deemed the information too prejudicial for a jury to learn. So to allow me to question West
about his 1974 conviction, Judge Carey ruled, would only be
telling the jury that he has the "propensity" to commit sex
offenses. He couldn't be convicted of being the Midtown
Rapist of 1985 just because he had been the Midtown Rapist
of 1974!

So the Court decided that if West took the stand in his
own defense, I could inquire as to whether or not he had
pleaded guilty to a number of felonies, but I was barred from
any mention of the specific crimes involved.

We were ready for the opening statement in the trial.
This is the presentation to the jury of what the People will
prove at the trial, with an outline of the evidence the prose-

cution expects to present. The defense chose to waive its
opening, and we were on to direct examination—the testimony of the witnesses.

The cases of the four women would be presented in
chronological order, the clearest way for this to unfold as a
narrative, building as an investigation the same way it did for
the detectives. Lois Lusardo, clearly ill at ease but relieved to
see that the courtroom was not crowded with spectators, appeared before the jury in a softly tailored business suit. She
held herself up with great dignity, which belied her youthful
age, as she sat less than twenty feet directly in front of the
man who had so savagely attacked her. Her answers to my
questions about the attack were clear, certain, and concise,
and she directed them to the jurors.

Abrams's cross-examination, which reflected his experience and intelligence, exemplified a solid effort that has become the style today among defense attorneys in stranger
rape cases. He knew there was no point in attempting to bully
Lusardo, make her uncomfortable, or challenge the occurrence of the crime. Quite the opposite, which is the smarter
approach, he began, "Miss Lusardo—I know and I am sure
the jury knows that it is a difficult thing for you to review and
relive the events you have described. . . . I am going to try to
make this as painless as possible." As I had assured Lois, my
adversary asked fewer questions about the details of the sexual acts than it was necessary for me to.

Instead, in a polite but determined manner, Abrams
questioned the young woman about the seeming inconsistencies between the descriptions recorded in the police reports of
May 24, 1985, and the testimony she gave on the direct case.
Those minor variances are the critical points in every identification case, for they allow the defense to say that although
the witness had indeed been the victim of a brutal crime, she
was simply mistaken about his client's participation.

With Lusardo, Abrams chipped away at the facts that
she had described her attacker as several inches shorter than
West, several years younger than West, and had even called

the police a day before the suspect's arrest to say she had seen the rapist on the street. Had it been West? She couldn't say.

As with any identification case, Abrams worked on Lois's ability to see her attacker. "Would it be fair to say, out of fear," he asked, "that for some of the time you were not looking at your attacker's face?" That was right as to some of the time, she responded, but she came back strongly when she explained that the encounter had been a lengthy one, and for much of it she had looked him right in the eye and could remember everything about him.

Lois Lusardo's answer goes to the heart of what makes sexual assault cases so much stronger to present to a jury than any other kind of identification case—even without a single shred of other corroborating evidence. The length of time of the victim's exposure to her attacker, and the intimate nature of that exposure, combine to make her ability to recognize the assailant much more solid.

Once the defense cross-examination is under way, the prosecutor's role is a more limited one. Lois Lusardo was prepared for Abrams's questioning and remained composed and responsive. Had he begun an irrelevant or abusive grilling, which he did not, it would have been my role to object and request rulings by the Court. Lusardo never budged from the certainty of her identification throughout the cross, and on my redirect, it was simply my job to assure that any openings that may have been made in her testimony were tightly closed.

In all, Lois Lusardo was on the witness stand for less than ninety minutes. Beyond the telling of her ordeal through my examination, she was the first to acknowledge that the experience was cathartic—she had courageously faced her attacker and accused him with confidence and with dignity. No one had humiliated or debased her, and none of the "myths" of a complaining witness's ordeal had befallen her.

The afternoon court session followed with evidence of Ms. Lusardo's medical examination at Bellevue Hospital. As in the majority of sex offenses in which the survivor has wisely submitted to threats of injury, there were no signs of any physical trauma, either external or internal. The physician had, however, observed the presence of motile sperm in the vaginal vault of the complaining witness.*

Detective Anthony Lombardo, a seventeen-year veteran of the NYPD assigned to the Crime Scene Unit, took the stand next to explain how he had processed the first assault scene for the presence of latent (not obvious to the naked eye) fingerprint evidence. With more than sixteen hundred such investigations under his belt, he described how he and his partner "caught" the Lusardo case and went to work in the sixteenth-floor ladies' room in the Fifth Avenue office building.

Lombardo explained how we come to leave our distinctive prints on objects. Our bodies secrete oils, he explained, and when we make contact with nonporous objects (porous ones absorb the oils and leave no clear traces) we transfer the oils to those objects. There were many surfaces conducive to retaining prints in the cold interior of a bathroom: the metal entrance doors and stall doors, the mirror, the porcelain sinks, the tiles, and even the metal towel racks. So Lombardo had used his ostrich feather brush to coat the potential print areas with his white and black powders (contrasting colors to surfaces being "dusted"). And then he watched as the outlines of eight partial prints became visible on the surfaces he had dusted—seven from the door of the toilet stall into which West had herded his terrified quarry and one from the stainless steel towel rack.

Next, he placed smooth, transparent tape over the powdered prints, lifted it, then placed it on a color-contrasted card, thus preserving the telltale prints. The detective had put his lifts in an envelope for forwarding to the Latent

---

* Today, that evidence, if present in sufficient quantity, would be analyzed by a laboratory for genetic fingerprinting, or DNA testing. But this testing is not possible in every circumstance, as I discussed in Chapter 15, and was not performed in New York in 1986.

Fingerprint Section of the NYPD, whose members then began the comparisons and search for Lusardo's rapist.

Abrams's cross-examination of this witness was excellent. As experienced as Lombardo was, his questioner dem-
onstrated a sound and substantive mastery of the subject
matter and made it clear to the jury that he didn't want them
to believe in the magic of the latent fingerprint process.
Abrams could be much tougher with a police witness than a
rape victim (unlike the old days, where such distinctions were
rarely observed), and his knowledge displayed itself ably.

There were minor jabs at Lombardo's qualifications—
that he was qualified only to lift prints, not to compare or
categorize them. And there were attempts to make the jury
think that his job had been inexpertly done—that he should
have removed the toilet door from its hinges because the
effect of gravity would have caused the graphite dusting powder to fall between the friction ridges of the fingerprints and
create "false ridge endings" and therefore inaccurate results.
There were several testy exchanges as Lombardo defended
his techniques before the jury until Abrams finished with
him, hoping to have sown some seeds of doubt in the minds
of the jurors.

The next day our lead-off witness was Marina Lamb, a
lawyer on the less comfortable end of questioning: the witness stand. More than fifteen years older than Lusardo, more
mature, and with several graduate degrees, she nonetheless
sounded much like the younger woman as she echoed a familiar narrative.

This time too, there was a striking difference in the tone
of Abrams's cross-examination of Ms. Lamb. Again, he
veered away from any discussion of the violent assault, especially after Lamb assured him that she had spent most of her
time looking directly at Russell West, hoping that she could
make some kind of "human contact" with him that would
urge him to spare her life. But the lawyer picked with more
aggression at the woman's delay in the lineup identification,
the lighting conditions, and the single photo she had seen

during the investigation that most resembled her attacker. Although she held her ground, Abrams did seem to be pushing and needling her more than he had Lusardo. Eventually, when I asked him why, the answer he gave me was "She's a lawyer, that's why I gave her a harder time—I thought she could take it." To me, he had come dangerously close to aggravating the jury by confronting Marina Lamb in such a snide tone.

Again, when the witness had been examined at Bellevue Hospital, there was no evidence of physical trauma.

The next day the jury heard from both Sylvia Becker and Tanya Johnson, the two attacked on the same afternoon a year earlier. By this point the similarities in the cases must have seemed overwhelming to the jury, and Abrams appeared just as anxious to get the witnesses on and off the stand quickly as they themselves seemed to be. More medical evidence and crime scene work filled the morning session.

When the NYPD's latent fingerprint examiner, Jose Vasquez, was called to the stand, Judge Carey made a novel ruling, at Abrams's request, which created a small fiction around which we had to work. Vasquez was trained in the classification and identification of fingerprints, so the job of comparing the lifts from the various crimes scenes to fingerprints of individuals "known to the department" (that is, criminals with arrest and conviction records) fell to him. The point raised in advance of his testimony by Abrams was that if Vasquez testified to the truth of the matter—that he had matched the crime scene prints to those of Russell West on July 25, the day *before* West was arrested—it would be apparent to the jury that West's fingerprints were on file with the police department, and therefore, that he had a criminal record.

So the Court directed us to create a little legend, and Vasquez was told to omit from his testimony the date the comparison was made in order to not prejudice the defendant. As it turned out, Vasquez was on the stand far longer than any of the victims who testified, as he explained and illustrated for the jury the painstaking nature of his assignment.

The classification of fingerprints, he explained, is made when you roll the ten fingers of a human being, coated with ink, onto a card and observe the pattern or formula made by the fingers. Once the formula is determined, the prints are filed according to that particular formula. Identification is made by examining the lifted print to pick up details, which must then match in the same order, fashion, and relative position the one in question on file. According to the training Vasquez received, he testified that if at least eight to ten points are identical on the prints being compared, then a match can be declared.

Since the information was critical in this case, the jury learned a lot more about fingerprints. They are constant throughout our lives, he told the jury, developing early in the fetal stage and never changing. No two individuals have ever been known to possess the same fingerprints.

Vasquez, who is a civilian technician and not a detective, carefully described the different types of lines, or ridges, that compose a print. He used words like "bifurcation" and "dot and ending ridge," which he later illustrated to the jury with enlarged photographs he had mounted to depict the evidence in this case. He was able to testify that in the weeks before July 26, he had worked on the crime scene lifts from the Lusardo and Lamb cases and had compared them to fifteen hundred individuals without ever being able to match them to a suspect.

Finally, Vasquez described the distinctive markings that had enabled him to identify three of the latent prints from Marina Lamb's crime scene as belonging to Russell West. Pointing to his enlarged chart, the patient technician traced the ridges on the defendant's "number four finger," outlining point by point the unique characteristics: "We stay right from ridge number four and count up two lines and we have what looks like a pair of glasses—actually it's two islands to-gether; and we go right above it and we have a single enclo-sure. . . . "

Once Vasquez had matched nine characteristics on each finger, one more than the accepted number for a valid match, he had declared a positive result. He went on to compare the prints to the Lusardo evidence and, again, matched two of the prints from the toilet stall door to the fingerprint card of the defendant, Russell West.

Abrams began a testy but knowledgeable cross, starting with the fact that the technician's classification was really an "art," based on subjective determinations and not a comput-erized system. Vasquez agreed with Abrams that almost 70 percent of the population exhibits the "loop pattern" classi-fication that West displayed. And Abrams vigorously at-tacked the technician for halting his comparison at nine points of similarity between fingerprints, since that is about the minimum acceptable level in such a subjective field. (In fact, as Abrams highlighted, the FBI required twelve points of similarity in order to declare a match, and Scotland Yard worked with no fewer than ten.)

So Vasquez fought back and insisted that he had actually found eighteen similarities on each inked finger and latent lift, but he had charted only the nine most obvious for pur-poses of the clarity of the exhibit. Also, he noted, there were *no* points of dissimilarity among any of the matches he had declared.

The prosecution ended with a string of police witnesses, who testified to their roles in the investigation, arrest, execu-tion of the search warrant, and vouchering of West's clothing.

Both sides rested—the defense called no witnesses—and we were ready to begin our closing arguments the next morning.

Geoff Abrams, having little to work with, still tried his case with grace and energy. He presented an eloquent ser-monette about the prosecution having the burden of proof. He acknowledged the traumatic victimization of the four women and urged the jury to consider that Russell West had been mistakenly charged—because of inconsistencies in witness descriptions, too much precision and coincidence in testimony, and faulty police training and techniques in collecting evidence—all leading to the State's failure to prove guilt beyond a reasonable doubt.

My summation followed, as I recounted the four stories to the jurors. Each woman's testimony alone, if credible, was sufficient to convict West of the crimes he had committed. And each act was more obscene because when he committed it he held in his control, at the tip of his knife, the *life* of each one of his victims.

The sad irony was, as I reminded the jury, it was exactly one year earlier—July 9, 1985—to the very day that the life of West's last victim was so tragically interrupted. The question they had to ask themselves was not, as Abrams had suggested, how the four survivors were able to recognize and identify Russell West's face, but whether or not there were any circumstances that would allow them *ever* to forget him.

The Court concluded the proceedings with detailed instructions to the jurors on the definitions of the penal law charges before sending them into the jury room to consider the evidence and attempt to agree upon a verdict.

Within several hours, the group of twelve men and women came in to announce the outcome: Russell West stood convicted of each of the attacks with which he had been charged.

Several weeks later, Judge Carey sentenced the Midtown Rapist to a prison term with a maximum of sixty years, and a minimum of no less than thirty years. Russell West will not be considered eligible for parole until he is in his mid-sixties, and in all likelihood will serve closer to the maximum of the recommended term.

CONCLUSION

THE ACT of rape results in the most violent and intimate violation of its victim—physically, emotionally, and psychologically. It is an offense that can radically alter the life of its survivor, both by the trauma experienced during the crime and in the lengthy recovery process that inevitably follows.

Not a week goes by that newspapers across the country do not have accounts of sexual violence, stories detailing the victimization of women, men, and children. They range from the assault on a teenage beauty pageant contestant by Mike Tyson in Indiana, to a mentally handicapped woman attacked by eight high school athletes in an affluent suburban community in New Jersey, to a priest's admitted molestation of scores of his adolescent parishioners in Massachusetts, to the allegations of the systematic rape of thousands of women and children in war-torn Bosnia. While the obvious goal must be the elimination of sexual assault crimes, we will never progress in that direction until we understand more about the different methods of assault and the pathologies of the assailants. The cases I discussed here reveal quite clearly that there is no single profile of a rapist—rape is committed by

269

men of every socioeconomic class; of every racial, ethnic, and cultural background; and a wide range of age and educational levels. The only shared trait seems to be that they thrive on the intentional humiliation, degradation, control, and powerlessness of the victims they choose to strike.

So while these crimes continue to flourish in our society, we must continue to excercise the one thing we can control— improving the way we respond to the survivors of sexual assault. Despite the significant legislative reforms of the 1960s and 1970s, sexual assault crimes remain the most under-reported cases within the criminal justice system. Most professionals estimate that more than half of the sex offenses committed still go unreported today. While some of that reluctance is attributable to the victims' fear of reprisal by the assailant or embarrassment because of society's attitudes, victims most often cite their lack of confidence in the system— police and prosecutorial agencies—as the reason for their decision not to report. The manner in which rape cases are investigated and prosecuted has a profound influence on the enormous number of people who are victimized by sex offenders.

Throughout this country, despite the efforts of the feminist movement against and responsible media attention to violent sexual crime, the services devoted to sexual assault victims have been shockingly inadequate. First, there is a desperate need for the development of appropriate medical services to be available to survivors. Whether or not victims report the attack to law enforcement officials, most recognize the need to seek medical care. In some jurisdictions there are victim service agencies that will cover the costs of examinations, but there are thousands of women who fail to get the necessary treatment for the tragic reason that they cannot afford the clinical fee. Further, if pregnancy results or a terminal illness is transmitted, it is rare in the first instance and nonexistent in the second for any government agency to cover the cost of the care.

Also consider this: In a major medical center in New

York City in 1992, a woman brought to the hospital at three o'clock in the morning for treatment after a rape had a gynecological examination performed by an oral surgeon because no qualified physician was available to see her. (Of course, we were unable to qualify him as an expert witness, since he had never performed an internal examination before that night.) What occurs in smaller cities and towns across the country echoes that experience and highlights the need for the establishment of effective medical protocols for rape survivors.

Another critical area needing attention is counseling services. It was as late as 1974 that Burgess and Holmstrom published their landmark study describing "rape trauma syndrome," the two-phase behavioral and psychological reaction exhibited by many survivors to the life-threatening occurrence of forcible rape. The acute phase immediately follows the attack; the long-term reorganizational phase is of indeterminate duration and frequently results in major changes, whether in relationships, residence, or employment. Many victims need the support of professionals to aid in their recovery process. Again, as is medical treatment, that support is available only in a handful of communities, funded by social service agencies, often for only a designated period of time.

In the acute phase right after the attack, the lifeline for many survivors are the rape-crisis advocates who staff telephone "hot lines" to dispense advice and who participate in the emergency room treatment in some hospitals, by comforting and escorting the victim through the clinical procedures. It is appalling to know that in almost every instance, the extraordinary work of this advocacy is carried on by unpaid volunteers. Many are themselves survivors of sexual assault, trained by other volunteers for their roles, and are available on twenty-four-hour call, even though they have other full-time professional responsibilities. Most hospital advocate programs exist on shoestring funding, fighting to remain alive in the face of administrative budget cuts. There must be government initiatives undertaken for the funding of crime victim advocacy and long-term counseling costs for the severely traumatized victims of these crimes.

The third area that must be improved is the response of the law enforcement community. With adequate medical and psychological care, the overwhelming number of rape survivors recover from their assaults quite well. But the provision of services in those two fields does not mandate a survivor's participation in the criminal justice system. Only when we can make the survivor comfortable in the system will we be able to defeat the problem at its source: to identify the rapist, to convict him in the courtroom, and to isolate him from society for as long a period as the law allows. Our criminal justice system must recognize that many of the sexual predators—the repeat offenders whose behavior cannot be modified—must, in appropriate cases, be sentenced to life imprisonment without the possibility of parole.

These crimes *do* present unique issues for those who investigate and prosecute them. While some legislative changes need to be implemented throughout different states, most of the laws have been in place for the last two decades to allow the aggressive prosecution of these cases. Once again, in too many counties nationwide, there has been a failure to commit financial and human resources to sexual assault cases, and to ensure that victims of these crimes be made more comfortable in the process.

As we struggle to put in place the essential services— medical, counseling, and legal—the other critical need to which attention must be devoted is the education of the public. Every archaic stereotype and myth about rape must be exploded, from the moronic platitudes that blame the victims for their plight to the misconceptions that rape is an impulsive expression of lust rather than deliberate violence, to the equally pernicious falsehood that we cannot win these cases in the courtroom.

The people who cling to the myths about rape are, like the rest of us, among people all over this country who are called to serve as jurors on rape cases everywhere. When they enter the jury box with the biases enforced by their experience and misinformation, if they persist in judging the victim and not the offender, the verdicts will reflect their ignorance. The effort to educate about sexual violence must begin in our schools and continue in every forum available. Until we can eradicate crimes of sexual assault, we must respond to their survivors with respect, compassion, and an effort to treat them with dignity when they seek justice from a system that denied them access for hundreds of years.

For me, this work has been enormously rewarding. Survivors come to the criminal justice system not expecting that it will serve their needs because of the history Brownmiller documented so brilliantly twenty years ago. But my colleagues and I have participated in a system in which extraordinary changes have taken place—changes that enable us to achieve justice in a remarkable number of cases and to make survivors more comfortable throughout the process. Those crime victims I have met—women, men, and children; the smart, warm, dedicated, and good-humored people I have had the pleasure to call my friends, in both the Manhattan District Attorney's Office and the New York Police Department; and the incredible support, quiet generosity, and trust given to me by Robert Morgenthau have made this job the most wonderful place for a woman like me.

ACKNOWLEDGMENTS

NEARLY thirty years ago when I arrived for my first day on the campus of Vassar College, I had the great fortune to be assigned a roommate named Alexandra Denman, who remains my dearest friend to this day. When she met and married Ben Stein, I gained another loyal and devoted supporter.

It was Ben who encouraged and persuaded me to write this book, brought me to the people at William Morrow, sat in the courtroom with me every day throughout the trial of Russell West, structured and framed the focus of many of my anecdotes into the form of a book, and continued to hearten me throughout the long years it took me to complete the task I had undertaken.

No editor could be more patient than Adrian Zackheim, who has committed his interest and energy to every aspect of this project, and who has lived through many of these cases with me with great understanding and compassion, even as they delayed his delivery date. His kindness to me has been immeasurable.

It was the combined generosity of spirit of both Ben and Adrian that convinced me I could, indeed, write this story myself—a dream I had not expected to fulfill.

ACKNOWLEDGMENTS

In the final stages of the process, Esther Newberg offered friendship and guidance, for which I am immensely grateful.

I am indebted to my colleagues, the women and men who have been members of the Sex Crimes Prosecution Unit and worked on these cases with passion and devotion, judgment and balance. John Dalton and Maureen Spencer are the backbone of the unit and their friendship has added an extra dimension to the work we have done together. And my special fondness is reserved for my teams of trial preparation assistants—amazing pairs of talented young women who have come to work with me over the last decade—on their way to becoming lawyers, doctors, filmmakers, and mothers.

My inspiration for this book has been the courage of the victims of sexual violence who have chosen to participate in the criminal justice system. I look forward to a time when their number will decrease, and when all who seek justice in our courts will be treated with dignity.

My mother and father gave me the great gift of believing I could accomplish any goal on which I set my heart, and taught, by their example, the enormous rewards of public service and doing things for others—loved ones or strangers.

And it is my beloved Justin who has lived through every moment of the writing of this book with me, in our beautiful home on the Vineyard, summer after summer. He has been my strength through the dark hours of my work in the office and the courtroom, and calmed my tantrums whenever the word processor devoured whole chapters of my text as I tried to tell these stories. Most of all, he encourages me to continue to do the work that I love, and to write about it.

INDEX

INDEX

INDEX

INDEX

Joey (undercover police officer), 161–162

John (rapist), 211–212, 213

Johnson, Lyndon B., 103

Johnson, Tanya (fictitious name):
at grand jury presentation, 248
at pretrial hearing, 255
Russell West identified by, 245
sexual assault of, 78, 231
as trial witness, 264

Jonelle (rape victim) (fictitious name), 93–94

Julie (sexual assault victim) (fictitious name), 176

jurors:
in acquaintance rape cases, 134–136, 258
crime victims as, 151
personal sexual experience of, 102
rape motive not understood by, 81
research on biases of, 134
selection of, 257–259
sex of, 258
societal misconceptions held by, 81, 99, 258, 273
unanimous verdict required of, 41, 91–92
victim's credibility and, 207, 208, 211, 216

Justice Department, U.S., criminal justice projects funded by, 80

Kalick, S. Michael, 132

Karen (acquaintance rape victim) (fictitious name), 143–148

Karen (married rape victim) (fictitious name), 213–216

Kearney, Charles, 144

Keenan, John, 104–105

Kennedy, John F., 103

Kids Will Be Kids Company (fictitious name), 19

Kilabru, Ida, 241

King, Steve (Steven Davidson), 195–197

King Productions, 195–196

Koch, Edward, 62

Koplik, Benjamin, 167–169

Koplik, Michael, 169

Lamb, Marina (fictitious name), 265
as attorney, 255, 263
grand jury testimony given by, 247

at pretrial hearing, 255
Russell West identified by, 244–245, 263–264
sexual assault of, 113–117, 231, 235, 240
as trial witness, 263–264

Landau, Sybil, 46–47

larceny, sexual scam vs., 191

Latent Fingerprint unit, 238, 262–263

"laughing gas" (nitrous oxide), 167, 168

Law Enforcement Assistance Administration (LEAA), 80, 120

Lee, Vaughn, 148–151

Legal Aid Society, 25, 246, 248

legislative reforms, 14
acquaintance rape prosecution facilitated by, 134
on corroboration requirement, 16, 79, 82, 121, 122, 126, 134, 142, 199
on earnest resistance standard, 110–111, 121, 126–128, 134
need for, 7, 8, 79–80, 120
on victim's personal life as evidence, 122–126, 247

Lenox Hill Hospital, 29

Leslie (Lusardo's coworker) (fictitious name), 19, 24

Leval, Pierre, 103

Levin, Jennifer, 125–126

Lifecodes Corporation, 182–183

lineup identifications:
pretrial hearing on, 247, 254, 255, 257
of Russell West, 243–246
security procedures for, 120, 242–243, 257

Lizio, Paul:
lineups conducted by, 242, 243, 244, 245, 254
suspect's background investigated by, 238–240
testimony of, 254

Lombardo, Anthony, 262–263

Louisa (false rape victim) (fictitious name), 217–222

Lusardo, Lois (fictitious name), 19–24, 28
attacker described by, 260–261
fingerprint evidence and, 265, 266
grand jury testimony given by, 247–248
photographs viewed by, 232–233
police inquiry and, 231–233, 234

INDEX

INDEX

INDEX

INDEX

rape laws:
  earnest resistance required by, 110–111, 121
  see also legislative reforms
rape shield laws, 121, 122–126, 134, 247
Rape Trauma Syndrome, 131, 271
rape victims:
  anonymous hot line services for, 82–83, 271
  assertive attitude developed in, 121
  bail decisions and, 35, 86
  blaming of, 13, 132, 133–134, 258, 272, 273
  courtroom appearances by, 37–38, 88, 89, 90, 92–95, 100, 137, 150, 152, 199, 206, 246–248, 249, 254–255, 260–262, 263–264
  District Attorney's Office interview procedures for, 56–57, 81
  earnest resistance standard for, 110–111, 121, 126–128
  elderly women as, 58–60
  evidential use of personal history of, 122–126, 247
  financial benefits for, 228
  grand jury appearances of, 36, 66–68, 246–248
  as hostages, 110–111
  illegal drug use concealed by, 205, 206, 207, 211, 213
  jurors' assessments of, 79, 134, 273
  medical services for, 14, 58, 77, 145, 152–154, 261–262, 270–271
  one-on-one interviews with, 63
  physical injury to, 57–58, 152, 153
  pregnancies of, 124, 270
  previous prostitution convictions of, 123–124
  prior chastity of, 124
  psychological counseling services for, 14, 77, 93–94, 140, 149, 223, 271–272
  reliability of identification by, 201–205, 261
  reluctant reporting by, 59, 82, 138, 139–140, 149, 152, 218–219, 270
  self-blame of, 132
  single prosecutorial contact maintained for, 57, 103, 120
  special police services for, 82–84

stigmatization of, 7, 13
venereal disease contracted by, 58, 77, 124, 152, 270
see also acquaintance rape victims
rapists:
  citywide behavior patterns of, 82, 83
  normal domestic lives maintained by, 136, 240
  physical appearance of, 135–136, 155
  prison sentences for, 42, 44, 94, 95, 183, 267, 272
  in professional consultation circumstances, 155–170
  recidivism of, 27, 43, 44, 272
  serial, 60, 90, 231, 233–235, 237, 249–250; *see also* West, Russell
  stereotypical images of, 134–135, 155, 269–270
Raymond (Lusardo's coworker), 19, 24
recidivism, 27, 43, 44, 272
recording devices, hidden, 158, 159–162, 164, 167–168, 169
remand decisions, 87
Reskin, Barbara, 134
Richards, Hugh, 191–194
Riker's Island, 25, 246
robbery:
  felony trials for, 98
  sexual scam vs., 191
Robbery Squad, 233–234, 240–241
Roosevelt Hospital, 223
Rose (sexual molestation victim) (fictitious name), 168–169
Rosenblatt, Albert, 194
"rough sex" defense, 146
Rovins, Jeffrey, 61
Ruiz, Iraida (fictitious name), 62–64

Safe and Loft Squad, 236
St. Luke's Hospital, 149
St. Vincent's Hospital, 140, 149
Saracco, Steve, 141, 190, 196, 216
scams, sexual, 185–197
  consent issues connected with, 190, 194, 196
  defined, 185
  employment offers as, 195–197
  by health therapy practitioners, 191–194
  in professional training programs, 185–191
SCAU (Sex Crimes Analysis Unit), 82–83

INDEX